CULTURE SHOCK!

A Parent's Guide

Robin Pascoe

Graphic Arts Center Publishing Company
Portland, Oregon

In the same series

Australia	Hong Kong	Philippines	London at Your Door
Bolivia	India	Singapore	Paris at Your Door
Borneo	Indonesia	South Africa	Rome at Your Door
Britain	Ireland	Spain	
Burma	Israel	Sri Lanka	A Globe-Trotter's Guide
California	Italy	Sweden	A Student's Guide
Canada	Japan	Switzerland	A Traveller's Medical Guide
Chile	Korea	Syria	A Wife's Guide
China	Laos	Taiwan	Living and Working Abroad
Cuba	Malaysia	Thailand	Working Holidays Abroad
Czech	Mauritius	Turkey	
Republic	Mexico	UAE	
Denmark	Morocco	USA	
Egypt	Nepal	USA—The	
France	Netherlands	South	
Germany	Norway	Vietnam	
Greece	Pakistan		

Illustrations by TRIGG

© 1993 Times Editions Pte Ltd

This book is published by special
arrangement with Times Editions Pte Ltd
Times Centre, 1 New Industrial Road, Singapore 536196
International Standard Book Number 1-55868-425-5
Library of Congress Catalog Number 98-86356
Graphic Arts Center Publishing Company
P.O. Box 10306 • Portland, Oregon 97296-0306 • (503) 226-2402

Printed in Singapore

To Rodney, Lilly, and Jamie
with all my love

CONTENTS

Introduction by Dr Kirsten Herh **9**

Historical Parallels...Different Concepts Of What Is Real...Parents'
Attitudes, A Child's Insecurity...Anxiety And Stress Of Life
Overseas...Pressures Of International Schools...Learning Another
Language...Children And Native Care-givers...Learning
Disabilities...Common Types Of Children...Accepting Your Child

Chapter One **27**
GLOBAL KIDS

Chapter Two **35**
YOU'RE RUINING MY LIFE!
Getting Ready to Move Abroad

Accepting The Idea Of The Move...Telling Your Children About
The Move...Answering Their Questions...Holding Back
Information...Dealing With Emotional Upheavals...Discussing Your
Children's Fears...When To Consider Boarding School...The
Boarding School Option...Strategies To Get Everything
Done...Getting Ready To Go With A Baby...Saying
Goodbye...Quick Tip Summary

Chapter Three **63**
LEAVING ON A JET PLANE
Your Bags Are Packed: You're Ready To Go

Countdown To Takeoff...Arrival: You Made It!...Early Survival
Tips...The Best Is Yet To Come...Quick Tip Summary

Chapter Four *80*

FAMILY CULTURE SHOCK

And How Mommy's Own Shock Affects the Kids

Jet Lag And Culture Shock...Family Culture Shock...Why Is
Mommy So Shocked?...Culture Shock Denial...What Causes A
Child's Culture Shock...Who Is Most Susceptible?...Signs That
Your Child Is In Shock...Help Everyone Get Through Culture
Shock...Keeping The Proper Perspective...Quick Tip Summary

Chapter Five *104*

THE NEW LIFE OVERSEAS

Getting Used to a Different World

Secondary Culture Shock...It's A Different World Overseas...Second
Language Problems...Behavior Problems When Issues
Explode...How Can Parents Alleviate Problems?...Communication Is
The Key...What Exactly Are You Communicating?...Your
Children's Family Life Will Be Different From Your Own...A Goal
Of Making Children Feel Secure...Quick Tip Summary

Chapter Six *132*

INTERNATIONAL SCHOOL DAZE

Getting a Global Education

Be Prepared To Adjust To An International Education
System...International Schools...Fewer Social Services And Limited
Special Programs...The Language Issue At International
Schools...Impact Of Local Culture...Over-achieving
Parents...Higher Academic Standards...An American Bias...Fewer
Disciplinary Problems...Getting High On Grades...Politics In The
Classroom...Servants And Student Behavior...Sex
Education...Emotional Problems In School...What Other School
Options Are There?...Pre-school Issues...A Greater Role For
Parents Overseas...School, The Center Of Your Child's
Universe...From The Mouths Of Our Babes...Quick Tip Summary

Chapter Seven *160*
THIRD CULTURE KIDS
Understanding the Neighborhood Friends

How Did The Notion Of TCK Start?...What Is A TCK?...The
Third 'Expat' Culture...Where Are You From?...Where Is
Home?...Home Vs. Nationality...What Are The Characteristics
Of A TCK?...Other Important TCK Issues...It Can't Be Too Bad
A Life

Chapter Eight *179*
KEEPING THE MINDS AND BODIES SOUND
Health and Safety Issues

Know Your Emergency Procedures...Keeping Emergencies At
Bay...Preventive Medicine...Treating Common Illnesses...Going To
The Doctor...If Your Child Must Be Hospitalized...First Aid...First
Aid Kits...Having A Baby Overseas...Mental Health Issues And
Children...Your Child's Mental Health...Signs The Child Isn't
Coping And How You Can Help...Seeking Help From
Professionals...Books To Help You Double-check...Quick Tip
Summary

Chapter Nine *213*
HOME LEAVE AND OTHER HOLIDAYS
Kiddie Wanderlust

Travel Is A Fact Of Life...Different Types Of Journeys...Keep It
Simple...Too-high Expectations Of Children...The Importance Of
Rules And Routines...Preparing Them To See Family...Where To
Stay...Home Leave Culture Shock...Reverse Culture
Shock...Appointments For Your Children...Setting Limits On
Shopping...Children Traveling Without Parents...Other Travel
Tips...Parents Traveling Without Children...Major Holidays
Celebrated Abroad...Creating Travel Memories...It's Worth
It...Quick Tip Summary

Chapter Ten *235*

THE SHOCKS OF RE-ENTRY

Helping Your Children Return Home

Going Home As Different People...Making The Decision To Go
Home...Parents' Re-entry Attitudes Affect The Children...Re-entry
Can Be Harder Than Moving Abroad...Re-entry Comes In Three
Stages...Teenagers And Re-entry...Why Does The Teenager Take
Re-entry So Hard?...Issues Parents Of Teenagers Must
Face...Helping Children Of All Ages Adjust To Re-entry...Helping
Teenagers In Particular To Adjust...As Parents, You Will Be
Adjusting Too

The Author *265*

Index *266*

Dr. Herh has specialized in child psychology for eight years in Denmark and for the past five years in China. In China, she has been consultant for both the International School of Beijing and the resident foreign community. With a school population of 350 students, she has had numerous requests for a broad spectrum of traditional psychological help. She has administered clinical tests, worked with teachers, and where necessary, worked privately with students and, often, their parents.

When this book was written, she was the only psychologist available for consultation in Beijing for the expatriate community. She thus worked without benefit of colleagues with whom to consult which is the common practice. At the same time, the circumstances provided her with a rare opportunity to gain a broader understanding of the many diverse problems facing children growing up in an international environment or setting, an opportunity she would not have had working in the more highly specialized clinical environment in the West.

Dr. Herh is the mother of two children – a girl and a boy who were respectively 9- and 2-years-old before her family embarked on their five-year assignment in China. Her own children's contributions to her understanding of children's adjustments overseas have been invaluable.

INTRODUCTION
BY DR. KIRSTEN HERH

The study of children who grow up moving from one foreign country to another adds new dimensions to the field of child psychology. Children who move internationally every few years experience extreme social situations. A closer examination of how they handle those situations will definitely have wider implications for an ever increasing mobile population.

For my colleagues in the field of child psychology, a study of the reactions of these internationally mobile children enhances our insights for later application to the general population of children. And for parents either currently living in a foreign country with their children, or about to leave home for one, my experience and observations will, I hope, provide both assistance and reassurance.

HISTORICAL PARALLELS

International culture provides a framework for the interaction of all the cultures of the world. As one example, take the immigrants to America at the beginning of this century when many different cultures converged on cities like New York. Whether or not one can make historical parallels between the modern-day expatriate culture and those immigrants to the New World, I have nevertheless found one theme expressing itself in both instances.

Despite the cultural melting pot into which they were thrown, most adult immigrants worked hard to maintain their own culture. Their children, on the other hand, reacted differently. They moved quickly to integrate, to put the old countries and the old ways behind them, to become Americans as quickly as possible.

As a psychologist looking at this theme, I believe the difference between the two generations rests less with cultural identity, and more with the coping strategies the two groups devised to help them adapt to a new, unfamiliar environment. In many ways, the same strategies apply to expatriate adjustment today. While there is a long history of expatriates – from the days of the Roman garrisons to the colonial administrators of this century – today's expatriates live in a much faster-paced environment. In such instances, it is almost certain that parents will choose to hold back – to maintain the old, familiar ways, to hold on tight to their national identities – while their children will choose integration as their path to survival.

DIFFERENT CONCEPTS OF WHAT IS REAL

The difference in coping strategies rests with the different concepts of reality. Most adults living abroad, especially those posted to vastly different Third World cultures, perceive life as a sort of waiting station until the next posting. It is a fairly common phenomenon that well-educated expatriates will talk about their current life as something superficial when compared to the 'real life' at home. In fact, it seems to be a fashionable lifestyle in international communities for individuals to put a fair amount of distance between themselves and the realities of daily life. This is understandable when life conditions change so often and so quickly. This psychological distancing is a natural defence against the confusion of moving around. It works sufficiently for adults who have the ability to abstract from what they are experiencing.

But children can't do that. Children define themselves and place their identity in the here and now. They think in concrete terms and only gradually develop the adult form of abstract thinking, which is a direct function of the development of the brain during childhood.

While a 7- or 8-year-old may have language skills that suggest a more mature, adult-like understanding of the world, at a basic level that child still operates on an entirely different plane. It is only when children become 12 or more that they can understand the sort of distancing their parents engage in, or the abstract idea of belonging somewhere other than where they are living at the moment. Children are in the process of developing a self-identity, and are unable to separate themselves from the culture around them. For them, 'real life' is the here and now. It is not something far away that exists only as a vague memory.

A child might learn to say, "I don't really live here, I come from France." He might even learn to imitate his elders in criticism of the local culture, often in harsh terms. But he does so with the radical consequence of undermining his own self-confidence. Just as children have the need to love and admire their parents as they develop a self-image, so do they thrive on loving the world around them during their moral development.

PARENTS' ATTITUDES, A CHILD'S INSECURITY

When the authority figures in a child's life are critical of their surroundings it provides fertile ground for all sorts of insecurities to grow in the child.

Take the case of a 7-year-old boy I met by the name of Michael. (I have changed the names of the children I describe to maintain confidentiality.) Michael was uncomfortable in China because his hair was white and curly and this caused the Chinese to touch him incessantly. He was offended by this because he took this touching as an unfriendly act. In a misguided show of support, and for reasons of self-defence, his parents gave air to their own prejudices about everything in the local culture. The result was a very unfriendly approach to the host culture by the family.

Still, it was local people who helped in the house by cooking and babysitting. And while the parents could differentiate between their concrete relationships with the people in the house and their irritation toward the host country in general, the child could not. For him, an idiot would always be an idiot, whereas calling someone an idiot might be only an expression that an adult allows to slip at the end of a frustrating day.

At 7 years of age, Michael was in the process of exploring the world in order to understand it. Being surrounded by 'idiots', to him, was narrowing his own potential for personal growth. Such intangible limits create blockages and anxiety. So in the end, despite the parents' good intentions of lending support to their child, they effectively transmitted their own anxieties and attitudes onto their child.

I have seen this transference of the parents' anxieties and attitudes in other areas as well. I have especially witnessed it in regard to international schools. For instance, the culture shock experienced by a European child arriving in a city like Beijing for the first time may be a minor problem when compared to the more substantial shock of attending an American-focussed international school for the first time. If a child has never attended a school which has major testing, never experienced competition as a major factor of motivation, never seen a multiple-choice examination, or never heard of the term 'honor roll', that child will have to take more than a few deep breaths to regain his self-confidence.

Eventually, of course, it turns out that the teachers are human and competition can be fun. The child will realize he is not alone and there are other non-Americans at the school as well. But in the beginning, it can be a frightening situation for the child and naturally he will engage in a lot of hostile criticism.

If the parents reinforce that criticism, it can lead to trouble. When children hear their parents lashing out with strong, opinionated criticisms against their school, their learning will definitely be impeded for they will eventually absorb their parents' anxiety. It takes a strong father or mother to put his or her anxieties aside, and reassure a child that he will do just fine. In the traveling lifestyle, where families move from country to country, there is no choice for parents but to adopt a basic acceptance of the surroundings and actively focus on the positive aspects. Clearly, this positive stance will apply in other areas of the child's life as well.

ANXIETY AND STRESS OF LIFE OVERSEAS

Children with easily provoked nervousness or anxieties will often have difficulties going through major changes in life. Moving from country to country definitely qualifies as a major change. Nervousness tends to become magnified by an overseas move. And with good reason: for a certain period of time, life becomes uncontrollable and unpredictable, precisely the conditions which provoke the nervous child.

Working as a psychologist at an international school, it is fairly common for me to see children expressing anxiety at a level which, had it been seen in a secure environment, would have been diagnosed as serious. But given my experience with children constantly on the move, I have learned to begin every treatment with the assumption of a crisis reaction at the back of my mind. My reasoning should be obvious: moving around the world every second or third year provokes serious stress – a reaction to the crisis of the move – in every child. Some children cope with it better than others.

Eleven-year-old Anna is an example of a child who did not handle the stress of moving easily. After she had lived in Beijing for almost a year – the typical settling-in period – Anna was referred to me by her teachers because she was not performing well in class. According to her school records, she had never had academic difficulties before, and she had done well in the psychological screening process for learning difficulties.

But when I interviewed her, she revealed to me that she was frightened by her teachers. She was convinced they did not like her and that she should never turn her back on them or she would come to some harm. Anna was at such a stage of advanced anxiety that she could vividly describe to me situations in which she was convinced her teachers were waiting to grab her and do her harm.

As a first step in helping Anna, I allowed her to express her fears openly, instead of simply telling her she should not feel what she was feeling and think what she was thinking. Anna had been put in a difficult situation – moving to China – so I reassured her that she did, indeed, have reasons to react the way she did. The reasons might be difficult for an adult to understand, but it is still her right to think and feel her own thoughts.

It is always difficult for a parent to deal with a child's anxiety, but this is especially the case when the family is living abroad. In an international setting, the child's anxiety often provokes the parent's ever-existing sense of guilt over the decision to move abroad in the first instance. Parents easily jump to the conclusion that, in one way or another, they have created the anxiety in their child.

In Anna's case, her mother felt guilty. She overdid the consolation: she spent too many hours comforting her daughter. When Anna couldn't fall asleep, she would stay with her until she did. She felt sorry for her daughter so she couldn't say no to any of Anna's requests. The resulting situation was not a healthy one for Anna, as most limits simply vanished.

Parents cannot take over their child's anxiety, although to attempt to is a typical parental response. It's natural for parents to feel responsible for creating anxiety, but ultimately they do the child more harm than good if they try to place the burden of the child's anxiety onto their own shoulders.

Anxiety often expresses itself when a child is having an identity crisis and is struggling to separate herself from the parent. In Anna's case, the mother would have helped her daughter more by helping her build up her own identity; by imposing limits rather than taking them away. The anxiety was Anna's, not her mother's. She needed to be able to deal with it on her own, by expressing herself freely.

PRESSURES OF INTERNATIONAL SCHOOLS

My Scandinavian heritage may be reflected in the following story which makes the rounds of international schools, but I feel it is useful in illustrating several of the points about the international school system which I would like to make. The story goes like this: When American parents meet a teacher for the first time, they ask: "What is my child learning?" When British parents are introduced, they ask: "How is my child behaving?" Scandinavian parents simply ask: "How is my child?"

Simplistic as this story may be, it demonstrates the difference in national attitudes towards expectations for children in a competitive academic setting.

I believe that stress is created for younger children at international schools which favor an early introduction of reading and writing skills. Some children are simply not mature enough to learn to read and write at the age of 4. Every kindergarten teacher knows that. Too many children are left behind by such an exercise and, in the end, whether a child learns at age 4 or slightly later doesn't mean much. A comparison can be made to the child who walks early. Whether they walk at 8 months or 18 months does not ultimately affect their ability to walk. It is a direct result of their physical development. Likewise, reading and writing are based on very primitive brain functions, such as pure visual recognition and memory. So whether a child learns to read and write early does not necessarily have much to do with intelligence but with the rate of their development. It was proven a long time ago that early reading and writing does not necessarily lead to better readers later on.

Many teachers are very good at letting children learn according to their maturity. But even in a class with a good teacher, the child who is late maturing will feel lost when he senses that the main purpose of his school is to produce children who can read and write at an early age – and that he can't attain that goal.

I believe that a class of 4- to 6-year-olds should follow the level of the late readers in reading and writing. The rest of the time can be filled with creative subjects, allowing the children to develop along with their peer group without loss of self-confidence.

Similarly, I feel that high school students are exposed to too much academic stress at the expense of their emotional development. High school students at international schools often complete college-level assignments. I have no quarrel with their intellectual abilities to perform at grade levels above and beyond their years, but the question is, how does this affect their personal development? It is my belief that the hours devoted to researching and writing too difficult assignments would be hours better spent in the development of a teenager's emotional and spiritual maturity. In my professional capacity, I often see high school students who may be capable of presenting articulate arguments about the geopolitics of a region of the world, yet they are inexperienced in matters like how to relate to and learn from others.

The high school years provide a critical period for the formation of character. I believe the teenage years should be an introspective time of life, exploring feelings and human relationships. I don't dispute that adolescents thrive in the learning process – and that education should be a major occupation – but there is a very fine line between learning only for the sake of academic purposes and learning that recognizes the need for personal growth.

This theme becomes especially crucial in the international culture that provides limited room for spiritual growth, which normally develops at 'home' through family relationships and an intricate network of friendships. In an overseas environment, room has to be created for that spirituality to flourish. Adolescents, through their exposure to and integration with numerous cultures, have an excellent opportunity to benefit from such inner growth. They won't have that chance, in my opinion, if they are constantly distracted by academic assignments that do not correspond to the needs of their age.

LEARNING ANOTHER LANGUAGE

There is a belief that it is easy for a child to learn another language. It's possible for toddlers to easily parrot the correct tones of another language. And it is impressive when a child becomes fluent in a second language before the age of 3. However, nobody should think this fluency comes without cost.

In the first instance, it is as difficult for toddlers to learn Chinese, for example, as for them to learn English. They do not learn it unless they have a Chinese care-giver for long periods of the day. It comes after hours and hours of trying out new words, and being corrected over and over again. This is an exercise children do not necessarily dislike, but it is stressful for a toddler who finds he is not understood by everyone when he uses one language. For a 2-year-old, being able to communicate is a major step in his development, in the mastery of his world, and in the formation of his self-confidence. I believe, and I think I have seen it in my own professional experience with overseas children, that when a child is exposed to too many languages at an early age, it can hamper the development of his identity.

Older children definitely face difficulties with language acquisition. Before the ages of 7 or 8, it is easy for children to learn a language using the proper pronunciation and to become as fluent as a native, but at the same time, the language is easily forgotten. After this age, it becomes more difficult to speak a new language without an accent, but once it is learned it seems to last a lifetime. This is due entirely to the development of the brain. Around age 8, the areas of brain used for language acquisition are developed, but at the same time, the learning process seems to become more complicated.

A child over 12 will learn languages basically in the same manner as an adult. If anything, it is more difficult for the child to learn a new language since he does not have the experience and self-knowledge to know how to learn. When parents want to understand what a child of 12 or more is going through to learn another language, they need only think of how they themselves would fare. This is of particular interest to parents who place their children in English as a Second Language programs at international schools. The child will spend the entire day having to communicate with people he does not understand very well. He has to listen carefully at all times, an exhausting process but critical since communication is essential for social interaction. ESL children are exhausted by the end of a school day. This certainly has to be considered in the assignment of homework.

There is a variety of opinions among language professionals as to whether or not a child will remember a language once spoken fluently. Most professionals believe that if a child has been bilingual in early childhood, then the language area of the brain has been highly stimulated during growth and he will tend to learn languages easier.

But in the matter of a language once fluently spoken but forgotten, there is little evidence that that particular language will be any easier to re-learn than learning an entirely new language.

CHILDREN AND NATIVE CARE-GIVERS

Children do not relate to servants in the same way as adults. They do not have a fully developed sense of themselves and are in the process of building their identities through their identification with their adult care-givers. This theme becomes particularly critical in the case of younger children left in the charge of native care-givers all day, for they cannot clearly see the other person as someone from a different culture, speaking a different language. They do not have the cognitive tools to understand that they should withhold the identification process until their parents return at the end of the day. They are naturally going to assume many of the character traits of the care-giver.

If a child is left all day with a care-giver, he will become in many respects like that person. That is all right if the care-giver is a sweet person, but parents should consider if they are ready for the child to develop the traits of a person so different from themselves. Care-givers in one's own country usually come from the same culture. Overseas, a different situation is created which must be considered thoughtfully by parents.

Some parents can move around and their children have many different care-givers and still remain psychologically healthy. This occurs because the parents have a natural talent for maintaining contact with and understanding their child. Perhaps the child is born with enough psychological strength to cope with the changes.

But leaving a child during his early childhood for prolonged periods in the care of ever-changing care-givers, speaking different languages and coming from different cultures, can, I believe, be a dangerous flirtation with the child's destiny. I believe a great majority of children cannot go through such stress without being hurt in one way or another.

The case of a young boy named Robert illustrates this point. Robert spent his first two and a half years in India, closely attached to an Indian care-giver who lived in his backyard with her family. His first words were Hindi and he developed some fluency in the language. His father was then posted to Europe where the family stayed with his grandparents for most of the time. Naturally, he quickly forgot his Hindi words. When Robert was 3-and-a-half, the family moved to China. He had a Chinese *ayi* looking after him all day, and his parents were naturally impressed when Robert quickly learned to speak Chinese within the first year. The parents always considered their son to be a very bright boy and a fast learner, especially as his early childhood was essentially trouble-free except for typical pre-school behavioral problems.

I met Robert when he started school. He was 4-and-a-half at that time. He was referred to me by his teacher because he had learning difficulties which did not show up in any academic or IQ testing. The results showed he was a bright boy with no cognitive problems whatsoever. His personality was very sweet, and he was an easygoing boy.

But in class, he was unable to follow directions. He would sit dreaming in his own little world. As I came to know him better, I realized he was quite a disturbed little boy, wearing only a veneer of adjustment that hid an inner life of confusion and anxiety. The family was forced to move back to Europe to seek further professional help.

No one can say whether or not Robert would have turned out the same way had he lived in a stable environment. But it is my personal belief that Robert is by nature more sensitive than other children, and that all the moving around and being looked after by care-givers speaking different languages had been a disaster for his development.

LEARNING DISABILITIES

It is a fact that moving to another country inevitably leads to some form of crisis for a child. When a child is in crisis, both the strengths and the weaknesses of his personality will be magnified. Minor problems will be blown up to a degree almost unrecognizable. In such instances, parents will find themselves dealing with problems they were either completely unaware of, or which they believed to be minor. Overseas, everything becomes magnified as a general rule of thumb. Suddenly a minor problem at home becomes the major problem of the day.

I would like to use my own personal family experience to illustrate my point. My daughter Marie had what I thought at home to be a minor hearing disability. She was very late in language development, but that didn't seem to present any major problem. She made minor mistakes in pronunciation of her native Danish, but one could hardly hear them. When Marie was 9, we moved to China. I was convinced there were no problems to worry about. I was soon to think otherwise.

The first thing she had to do was learn English. She was not admitted to the international school because she couldn't speak English, so I enrolled her in a local prep school to bring her English up to an acceptable standard. This particular school had several classes all together in one room, so naturally it was very noisy.

Under normal circumstances, noise doesn't bother children much. But as my daughter had difficulties with auditory discrimination, she could not understand a single word. In fact, as time went on, I found she was virtually getting nothing out of her school day.

I am not a native English speaker myself, nor am I a teacher, so even though I tried to coach her for hours after school, it wasn't good enough. I engaged professional tutors and structured her day so that she could hear English being spoken as much as possible. Yet the language development continued to move slowly. I suddenly found myself with a daughter who had never seemed to have problems, placed in the worst possible situation for her. As a child psychologist, I was not at all proud of myself for not having foreseen this.

Marie's case illustrates how a little problem can become magnified in a move overseas. In my professional experience, her case is hardly exceptional.

I am presented often with another major problem with rather large implications for learning: children with inadequate organizational skills. These children may be very well structured within the context of a stable home, but are provoked during a move. This happens because everything in their daily life has to suddenly be restructured. The outer world becomes unpredictable, which can be difficult enough for an adult, but disastrous for a child with limited organizational skills.

Trouble also typically befalls a child with specific memory problems. It's true that school work anywhere in the world must be memorized, but when everything around a child suddenly changes and everything from streets to names must also be memorized – in a new language – the result can be unsettling.

I recommend that parents do not bring children overseas if there are any indicators whatsoever of learning disabilities. These children need continuity and experienced professionals to help them, and such individuals are in most instances not available overseas.

COMMON TYPES OF CHILDREN

When I think about the psychological implications for children living overseas, I find it almost impossible to think of children as a single group since they are so different and react so differently to the various situations. I find it more natural and practical to talk of different groups of children, or types, according to various dominant personality traits. That is, are they sensitive? Are they active? Are they young intellectuals?

At the risk of over-simplifying the wide variety of children, I feel that a summary of the most common types of children could give parents the opportunity of knowing their own child better.

The 'Intellectuals'

The group of children whom I like to identify as the 'intellectuals' are those whose strength lies in being academically alert. They are fast learners, often from the very beginning of school. These children are not necessarily more intelligent, although some might be. I'm speaking of those children who are just naturally interested in academia. They love school; they are alert in class; they are the first ones to raise their hands to answer a question. They take part in everything, listen carefully and are enthusiastic about projects.

These intellectual children are survivors in an international setting. An early school start and high academic demands, combined with an international school culture that values academic performance, certainly give these children a head start compared with other children. The demands of an ever-changing school system and those associated with moving around the world are easily met by these children with fast and flexible thinking.

But these children are not perfect, and while their portability within school is definitely a plus, that can also create an imbalance with their emotional development. Low self-esteem, followed by a lack of respect for others, are just two of the negative psychological situations created by intellectual dominance.

Barbara moved from England to an international school when she was 11-years-old. Considering that it was her first time living abroad, she settled in incredibly fast. Everything was so different from her culture at home, but she did not seem to mind much. She just did everything, including going to diplomatic receptions, as if she was already a woman of the world. She adjusted from her former life in the country to life in the city as if it only meant a change in the appropriate clothing.

Nobody, of course, does all of that kind of 'adjusting' without a reaction of some sort. Barbara still reacted as she always had to frustration. She became compulsive about her homework because it gave her respect in a school system which credited Honor Roll students with unreserved enthusiasm for their academic progress. She also became dominating and bossy, which nobody liked, but accepted because of her academic sovereignty.

The school culture obviously valued fast adjustment and academic progress over behavior, so Barbara had no need to change. And she didn't change much during her four years overseas. That was unfortunate. She was not challenged to develop other parts of her personality, as her survival in the international school culture did not demand that.

The 'Feeling/Sensitive' Child

Unlike the 'intellectuals', the 'feeling/sensitive' child who becomes a traveling child usually has trouble moving around. It takes that child a long time to settle down as he tries to sort out his feelings about the moving experience. He prefers deeper contacts with people, so that making a quick, superficial connection – more typical overseas where no one stays anywhere long – is not his strength. He can stare out of the window, or look at children playing in the playground without feeling compelled to run and join in. He is simply out of touch with instant friendships.

This is the type of child who does best in a school system in which he will have either the same teacher for a length of time or, at the very least, remain in the same school.

David is an example of this type of 'feeling/sensitive child'. Like Barbara, he comes from a similar Western country and school system. But he had many difficulties settling down in his new surroundings. He missed his friends and everything he had left at home, and spent a good deal of time daydreaming, writing letters, and looking at the pictures and memories he brought from home while feeling empty within his new environment.

During the first six months of school, he was in a very low mood. He spoke of a 'glass wall' which he felt separated him from the real world. At school, he did everything very slowly in the beginning. Small variations in the teaching system caused him many problems. For instance, he failed whenever there was a multiple-choice test because he had to think carefully about every choice. As time went on, though, he caught up. He slowly developed self-confidence in his new environment. Luckily, he stayed for four years, which gave him exactly the right amount of time to prove to himself that he could deal with the situation successfully. Had he moved before that period was up, he might have thought of himself for years as incompetent and stupid, despite the fact that he is a very intelligent boy.

The 'Active' Child

Some children express themselves more than others through sensations. They have a strongly developed set of senses. They like adventures and overcoming material obstacles. They like handling facts. They wanted to go see the world before the parents even started to think about moving overseas. These children are not intellectual in that they don't choose to occupy themselves over long periods of time with paper and pen.

The parents of these children always have to find something 'real' to do, like planting seeds, washing clothes, or hiking. Teachers tend to feel these active children lack the ability to fantasize because they are not interested in creating stories. They would rather live them. They are also not that interested in school work, especially at the younger ages. They may be slow learners in the early grades, which statistically is not a true measure of how they may do later in their school careers, for children differ greatly in the speed with which they learn to read and write.

The danger for the active child overseas will be deprivation of sensory stimulation. No playgrounds, no opportunities to ride bicycles, sitting in classrooms without windows – these are the 'stressful' situations for active children. Parents of this child will not win by forcing their child to practice writing or reading after the school day has ended. If it is important to do so, then strict time limits should be established after consulting the teacher.

ACCEPTING YOUR CHILD

No child is a purely 'intellectual', purely 'sensitive' or purely 'active' type. I'm speaking of the dominating character traits when I make those classifications. But I feel strongly that children can find and use their less prominent or even hidden traits if given the right opportunity.

If parents want to help their children realize their full potential and develop all facets of their personalities, they must first and foremost understand and accept their child for who he is, at any particular stage of his life.

To accept a feeling, sensitive child is to appreciate the quality of the way he feels and to help him find ways of expression. Books, music, and art are natural expressions of feelings. To accept a child who does not make friends easily, is to accept that being alone or together with only family is not the worst thing in the world. Certainly it is preferable for a child to have friends of his own age, but if he doesn't make them easily, it is not the end of the world.

Everybody experiences difficult periods in their lives, and sometimes one is thrown into a situation that does not capitalize on one's particular strengths. That is the time for introspection and for free examination of the conditions surrounding an individual. Eventually, the child will expand other areas of his personality, and cope the best way he can.

We do not know why, but if parents do not know and accept the child's starting point, then the child is bound to stay there for a much longer time than necessary. That is a psychological rule.

Chapter One

GLOBAL KIDS

On the surface, they look like typical middle-class children anywhere. They board a school bus near their home, kick a ball around a playground, or sit behind classroom desks pondering the complexities and futility of studying algebra. There is a twist to this story though. For children who move from world capital to world capital, home is not always a three-bedroom house in suburbia. It can be a diplomatic compound or military housing complex shut off completely from the local society, or a towering, luxury European-style apartment building. The playground might be neither green nor safe, a segregated enclave where local children may never play, or a concrete parking lot. Or it could be the most lavish Western playground a Third World child has ever seen. And the fellow classmates struggling with mathematics? They are usually multicultural, hailing from two dozen or more nations from all corners of the planet, or students of an exclusive boarding school where royalty sharpens pencils with ordinary folk.

Call them global nomads, mobile children, expat kids, military or foreign service brats, or third culture kids. Their collective name matters as little as their concepts of borders, which are significant merely as signposts for a lengthy wait at an immigration control booth at some hectic international airport. They take such bureaucratic frontiers in stride, almost ignoring them, just as they overlook another's accent or skin color. It is no wonder that the experts studying internationally mobile children hail them as the future mediators of the world.

For these offspring of diplomats, business people, soldiers, teachers, foreign experts, missionaries, journalists, or a variety of other international consultants, the world is a series of flights – long-haul flights in many instances – where the travel day ends in a new bedroom or hotel room. A few days later, there's usually a new school to check out, with unfamiliar teachers, students, and lunchroom. Sometimes, the new school is local, or one which is limited to their own nationality or religious persuasion; other times, it is open to the international community. Regardless, it is all new and strange, exciting and frightening at the same time. Their previous experience sometimes helps; they know a new place can be conquered. It can become familiar. For a year. Maybe two or three this time. Seldom longer than four years.

There are many reasons for living abroad. As a parent, never fool yourself into thinking that your decision to opt for an international life over a domestic one will not directly affect your children in very profound ways, both positive and negative. If a love of foreign languages and cultures has pushed you out into the world, your children will likely end up sharing your passion, especially if you make them active participants in your own learning experiences. When a parent seeks out better professional opportunities abroad or a higher quality of life, the child may also want to enjoy the same perquisites when he or she reaches adulthood. A commitment to improving standards of living for citizens of underprivileged Third World nations may equally be passed on to children who will forge second and often third generation careers in international development.

Likewise, parents who move overseas to run away from home and families – for whatever reasons, and they may be good ones – must recognize that too will have an influence on your children. When parents move abroad with the intention of never going back home on any regular basis, they are pulling up stakes for their children too. They will lose out on the stabilizing factor of a permanent home – even if it's just a summer cottage, which *they* may need even if *you* don't anymore. The emotionally charged issue of rootlessness and the concept of 'home' for a traveling child are just two of the many issues which will be addressed in this book.

Today's global children appear to shake off jet lag as easily as they change their clothes, yet they are in a constant state of adjustment. When they are young, they are extremely portable. They can be easily distracted from the troublesome aspects of an adjustment period which their parents may not be able to ignore. Every day may spawn a new adventure for the youngster: a long plane ride to an unknown but exciting destination with a flight attendant handing out presents; a hotel room, a luxurious coffee shop, or a room service tray on which their hamburger and french fries may be served as frivolously as haute cuisine; a new apartment building with local characters to be met, hallways and stairwells to be explored. Even a teenager, in the midst of the trauma caused by being yanked away from friends, will find something exciting in the new environment faster than his parents.

Numerous opportunities for exotic travel also motivate many foreign service and other international families. These adventures provide memories which I believe will stand the test of time. They say a child's memory is short, but I will be amazed if my daughter Lilly will ever forget the experience in Chengde of gliding for 15 torturous minutes up a Chinese mountainside in a rickety, open-air chair lift which looked like it had last been serviced in the time of the Qing emperors – for whom the imperial retreat of Chengde was created. She was 8-years-old at the time. Up we went on this flying park bench, shakily gliding over steep canyons and ravines, ostensibly to relax from our hardship posting in Beijing. Lilly and her father were in the first chair. In the rear, her brother Jamie, four years younger, shrieked in his chair while I sat gripping him in a kind of vacant way, too frozen to even lift the video camera at my side. My purse was slipping out through an open slat behind me, but I was immobilized with fear. All this trauma, merely to check out the 'Sledgehammer', a weird-looking rock formation, a tourist site for which the area is noted.

"That was the *tensest* experience I've ever had in my entire life," she informed her equally tense mother when the last canyon had been crossed and the chairs were mercifully on their way down the mountain without us.

"I'm walking down. I don't care how long it takes. I'm not going to die in Chengde!" Her mind was definitely made up on this one.

Naturally, she relented – and coped – less than half an hour later and enjoyed the voyage down. I wish I could report making the same adjustment, but in my view, a canyon is a canyon, just as dangerous-looking on the way down as on the way up.

Traveling children experience childhoods radically different from the ones their parents may have led as children. I certainly never glided over Chinese canyons on a chair lift growing up in the heart of a Canadian city like Toronto. It was a big thrill if we went across the border to Buffalo, New York, for a day of shopping, returning at dusk wearing five layers of new clothing which didn't fool customs officials for a minute. While your own mobile kids may have crisscrossed the globe many times even before they were old enough to go to school, and lived in cultures as startlingly different as East is from West, you may never have strayed from your own street or neighborhood until high school. A global child may be born in one foreign capital and never have lived in the country stamped on his passport until he begins school. His father or mother may never have been on an airplane until adolescence. Moreover, the lives of mobile children can't – and shouldn't – be compared in any way with those of their friends and relatives back home who have never traveled or moved anywhere before.

As an adult, you may secretly envy the ease with which your children adapt to their new surroundings. Adults cannot surrender themselves with quite the same wide-eyed abandon their children can. A parent's national identity is too ingrained to relinquish so easily. But don't be fooled by the superficial veneer of adjustment which many children put on to please their parents. Behind their smiles may lurk anxieties which should be dealt with right away.

Parents can easily provide the comfort and emotional support which makes possible their child's smooth transition from culture to culture – and a continuing healthy climate for their child's natural development. Parents can also provide suitable positive role models from which their children can take their cues.

Best of all, when living overseas, parents become their child's teachers outside the confines of a classroom. I might have been scared witless sitting in a shaky chair lift over a vast expanse of China, but my fear was a minor sketch in the larger canvas my children were viewing. My husband and I were introducing them to new sights, sounds, and smells. On that day in Chengde, the lesson was on a particular region of China; on other days, on other trips, we roamed streets and markets and met other people, witnessed other ways of living. Wherever we saw something they didn't comprehend, or found frightening by its difference, we explained so they could understand and appreciate how other cultures live. When confusion reigned, we could enlighten as best as we knew how. Not an easy task, but an excellent opportunity not many parents have, and an unbelievably enriching process for everyone.

This book is designed to assist parents – especially mothers who shoulder the majority of day-to-day responsibilities – who are preparing for an international move or currently raising their children while on overseas postings. Children living abroad will require different nurturing and support from that which their non-traveling parents needed when they were growing up. This support will differ for each stage of childhood and adolescence.

While this book can't possibly claim to include each and every issue associated with child rearing overseas, it will offer guidance on some of the most critical ones. Based on first-hand experiences of children, parents, educators, and medical resource people, *A Parent's Guide* will provide practical advice and emotional reassurance to mobile parents traveling the globe with children in tow. Hopefully, for every question I am unable to answer due to the limitations of space, my words will trigger other important questions which parents need to ask not only of the corporation or government assigning them overseas, but of themselves as parents. Do you know your children well enough to make the decision to go abroad? Do they have a learning

disability which won't be catered to by an international school? Are you setting your child up for loss of self-esteem? An unsuccessful adaptation? Parents need to develop their own checklist for knowing and understanding how their child will cope with an international move.

My own opportunities to research this subject and offer observations and advice obviously come from two subjects being observed from close range – my own two children who travel as a result of their father's career in the Canadian foreign service. Both children are examples of mobility and portability, especially when it comes to schools. Lilly was born in Bangkok in 1983, began kindergarten in Canada, attended first grade at Taipei American School, and second and third grades at the International School of Beijing. She's currently back at the same Canadian school where she attended kindergarten. Jamie was born in Ottawa in 1987, attended nursery school at the tender age of 2 while living in Taiwan, and an all-day pre-school in Beijing just after turning 3. Returning to Canada for kindergarten was like another posting to him. Watching their development – both scholastically and more important to me, emotionally – has provided insights, many of them humorous although not perhaps at the time, which I will be passing along in these pages. Much of my research on this subject has been by osmosis, after so many years of listening and learning from other international parents.

I believe that most of the issues I address in *A Parent's Guide* transcend borders. Whether it be Bangkok or Paris, children must cope with new surroundings and a new lifestyle which, to them, will bring confusion and unsettledness. Parents are the only constant in that cultural whirl so would do well to recognize what their children are going through in order to bring some order and security to their ever-changing world.

Raising happy, well-adjusted children is always a challenge for parents, regardless of where they live in the world. Parents of mobile kids have an even more daunting task when you throw in all the curves, unknowns, and dangerous looking canyons associated with life in another, often drastically different culture.

Parenting issues overseas are not that radically different from those that parents face if they stay in their own country. Overseas, however, all the issues are magnified because traditional life supports are absent. Grandparents or close friends are not around the corner to help out in an emergency, medical services may not be the same, and housing may be cramped or conversely so lavish that everyone loses sight of reality.

Above all else, parents should trust their instincts about what's best for their children. But it can't hurt to hear how other people have coped. Parents of teenagers may be reassured to learn that when their young adult screams, "You're ruining my life!" upon hearing news of a move, followed by, "I don't want to go," he won't be the first teenager to do so. Nor will he be the first to hide in a bedroom for the first months overseas, with headphones providing a wall of music to block out the new and unfamiliar environment. Other parents can assure you that gradually your teenager will emerge from his safe haven and start a new life. If he's been telling you how much he hates the post, try eavesdropping – just a little bit – on his conversations with his peer group. Rather than complaints, you may hear how much he actually is enjoying himself and appreciating the opportunity to learn and travel abroad. Parents of toddlers, who may be clinging to you for dear life, can take comfort in knowing that other parents have been through the same trying period. I know, because I spent a year in Taipei trying to detach a frightened 2-year-old boy from my body.

To mobile children, the concept of 'global village' is their reality. The world, and their broadened perspective on it, is truly home. Their parents' overseas careers, especially if combined with sensitivity to their children's unique upbringing, provide a passport to an extraordinary childhood with a lasting, positive legacy in their adult lives.

Chapter Two

YOU'RE RUINING MY LIFE!
Getting Ready to Move Abroad

"I was scared of getting blown away, basically."

—a young Canadian boy's pre-departure anxiety about
moving to a country with political problems

Despite the harrowing approach to its harbor-side airport, Hong Kong has always been my idea of a fantasy posting in the Far East. The notorious white-knuckled landing there, infamous among Asia travellers because of the close proximity between giant passenger jets and Kowloon clotheslines, supplies the perfect introduction to the life-on-the-edge attitude which permeates Hong Kong like the smell of its fragrant harbor.

I have always dreamed of living there. To me, its vestiges of the old colonial expatriate life, combined with an end-of-an-empire frenetic energy, make Hong Kong the quintessential foreign assignment.

So on the day my foreign service husband came home and announced his decision to study Mandarin (at the time, we were living in our home base near Ottawa between postings), I was absolutely thrilled. I knew we could count on living for one year in Hong Kong for his Chinese language training program before moving onto his assignment in Beijing. At last, I thought, my fantasy posting was about to come true!

Then, almost as abruptly as his decision to study Chinese was made, a second decision shattered my dream. On a wintry night months later, my husband returned home from the airport after several weeks' tour in China, shook the snow off his coat, and announced, "Forget Hong Kong. They want me to go to Taipei instead. For a year." With that, he finished taking off his coat and headed into the kitchen to make a cup of tea. As a throwaway, he added, "I think it will be better there for the kids."

Later, he would come to regret his decision. After a lightning evaluation of the quality of life in Taipei (he was there less than 24 hours to look around) he hardly had enough time to properly assess the Taiwanese capital with two young children in mind. If he had, he would have noticed the absence of parks, public recreational facilities, and the 18-month waiting list for the only expatriate club in town just for starters. And then there was the air, or complete lack of it, and the exorbitant price of absolutely everything, especially babysitters. Just the kind of place to be trapped at home with a contrary 2-year-old boy.

That bad news was in the future. Then, I had to wipe the despair off my face, slap on a smile and keep it plastered there during months of preparation for our move. There lies one key to a successful (or unsuccessful, depending on what you do next) beginning to an international move with children. I'm referring to the kind of assignment when you as the parent, especially the mother, aren't exactly thrilled about your destination. You must learn to do what I did: I had to very quickly get used to an idea which definitely wasn't my first choice.

ACCEPTING THE IDEA OF THE MOVE

I had two clear options on the day my husband informed me about the switch in destination: I could get used to the idea of moving to Taipei then and there, or I could get used to it eventually. There was clearly absolutely nothing to gain by pouting or constantly reminding him that his diplomatic skills of negotiation and consensus had somehow been misplaced. Everyone would have been off to a bad start.

With children of any age, parents must put the best face forward and avoid imposing preconceived notions, prejudices, and fears onto the younger generation. Parents – and especially the mother who is frequently the emotional touchstone before, during, and after an international assignment – provide important positive role models. Children of all ages take their cues from you. If you're giving off bad feelings, you know someone is receiving them loud and clear. Accept that you are moving, even if it's to a place which may not be your first choice, and then press on with your preparations. Watching their parents get on with life will not only help mobilize the children, it will also shape a positive attitude about the adventure from day one.

If your family is having a difficult time adjusting to the idea of a move, it may be comforting to know that all families, even professional traveling families who move every few years, often take the news of an assignment with a mixed bag of reactions. Families who have been at home base for several years may find the idea of moving a welcome relief. At last! We're getting out again! For others, who have only been home for little more than a year, the thought of another assignment is daunting – and exhausting. There hasn't been enough time to feel at home before hitting the international road again. Where it is the first time for an international move, the excitement is usually high, but combined with tension from a fear of the complete unknown.

Other families may be hearing of a cross-assignment. This can mean they don't even get to return home for a few years to recharge their sense of their own culture. Often, that news is not taken well either. The family may have just adapted to one new culture, only to find they must now switch gears and think about another one, perhaps on the other side of the world.

The wife of a British diplomat once confessed to me that her reaction to news of one of her husband's postings did not exactly thrill her. She'd seen the country they were headed for as a tourist and had not cared for it too much. But she had met her husband when he was studying the language of that destination, so as she put it, "where did she think she was going?"

The unifying theme to each and every move is your complete acceptance of what is to come – and your positive presentation of that acceptance to your children. If mommy and daddy are happy about the move, there is hope for the children.

TELLING YOUR CHILDREN ABOUT THE MOVE

Your children, especially older ones, will probably know long before it becomes official that a move is in the wind. The clues will be obvious to them: snippets of overheard telephone conversations about passports or visas, strange people coming into the house to estimate the cost of moving furniture or the value of a piece of art, a workman or two fixing up a long-standing broken toilet to make way for a tenant. These are all early signs of a pending move and will likely tip them off. They may also begin to feel a certain tension in the air while their parents begin to adjust to the idea of their marriage going international.

They won't be surprised when you finally tell them, but it's still best not to casually mention it while driving to school or the grocery store. An international move is a major life event. Treat it like one. Plan a family conference and gather everyone together so that there is ample opportunity to ask questions. Just about everyone I have spoken to on this subject agrees that the dinner table is the best place for announcements like these. Make it special. It's a big, exciting news event, and if you present it in a 'special' forum, the message will be conveyed to your children that it is not an everyday, casual event.

Children must also be made to feel they play a role in such a major decision as moving abroad. They need to know their opinions and feelings count, so hear them out. Their opposition to the idea may not necessarily change the circumstances; the decision to move still stands. They must now learn to live with that decision. But at least you have given them the opportunity to register their views which will lessen some of their feelings of loss of control over their lives.

Be prepared for a negative reaction from children past the first golden 12 years. "You're ruining my life!" will likely be the response if your teenager is in the middle of high school and reluctant to leave friends behind. Don't immediately respond with platitudes which your teenager will not listen to anyway. Let them sulk for a while. Sometimes an idea needs time to sink in. Give your teenager that time and space to digest the news.

Don't try to be cute and accidentally overwhelm your children. By that I mean don't decide that since you're moving to Thailand or Mexico you should announce the move in a local Thai or Mexican restaurant. There will be time later, before moving day, to introduce children to the culinary culture. At this point, spicy Thai soup or a Mexican enchilada may incite the child to riot completely against the move.

And one more tip: don't bother telling your children to keep the news a secret. It's pointless anyway. Within 24 hours, their entire school will know. In some instances, this news will give your children instant status so don't deny them their 15 minutes as a celebrity.

ANSWERING THEIR QUESTIONS

Before announcing the move, make sure you have done as much homework as possible. Come prepared to answer the questions you know your children may have. If it's possible, try getting brochures, a video, or some children's books (folk tales from foreign countries are terrific with younger children) to also have on hand for the grand pronouncement. Some people actually read travel brochures out loud like stories to younger children. Older children may enjoy seeing travel brochures of nearby areas where you may travel together as a family.

Regardless of age, children will have questions which fall into at least the following categories, so before breaking the news, try to have some information available to answer these questions:

- school: what kind of school? how big? how many grades? where is it located? is it American, international, or local? is it co-ed? is it hard? will there be a lot of homework? what about extracurricular activities? are there lots of after-school sports? is there a school uniform or is it a free-for-all designer school? is there a McDonald's nearby?
- house: where are you going to live – in a house or an apartment? in a compound or on an ordinary street? will they have their own bedroom? will there be servants? will there be a playground nearby? will they walk to school or take a bus? will they have a swimming pool?
- kids their age: will there be lots of potential friends? will there be kids of the same nationality?
- the new country: what is it like? how many people? what is the climate? how far is it from home? is it a democracy? are the people happy? is it a rich or a poor country?
- things to see: what are the sights? what's special about the country which we'll be able to see? can we travel a lot within the country?
- things to do: will there be swimming? sports? picnic places? movie theaters? radio stations? malls? discos?
- what people eat: what's the food like? will we be able to eat peanut butter? do we eat local or Western food?
- how do people live: will we have neighbors in slums? mansions? do they dress a certain way?

HOLDING BACK INFORMATION

Some parents actually prefer to tell their children very little beforehand and literally move to a post without advance information. A Dutch foreign service wife I spoke to said that before one of their postings, she and her husband simply announced at the dinner table to their young daughters (then aged 3 and 6) that they were going on a big trip but didn't elaborate on their destination.

There was a good reason for this, explained the mother. The year was 1986, and they were being posted from The Hague to their embassy in Manila, only months after Corazon Aquino and her People Power toppled the regime of Ferdinand Marcos. As she herself was getting astonished reactions from friends ("You're going to Manila?! Now?"), she decided it was best to play down where they were going and wait until they had arrived to fill in her daughters. She simply didn't want to overwhelm them.

Information given out beforehand can often just get lost in the emotional chaos which everyone is experiencing in getting ready to move. You can tell your children things, and they can hear, but nothing really sinks in. This is not much different from an adult pre-departure briefing where details get recorded in notebooks but aren't truly comprehended until you are actually in the country. As a parent, you alone can gauge the amount of information you feel your children are capable of absorbing. There will be lots of time to learn facts and figures about the country later. In the early days after hearing of your assignment, it pays to go slowly, and not over-stimulate children with information they can't process without getting upset.

Don't think you are doing your children any favors by withholding the news. Tell them as soon as possible, not so much because they hold veto power over the move, but because keeping them in the dark could fuel their feelings of resentment if they are not happy with the news. They will justifiably demand to know: "Why didn't you tell me sooner?"

To get everyone enthusiastic, make your talking points the fun things such as family adventures, decorating a brand new bedroom, or, if you're moving to a tropical country from a frigid northern climate, the joys of being able to swim or play tennis outside all year round. If the opposite is the case, extol the virtues of skating and hockey. Talk about the new culture and how exciting it will be to learn about it.

DEALING WITH EMOTIONAL UPHEAVALS

Despite careful efforts to avoid over-stimulating your children, emotional swings are still bound to occur. Everyone is in a high state of excitement and experiencing its partner, anxiety, and that's a breeding ground for mood swings. Every day may have a number of emotional peaks and valleys, for you and for your children.

Watch for obvious signs of a child's internal chaos. Insomnia is one of the most common indicators of a child's anxiety. Children of all ages will have the problem of falling asleep, and then waking up in the middle of the night to think about the pending move. Eating habits may also go awry; there is bed wetting or return to thumb-sucking in youngsters. Sullenness, outbursts of tears, and frustrations over things which don't normally frustrate will also point to some children's unhappiness and anxiety. You will ask them what's wrong, and they respond that they don't know. That's a sure sign of anxiety.

Younger children may cling to stuffed toys or anchor themselves to an obscure piece of your house like a chair. Teenagers don't want to engage in any conversation about the move. These and other behavior patterns you can't even anticipate will be the reactions and coping mechanisms of a child trying to deal with the idea of changing locales.

If your patience runs out because you're dealing with all the practical details of moving a household, try not to take your frustration with the moving company out on your family. As an adult, you can articulate your frustration. Children cannot. They will not understand how an international move is connected to the fact that they have an upset stomach. The parent must explain things again and again. You may find yourself repeating the same limited information about a new apartment or school over and over. But while you struggle to maintain your patience, just remember that each time you are repeating yourself, you are also reassuring your youngsters.

Watch for so-called perfect children who seem to be taking it all in their stride with no ill effects. That may be true. For now. But somewhere in their mind, thoughts are turning over, some of them fearful. Anxiety or fear may come out in some form, or find an outlet when you least expect it. Children are not robots.

Avoid placing extra stress onto an already overloaded emotional agenda. Some hectic, stress-producing pre-departure activities can't be helped, but others can be avoided by careful planning. For instance, don't move out of your house so early that you end up camping out for a couple of months in a relative's spare room. You are already packing up a major household. If you end up packing and repacking your traveling luggage half a dozen times before you even leave home, the entire family's stress threshold will simply burst.

DISCUSSING YOUR CHILDREN'S FEARS

"Will I make any friends?"

Of all the questions your children are likely to ask – and be gravely concerned with – new friends will seem to take top billing. It begins with their fear that they will miss, or be forgotten by, the friends they currently have. And then the fear transforms itself to making friends 'over there'.

Tackle each of their fears systematically. If they are worried about friends at home, or the current posting, suggest practical ways of keeping in touch. Letters are the obvious way, but videotaped letters, faxes, audio cassettes of conversations, and the occasional phone call (depending on the distance) can easily be done. Summer reunions or any future get-togethers can be suggested. The message to your children simply is that you as the parent will be doing all you can to help them stay in touch with their friends, but they also have some responsibility to this.

As for new friends, a lot will depend on the age of your children. Pre-school children will immediately be part of the play group or nursery school circuit if the mother dives right in and makes connections. School-age children will have opportunities for new friends from day one of school, but a lot will depend on both the personality of the child and the social interaction of the parents.

School friends, for some, will come easily. Outgoing children will turn to their neighbor in class or the person sitting beside them on the school bus and engage in instant friendship. Quiet children may need some help from their parents and especially their mothers. A Canadian friend of mine who moved to Washington, D.C., for her first posting couldn't believe what she had to do in order to make friends for her young children. As Washington isn't a Third World post where an embassy or local community club may welcome newcomers, she had to face cold-looking, closed front doors along a residential Virginia street. Out she went and started to knock on the doors where she had observed young children going in and out. She introduced herself, her children, her nationality, and other relevant information and set up play dates for her youngsters. If your child is worried about making friends, offer assurance that you as a parent are prepared to do what my Canadian friend did. Reassurance will go a long way to helping your child cope with that fear.

Friendship for the teenager is serious business. It combines not only social interaction, but the more critical issues of self-image and self-esteem as well. Making friends becomes part of how the teenager is being perceived, accepted, and even in which social set ('in' or 'out' crowd) he or she belongs. If it's possible before moving day, try to find an older teenager or young adult who has moved around a lot to talk to your own teenagers about finding their way around a new school – like finding the cool place to eat lunch – and making friends. This doesn't always work if you match up teenagers of the exact age because your teenagers may not to respond to someone their own age who has the confidence they may be lacking. Somebody slightly older, and thus non-threatening and non-competitive, may work better.

Fear of the unknown, not surprisingly, is the other big challenge for parents to tackle with their children. This category can include fear of the new school, bus, neighborhood, local people, culture, and so on. It helps if somebody in the family has traveled to your assigned country before. If that hasn't happened, and your children are particularly fearful, a case can be made for participating in what orientation companies call 'look-see' visits. These are essentially reconnaissance tours before moving day. One parent, often the father who is already doing business in the country, arranges to visit the school, the new apartment, and professional moving consultants. He talks to all concerned and often takes pictures to show his children. International school teachers report that it is not unusual for advance 'movies' to be made at the school, and they support such initiative when it is done to allay a child's fears.

Then there are political fears. I talked to a Canadian boy who was 11 when his family moved for the first time ever in his life – to a country in the middle of political turmoil. His father had gone ahead for a 'look-see' visit and got caught up in the political events. At first, the boy worried about his father's safe return. In the weeks leading up to his move, after his father had returned to Canada unharmed, he didn't worry about the fact that he had never been on an airplane before or had never been abroad. He was scared stiff of getting caught up in events at their new post, or as he put it, "I was scared of getting blown away, basically." He talked a bit about his fears to his best friend in Canada before he left, but for the most part, he had to wait until he was physically on the ground at their new post before he could put his fears to rest. Because his images of the place had come from television features filled with pictures of soldiers and tanks, just the sight of such normal things as "trees which were the same height" along the airport road helped calm him down. The unknown suddenly was in sight; the fears vanished.

Teenagers fear a temporary loss of independence – having to travel with and rely on parents again after several years of freedom of movement. Teenagers may be wondering: Does this move mean I have to hang out with my kid sister or brother? Will I be able to shop for my own clothes or will mom have to take me? Will I be able to get around on buses? Can I drive there? Any issue which pertains to teenagers' sense of separate identity from parents will most certainly be spinning around in their heads in the months before the move.

Anticipate these fears, have some answers for them, and openly discuss them with teenage children. It helps to have it worked out in your own mind just how protective you plan to be, which can be very difficult to do. Always leave the subject open to further discussion; you have not got all the facts yet. Reserve your final opinions until you have seen what it is like 'over there'.

Be sure to encourage every member of the family to share how they are *feeling* about the move. Don't just discuss logistics and practicalities all the time. Honest communication about feelings may be more useful in the long run than deciding what to sell or buy.

WHEN TO CONSIDER BOARDING SCHOOL

The question of boarding school will depend on several factors, especially on where you are being posted. If your children are teenagers and the local international school doesn't go beyond mid-level high school (or the city is not a great place to bring impressionable young adults), then you may be considering very seriously the idea of leaving your children behind in a boarding school.

Your nationality may also be pushing you in this direction. The British, for instance, appear to favor boarding school for their children. Your child's scholastic background could also force you to consider the boarding school option.

International schools are generally a lot tougher than the schools back home. Not everyone does well at them, and many students drop a few points in their averages. International schools also do not normally cater to students with learning disabilities. (There will be more on this subject in Chapter Six.) If you are aware of any handicaps which your children have exhibited so far in their school careers, listen carefully to what international school directors and guidance counsellors are telling you, not what you want to hear. Even they will be telling you not to bring your children overseas or to expect the schools to accommodate them if there is any disability.

I have heard the same comment over and over again when visiting international and American schools: they *do not* cater to students with learning disabilities, and parents of such children should seriously consider their decision to move their children abroad. This is a prime reason to consider a boarding school where the child's special needs will be addressed.

THE BOARDING SCHOOL OPTION

If this is the first time you are examining this issue, you may like to know that your emotional angst has been shared by many parents before you. From talking to parents, I have learned this is not a decision that anyone takes lightly, or escapes from without some feelings of guilt. The nagging question seems to be, "Are we doing the right thing for our child?"

At this stage of the posting cycle, when you are about to leave home while your child stays behind to begin boarding school for the first time, you can be sure that nobody, not you or your child, is very happy about life. We're back to that fear of the unknown. Your child will be wondering if he will make any friends, or like the teachers, the food, and the general living conditions of the boarding school. You are also wondering the same, along with feeling general anxiety about the quality of your child's education and if teachers or administrators will ever write you a single letter.

If you have done your own homework about the school, you should not allow your fears to run wild. If you are just beginning your research, here are a few suggestions.

Some schools allow children to spend a summer term as a trial run so ask about that possibility. How do you even find a suitable school? Word of mouth, according to most parents who have been through this exercise. Find other parents who have had successful experiences with various schools and talk to them about your fears and uncertainties. Other parents and their children often make the best guides through this educational maze. Follow up by contacting your government's ministry of education which may provide a state-wide, province-wide, or country-wide listing of all schools. Britain, not surprisingly, has an organization strictly for schools which cater to expatriate children.

Make sure you and your partner agree on the idea of boarding school. One parent displaying emotional uncertainty is just the opening an equally uncertain child will look for when he or she starts begging to remain with parents. Many parents, it seems, also prefer to send their sons to strict, highly regimented schools while selecting less disciplined learning institutions for their daughters. Try to reach an agreement on this issue as well.

Parents must present a united front. Children are naturally going to resist the idea at first, and may absolutely hate the experience in the beginning. Eventually, most children get used to it. If you are in the midst of this debate at this particular time in the posting cycle, stress that fact to them.

STRATEGIES TO GET EVERYTHING DONE

Make a plan. Any plan. But have one. I can't stress the importance of systematically organizing all the preparations you will need to complete before moving day. It's hard enough to think of everything when it's just two of you, but when you add children to the equation the list can become cumbersome. It can be manageable with proper planning.

Your children's pre-departure checklist easily warrants a separate notebook or file so if you haven't already started one, put down this book and get to it immediately. Your distraction level at this point is incredibly high. Writing things down, especially in some organized fashion, serves the dual purpose of reminding you of something which needs to get done, and physically forces you to take a few minutes to sit down, think, take a few deep breaths, and probably make note of something you have overlooked.

While there will certainly be preparations unique to your own situation, there are some basic ones which most parents will eventually find themselves thinking about. It is those areas of responsibility I can include here as a guide:

1. Contacting Somebody 'Over There'

Some organizations make this task easier. If you are moving to work for an embassy, a mission, a military base, a large multi-national company (as just a few examples), you will find there is somebody already stationed where you are going whose job it is to look after newly arrived (or about to arrive) families like your own. Write, fax, telex, or phone this individual as soon as possible with your list of questions about schools, housing, transportation, or any other information you would prefer to know before you leave. You may get a package of information about the place you're headed for if you give enough lead time.

When there isn't such a person in place, there are other alternatives. If you are outside the embassy community, you

could still try contacting yours to see if they can recommend any local consultants or individuals who may be willing to talk to you beforehand. If the embassy turns up nothing, try contacting the local Better Business Bureau or Chamber of Commerce. If you are a church-goer, contact the local minister or priest. They may have some suggestions.

Traveling with children, you also have one big advantage: you can contact the local international school or your own nation's school for information. (In every major post, there are separate schools for French, German, Japanese, and often Indian and other nationals.) When your children are about to enroll, the administration of these schools will in most cases go out of their way to help you with your questions. After all, it is in their best interests if it means your children will arrive relatively calm and cool having been forewarned and armed with advance inform- ation. If there is a private school in your city catering to children of diplomats, contact the headmaster or headmistress to put you in touch with the diplomatic parents who live in your city and send their children as day students to that school. You may match up nationalities and get great information.

If all of the above fails to put you in contact with someone 'over there', I suggest while still at home, you contact the embassy of the country you are headed for and talk to somebody there. Perhaps some official based in your home country can put you in touch with a fellow countryman willing to help.

2. Pre-departure Briefings

Once you have made contact with the other side of the world, look around your home base to see who can provide some briefing programs before you leave the country. Once again, embassies and international aid organizations are diligent in providing pre-departure briefings on the country you are headed for and on related international subjects like culture shock. Any company sending you overseas will also be able to put you in touch with professional briefing companies or individuals who may be able to give you a few ideas of what lies ahead.

Formal briefings for children are still quite limited as briefing programs seem to focus primarily on the employee and his overseas effectiveness. Briefings for the spouse and family, while offered by some briefing companies, are still limited in scope and, in my opinion, honesty. Nobody wants to hear anything negative. As a responsible parent, be sure to ask about the negatives as well as the positives. You aren't doing your child any favors by lying to them by omission.

In the absence of formal briefing workshops for children, here are a few exercises and activities professionals often provide for traveling children of any age:

- The Fresh Start Exercise: Point out to your children that absolutely nobody in the place you are moving to knows them or anything about them. While that can be frightening, it can also be liberating. It's like a child's joy at starting a new school year with fresh notebooks, free of doodling and markings, or making New Year resolutions. Remind your children that nobody knows they may have messed up an important test or a piano recital. Your children can set new goals for themselves in any area of their lives.

Give them a piece of paper and divide the space into two categories: I WILL TRY TO and I WILL TRY NOT TO. In this way, they can view the posting abroad as a fresh start to turn over a new leaf and better themselves as individuals.

- I'm Glad to Leave Because... Saying goodbye to people and places doesn't have to be a sad experience. There are some parts of life children can be glad to leave, whether it is the school bully or a piano teacher they have never liked. Once again, provide your child with a piece of paper with two titles: I AM GLAD TO LEAVE and I AM LOOKING FOR-WARD TO. See what answers they come up with and then discuss them.

3. Children's Pre-departure Tasks

Children feel a lot more involved in the moving process if they are assigned tasks. Not only will they feel they are contributing to the moving process, they may also take some of the burden off their mother. Here are a few suggestions which once again can be adapted for any age group:

- Return all borrowed items. Books should go back to the library, and toys and games back to friends. And if friends have borrowed something, now is the time to get it back.
- Update or start a good address book. Have your children compile a comprehensive, current directory of the addresses and birthdays of all of their friends or teachers with whom they may want to correspond. If your children give their friends a stamped, self-addressed postcard with the new over-seas address on it, they can be assured of some mail from home soon after arrival.
- Start a scrapbook or photo album which contains everything your children want to remember about their old school and neighborhood.

- Allow each child to organize his or her own goodbye party.
- Have your children organize belongings into things to give away, throw away, or take abroad.

4. Medical Examinations

Not unlike pre-departure briefings focused primarily on the employee, medical screenings that exclude children are another phenomenon which apparently crosses over nationalities. When an employee is assigned overseas, the employee and spouse may be examined by a team of medical experts – often including a psychiatrist – to identify any problems. Children, on the other hand, seem to be the parents' sole responsibility.

Parents must make sure they have thought of every possible pre-departure examination – from inoculations, to eyes and ears, and any other nagging problem which may become inflamed abroad where there may be only a village medical person and not a specialist. Don't forget to stock up on any prescription drugs your child may need. And visit the dentist too. You may not get a proper cleaning and X-ray for many months to come. Parents of teenagers wearing braces should find out if there is an orthodontist at the new post, or at least one easily accessible by air.

An international school nurse told me she was shocked to meet a large number of parents who arrived unprepared not only in the matter of proper inoculations, but also ignorant of both local medical facilities and emergency evacuation procedures. Embassy people are sheltered by their governments in this area; business people are vulnerable. If your assignment is corporate, do not leave home without some written assurances from your company for both medical coverage and contingency plans for unexpected emergencies. Don't take any chances when traveling with children. A broken arm, a burst appendix, or other emergencies may occur. Be fully prepared. There is more discussion on medical matters in Chapter Eight.

5. Passports, Visas and Legal Issues

First piece of advice – when moving internationally, make sure each of your children has a separate passport. If your child is listed on either parent's passport, you will not be allowed to leave the country alone. You will be stopped at passport control unless you have the child listed on your passport physically with you. And make sure you understand all visa requirements for the entire family. If you are planning a trip en route, be sure to check visa requirements for stopovers.

Second piece of important advice – when you have passport pictures taken, order extra copies. Those little passport pictures have a way of being useful in hundreds of ways you can't possibly anticipate, from school applications to future visa applications. So make sure you leave home with several dozen stashed away for future use.

Before you leave the country, meet with a lawyer or a family member to whom you have given power of attorney over your affairs while you are away. Make sure all emergency contingencies are covered in the event of accidents while traveling. Wills must be made out and, as grim as it is to think about, guardians for your children should be appointed before leaving home in the event of an accident while you are living abroad.

6. School Records

Copies of your children's scholastic records should be sent ahead with school application forms as quickly as possible to help the international schools make a proper grade placement for your children. The originals should be hand-carried when you travel in case the copies have gone astray in the mail. International school teachers I spoke to said it was amazing how many school records are 'stuck in the shipment' somewhere and actually never provided for the school's inspection.

At the same time as you forward school records, international school teachers also recommend you send either a class workbook or sample of a composition or test for your children's future teachers to examine. The work they have done the previous year often tells a much clearer story than grades do about where your child is academically, especially something handwritten by your child.

If your children's current teachers are not too overworked, you might ask if they would mind writing a personal note about your children which you can forward to the new school. The more information of this nature that you can provide the new school, the better able the new staff will be to help your children adapt.

7. Creating a Family History
One Canadian ambassador and his wife always decorate the family quarters of their official residence with a combination of the requisite Canadiana knick-knacks which our government provides as furnishings worldwide, and family memorabilia. Children's sculptures, drawings, paintings, and pictures are everywhere one looks. Their entire family history provides the decor in not only a colorful and pleasing way, but in a warm, familiar, almost soothing atmosphere. Their three daughters are all grown up now, but clearly the strong role they played in the international life of this family was important.

Not all mementos and pieces of art need be kept, but decide early to save highlights or particularly good samples of letters, photos, or even postcards so that everyone can participate in creating this portable family history.

Our own family started videotaping holidays and family reunions back in Canada. Everyone gets annoyed with me every time I pull out the camera, but how much we all enjoy looking back at these pictures, especially the children who grow at such an alarming pace that even a tape six months old seems dated.

Don't exclude your children from the creation of a family corporate history. Assign each child a task, as simple as saving his or her own paintings or keeping photo albums up to date each time a new batch of pictures are developed. Before leaving the country, ask your children what they would like to have a memento of and help facilitate it. We commissioned a neighbor who is an artist to give us a rendering of our panoramic view of the Gatineau Hills where we live outside of Ottawa. His pastel was on display for us in our Taipei and Beijing apartments and has provided many hours of nostalgic pleasure.

8. What to Pack

Pack this newly created family history collection for starters. When it comes to moving children halfway around the world, or even just down the street, it's important to move just about *everything* important to them. There may be people who disagree, but personally, I wish it were possible to pack up my children's rooms and put them on the plane with us wherever we are going.

Children's bedrooms are their sanctuaries. The more familiar things they see reappear in another country, the better they feel. Of course some household items just can't be moved. Moving a giant pinball machine, even if it is of special significance to a 12-year-old boy, is slightly ludicrous. I agree with the mother who consigned that item to storage.

When we moved to Taipei with our very culture-shocked 2-year-old son, it was only after our shipment arrived and we were able to put together a bedroom with his toys and 'friends' (stuffed animals) from home that his personality returned to any semblance of normalcy and happiness. Quantity is not the issue. You don't have to bring a lot of stuff so much as the items which are most precious to your children.

At a future date, you can redecorate bedrooms using local art and handicrafts, but for the adjustment period of the first six months, give your child a break and let him or her have familiar items around. Anything ultra-precious which is small enough to fit in a carry-on bag should accompany the child on the plane.

Books are a very important part of your child's traveling inventory. Make sure you bring lots of them in case the local library isn't well stocked. Try secondhand bookstores to save money when you want to buy in bulk. Also be sure to buy books about your own country, or ones written by your own authors. While you want to introduce your children to the literature of the country you're headed for, never let them forget where they come from. Books help. Be sure you include a child's atlas and if it's possible, your own country's encyclopedia. I can't stress how many times a last-minute purchase of a Canadian encyclopedia has come in handy for my daughter's school assignments.

Pack as many catalogues as you can: book catalogues, toys, clothing, even hardware store catalogues. You never know what you may need to order once you are 'over there'. Catalogues with pictures of various activities and sports in your own country also come in handy for school projects. By the same token, put in a few magazines that can be cut up for projects. While you're at it, arrange for airmail delivery of your local newspapers.

Sporting equipment is a must. We moved to Beijing without knowing that skating and hockey, popular Canadian sports, were offered on wintry Sunday mornings. A search for skates became our first winter's obsession, one at which we ultimately failed. Needless to say, during a home leave in Canada we put skates at the top of our shopping list. You never know what's available where you are going, so bring all the equipment you think your children may need for extracurricular activities. This may also include Boy Scout or Brownie uniforms, which are not always available in Third World countries.

Music, videotapes, or computer games, depending on your child's passions, may also have to be thrown into the shipment. You may end up hiring a cook who can whip up a culinary feast, but your children will demand macaroni and cheese. Try to ship favorite foods. And don't forget your Christmas decorations or any other holiday paraphernalia.

9. One Last Fling at the Mall

This discussion obviously leads us to an inevitable conclusion: you need one last major shopping spree before leaving. How this goes will depend a lot on where you are headed. Anyone departing for the Third World should get ready for major spending. I've had my own experience with this phenomenon and let's just say it left my credit cards smoking from so much use.

My advice is to return again to your master plan and make sure you have a 'things to buy' category. After listing everything you think you need to buy, cut the list in half by placing a priority on each item. That is, cut back to absolute necessities. Then, cut the absolute necessities in half by cutting back the number you think you need to buy. (However, never cut back on the amount of underwear you and your family will need if you are headed for a tropical climate. Buy lots.)

If you are moving with teenagers, give them a spending limit and then let them prioritize their own needs. Sure, every child would love to buy out a music shop, but we can teach them to exhibit some moderation. It's not as if you will never see civilization again. Remind your children, and yourself, of this fact.

Clothing requirements are much trickier to gauge. I was told to buy my children's clothing in Canada before moving to Beijing, only to find 'free markets' which offered items such as down-filled winter jackets (export quality) for less than $15 Canadian. Sweatsuits and other school clothes were also available, but buying good, sturdy running shoes became a major problem. China may make good running shoes, but they export them all. I discovered this fact one stressful day with my daughter. We spent hours going from market to market, department store to department store – only to finally find a pair a size too big. I was exhausted, and told my daughter to 'stuff it!' – the toes of the shoes, that is. My recommendation is to buy everything that you think you might need the first year. If worse comes to worst, you will have stockpiled clothing and other accessories which means you won't be cutting into a clothing budget over there. Everything will be put to use eventually and you don't have to spend frantic hours as I did, searching for items completely unobtainable in your new city.

Birthday and Christmas presents for your own children and for their friends can be handy to have in your shipment. Usually, books make ideal gifts so just buy extra at the bookstore when you're buying for children. Likewise, travel games and art supplies such as markers and crayons will always be put to good use. While you're at it, stock up on wrapping paper.

One last tip: while you are enjoying your last fling at the mall, let your children eat as much junk food as they want. Many young children I spoke with felt that before leaving home they had to eat enough junk food to last them the entire period of their stay overseas. A final blowout of eating will ensure they get sick enough to not want that junk for a while.

GETTING READY TO GO WITH A BABY

This scenario doesn't differ too dramatically from moving with older children. You must anticipate everything you could possibly need which is not available overseas, especially in Third World countries. If you think you are loading up excessively for your other children, their shipment will look like small potatoes next to a baby shipment.

Disposable diapers do take up a lot of room, but are so ridiculously expensive overseas it is worth buying ahead. But remember that depending on where you are going, you may have someone available to wash cloth diapers for you daily, so consider that as well as environmental concerns.

Formulas and cereals may also be available, but on an intermittent basis and too often in packages with expired usage dates. If your baby is still under the age of one, it's best to pack up his foodstuffs, including some dried foods (the kind where adding water makes an instant meal) because you are likely to use those while traveling. Jars of baby food are a personal decision. In some Third World postings, you will find you have a cook available to make fabulous baby meals from scratch. If you are moving to the First World, then you won't need the jars anyway. Bottles, nipples, and sterilizing equipment (preferably non-electric since a change in voltage can make things tricky) should be packed, along with cleaning paraphernalia like bottle brushes which may not be of the same quality where you are moving.

Make sure you take a year's supply of vitamins along with baby medicine for fevers. Whatever brand you prefer, pack lots of it which won't go out of date. Other serious medicines like antibiotics can travel in powder form, but I'm always leery of administering those drugs without a doctor's supervision so prefer to have those prescribed rather than bring them myself.

Clothing – especially sleepers – should be bought in bulk beforehand, bearing in mind the climate in your new location. Since your tropical home may have icy air-conditioning, bring warm sleepers regardless of the outside temperature. If you've been washing your baby's clothing only in some mild washing soap, bring along a good supply. The local version may be too strong and cause skin rashes. One other tip I can offer from my own experience with my baby daughter in Bangkok – bring along a lot of crib sheets. We seemed to go through those at a fast and furious pace, probably due to the combination of hot weather (my daughter would sweat a lot) and her amazing fluid intake in such a hot climate.

You may like to have your own baby furniture with you. Safe cribs and cots are sometimes hard to buy in small Third World countries. While you're loading up in the baby store, be sure to buy a portable crib for traveling. That way, you never have to rely on a hotel-provided crib, which vary in the safety standards they meet. All those other baby accessories – from bicycle seats to jolly jumpers, swings, intercoms, snugglies, and backpacks – should also be brought from home if you plan to use them.

Toys, especially crib toys, should also be bought beforehand. That is not to say that some foreign countries won't have wonderfully bright, decorative stuffed animals or wall hangings, but anything you think your child will be putting in her mouth should meet some safety standard, which often toys made locally in Third World countries, decidedly don't. And speaking of mouths – if you plan to use pacifiers (soothers), bring along several, especially the kind which won't ruin the shape of a child's mouth. Good quality pacifiers can be hard to find.

SAYING GOODBYE

Make sure your children say goodbye to absolutely everyone who is important to them. This 'closure' stage is critical if children are to truly feel they are moving away. Up until this point, the idea of the move may have seemed intangible and unreal. Farewell parties help ensure the idea strikes home.

Encourage them to say goodbye to places as well as people. If they have been library regulars or spent a lot of time at the local sports facility, make sure they drop by there to say their farewells.

Saying goodbye to pets can be painful. Be sure to recognize the unhappiness your child – and you, too, believe me – may be feeling over that separation. I couldn't believe my family's tears when we left our dog behind in Canada.

Farewells with grandparents can be fraught with emotional peril. As the parent, you may already have been accused of "taking the grandchildren away!" so your own parents or in-laws may not be in the best of moods during the countdown to your move and most especially on your day of departure. They may be controlling their own anger over seeing you go, and feelings of abandonment at a stage in their lives when they would decidedly prefer to have an offspring around in case they get sick. You face double duty: you need to pacify your own parents or parents-in-law while at the same time explain to your own children why granny is acting kind of cool, angry, distant, or just plain hysterical.

QUICK TIP SUMMARY

- Do present a positive attitude about the move.
- Plan a special evening or family conference to announce the news.
- Be prepared for negative reactions at first.
- Stress the fun part – family adventure and travel.
- Expect mood swings, insomnia, and regression in youngsters.
- Reassure children of all ages that they will make new friends.
- Consider the boarding school issue very carefully.
- Be sure to make a plan for getting everything done.
- Don't leave home without thorough medical examinations.
- Contact the local international school ahead of time for advice.
- If possible, do a 'look-see' reconnaissance visit.
- Ask your company for an air shipment allowance so that some household goods arrive before you do.
- Pack as many books and familiar items as space will allow.
- Be sure children say goodbye to people and places.

Chapter Three

LEAVING ON A JET PLANE
Your Bags Are Packed: You're Ready To Go

Question: How many classes of travel are there?
Answer: Two – First Class and With Children.

Traveling parents worldwide can freshen up that tired old joke with a new punch line. Along with First Class and With Children, must surely be added our own unique Third Class: expatriate parents en route to a new posting with freaked-out children, carry-on luggage way over any justifiable or rational limit, and possibly a drugged pet or two in the cargo hold. Having taken this form of 'luxury' travel on several occasions, I can offer my own testimonial to its merits.

The amenities are too numerous to list: stiff and swollen arms from lugging toy bags, diaper bags, knapsacks, strollers, and cranky toddlers who insist on being carried down endless airport corridors; stained clothing (the parent's) from at least one child's motion sickness usually in the first five minutes of a 12-hour flight; bruised ankles from where toddlers have attached themselves during some interminable wait to clear passport control; and the blinding headaches caused by exhaustion and resentment which cannot be cured by aspirin, but only by a knockdown fight between the marriage partners.

It is also a little-known medical fact that mothers forced to travel without the father apparently suffer from a contagious disease not yet described in any medical journal. I made this particular diagnosis after noticing the absence of sympathy a single mother arouses in fellow passengers who typically divert their eyes the minute they see a woman with children struggling down an airport hatchway looking as though she requires any kind of boarding assistance.

To any father ready to challenge what I have just written, I have a news flash for you: yes, you may feel equally hard done by if you are traveling alone with the children, but I personally have never had some beautiful, petite flight attendant (the kind who can't even reach the overhead rack) fawn all over me and insist on taking my troublesome child away. That's what typically happens when some 'poor single father' is spotted struggling with a diaper bag or child from hell who screams from the moment they step through the door of the airplane. A mother, on the other hand, has to settle for murderous looks or complete indifference.

Flight crews worldwide are also famous for offering advice and comfort to the single mother the minute she steps on an airplane with children and, worse still, sits down in the flight attendant's area. Crews will also 'advise' her to stow her child's airplane goodie bag (the one with all the distractions in it) in the overhead rack where it is completely inaccessible to little hands and try to arrest you when you reach for that same bag before the seat-belt sign has been turned off. And don't try heading for the toilet with a child about to wet her pants if that light is still on either. I have wanted to strangle the flight attendant who decides to wake up a finally, mercifully asleep toddler to offer food (usually not the child's meal you ordered months in advance, but something truly mouthwatering to a child, like hot and spicy shrimp) and the attitude that the meal can be eaten only at that precise moment, not a single flexible minute later.

Non-traveling mothers are in absolute awe of women who dare to take off for a 12-hour or longer journey across a major ocean or continent with only their wits and 12 pieces of carry-on luggage to keep the children distracted. I have been the recipient of this misguided admiration and secretly smirked about it, knowing full well just how fragile is my own brave, confident facade. Of course we know we will get through the ordeal (we survived the packing, didn't we?) but it's my belief that any woman with half a brain is neither brave nor confident: just petrified out of her mind not only about the fact that she may be moving halfway around the world to a foreign country, but that she has to safely deliver herself and her children there first.

COUNTDOWN TO TAKEOFF

Listen to me, and listen very carefully – don't leave home with children, especially young ones, without both parents. Yes, you would survive the ordeal as thousands have before you (and have a hysterical story to tell of the experience which is only funny in the retelling). But if there is a choice involved, do yourself and your children a favor and travel as a family. Trust me. And while you're at it don't leave home without two or more of everything else which, like parents, you may need along the way.

In short, your plans should most definitely err on the side of over-preparation. To be over-prepared does not have to translate into 80 tons of luggage to cart through 12 time zones. Being organized for the journey to your new home, whether it be a long or short trip, is really just a state of mind, albeit a weighty one. Of course, there are a few details to attend to first.

1. Planning a Holiday Along the Way

Whether it is your family's first time abroad or tenth, some parents feel it is a good idea to plan a vacation on the way to the new posting. There are several reasons for this, not the least of which is the fun aspect. A few days lying on a beach or touring around between pack-up time at home and arrival time 'over there', gives everyone a bit of breathing space. The holiday becomes free time to finally sit down and think about all that has happened and all that is to come.

Depending on where you are headed, short stopovers along the way also help pave the way culturally for the adaptation to follow (although just because a country is a neighbor to another does not mean there will be similarities). The age of your children will definitely affect the plans for these pre-posting holidays. If your child is in diapers, don't be overly ambitious. Likewise, toddlers have a short attention span so stick to something simple. Children between ages 5 and 12 are the best travelers because they are still young enough to want to travel with mommy and daddy, and can be so easily distracted by a zoo, a train ride, or a beach. I'd keep away from long tours of Gothic churches or day-long treks or hikes as they may not be suitable. Teenage children, in this day and age, will soak up culture only to a point, depending on their background. Try to combine a holiday which is culturally redeeming, with easy access to a shopping center or beach.

If you have never traveled *en famille* in any ambitious way, perhaps a trial-run holiday should be factored into plans somewhere. Families don't just automatically adjust to sharing hotel rooms and eating all their meals in restaurants together when they have never done so before. There is a certain rhythm inherent in traveling as a family and you might just need a rehearsal to set the tone.

Practical notes: do make sure you check out all visa and inoculation requirements before leaving home. A passport may not be enough to get you to some of the places you are going.

Also, talk to other families who have lived where you are going as they may have good regional travel suggestions for you. Other families may also suggest resorts or hotels along the way which are particularly good to stay at with children.

There are also travel agencies which specialize in holidays with children. Check in your city to see if one exists. They, too, may have some good ideas about where to go. They may also help you pre-determine other important issues such as the accommodation you select along the way. If there are hotels or motels with swimming pools available, book them. They are terrific when traveling with kids. Also ask if there are housekeeping rooms (the kind which offer a small kitchen or laundry facility).

2. What to Pack for Traveling

This is an entirely different exercise than your pack-up to move. Your luggage in this instance becomes your lifeline. And if you consider that your shipment may not arrive 'over there' for some time to come, the decisions you make about what to travel with will affect your early days in your new home.

With that fact in mind, it may be a good idea to pack one suitcase specifically for use when you arrive (it can stand idle along the way in hotel rooms). It doesn't have to be the world's heaviest suitcase – just filled with a few items you don't need while traveling but would like to have when you're stuck in a hotel room at your new posting for weeks. These items can include a few framed photos, photo albums, extra toys and coloring books, CDs and videos, and anything else which you want to save for later; and extra clothing you won't need while on holiday, especially if the climate you are moving to is different from your vacation spots.

Children of all ages should have their own piece of carry-on luggage filled with their personal life's comforts such as cuddly toys, favorite books, lots of paper and pencils or markers, and a few new items for distraction purposes on the airplanes. (Parents should have the equivalent of this comfort bag, although the mother's bag usually ends up filled with the overflow from her children's.)

One suggestion I was given when I first started traveling with small children, which I've passed on to many other moms, is to prepare a small, carry-on size photo album of children's friends and family, especially cousins they may not see for a while. I can vouch for the many hours of pleasure such an album will provide for your children. So try to pack one of those.

It is truly amazing how often professional traveling families over-pack despite years of experience which should have taught us the lesson many times over. Younger children usually prefer to wear one or two things over and over again, so why pack so much variety for them when it's pointless anyway? Hotel laundry or nearby laundromats have eliminated the need to pack a week's worth of clothing at a time when just enough for two or

three days will do. You can most definitely eliminate at least half of the clothing you may be considering packing. Now cut that amount in half again – and you'll still have unused articles.

If you're traveling with a baby or toddler (or both), it's hard to get away light. Diaper bags, toy bags, traveling beds, strollers, backpacks – it will be a veritable caravan. There is no way around it. Just remember what I said about packing two of everything – especially pacifiers if you are using them.

3. Watching the Moving Men

Parents offer mixed advice on whether or not young children should watch their house being packed up. Admittedly, if you have a toddler, it might be a good idea to have a friend look after him that day, if only to provide you with the space to deal with packers and movers. But I tend to agree with those who want their children to truly see that moving day is here. At the very least, children should see the house once it stands empty waiting for the next occupant. They will know there is no turning back. The family is moving.

Some children will absorb this information without any serious problems. They may see it as part of the excitement, and will run around the house into the empty rooms as part of a game. Other children – even professional traveling children – may be upset by the empty space.

As the parent, you will likely know long before that house stands empty just how your children will react to moving day. The child who doesn't want to move will have been showing signs of that displeasure all along, sometimes by refusing to participate in any pre-moving day cleanup or organization; or by removing items out of the boxes and putting them back into the drawers. An upset teenager may choose to be out all the time and never get around to sorting out what's to be taken. Be prepared for that child being upset when the movers have removed everything. You may be absolutely exhausted, but if you have anticipated an unhappy reaction from your child, try to arrange something special for the moment when it's all done, like trotting off to McDonald's or a movie or any activity which will take his mind temporarily off the move.

4. The Night Before Takeoff

Moving into a hotel often helps smooth over this unhappy transition period. A hotel, for children, is a fun place, especially if there is a pool or games room. You may only have to stay there for a night or two, but it's amazing how that night will stick in your children's minds for a long time to come. There's something about being on the threshold of an adventure which makes that hotel stay – even if brief – memorable.

Depending on where you are moving from and the time of year, there may be other families in the hotel also about to depart for overseas assignments. If you happen to run into any children in the elevator who look anywhere close to the same age as your own children, don't hesitate to suggest letting the children get together at some point in the next few hours. They may find they can confide their last-minute anxieties better to someone they've just met, than to their parents or close friends.

Do something special in the hotel on your last night – even if it's just ordering up room service because everyone is too exhausted to do anything else. Even if you have moved in with relatives or friends for the final night, plan something special.

One final tip: you can try to put your children to bed early, but don't count on them falling asleep quickly. Do you think you will just nod off peacefully? Your children are experiencing the same rush of adrenalin. Encourage them at the very least to just lie quietly and rest. And do the same yourself.

5. Boarding the Big Bird with Children

There are some airplane strategies which need to be carried out before boarding. If you are traveling with a baby, be sure to order a sky cot so the baby will be able to sleep. If your children aren't going to enjoy airborne haute cuisine, be sure to order children's meals from the airline beforehand. You do this at the time you make your reservation and then reconfirm at every possible moment. My husband thinks I'm crazy, but I've never trusted any airline to carry out any duty other than getting me safely to my destination (which, believe me, qualifies as major duty). However, when I'm traveling with my two children for more than eight or nine hours at a stretch, I like to know any requests I may have are indeed being looked after, so I bug the airline every chance I get. Special children's meals (you can also order special vegetarian, low calorie, even Kosher meals depending on your requirements) are truly a godsend. Not only are these meals child-friendly, they are also typically served first which means your hungry child is not waiting until the food cart makes its way to your end of the airplane.

Just because you know there will be food – even special meals – on board, is no excuse not to travel with your own emergency food bag. Juice boxes, dried cereals, raisins, and fresh fruit are all great toddler snacks (and meals if you end up waiting in airport lounges through endless delays). If you freeze the juice boxes the night before, they will gradually thaw and be cool for drinking during the flight. Pack lots of gum and suckers for ear problems (and distractions), and biscuits and crackers for upset stomachs. I always travel with my own bottled mineral water for my young children. Airplane water is potable, but the change from your own drinking water could well upset a child's stomach.

I never board an airplane without an emergency medical kit for both children and adults. Any kind of anti-nauseant medicine should be in that emergency kit, as should a thermometer, and medicine to bring down a fever. If you are planning on dosing your children with medicine to knock them out, be sure to pre-test it. Antihistamines are the most effective, according to some doctors and my own experience. They serve the dual purpose of keeping the child's ears clear and making them sleepy. Nevertheless, numerous mothers have reported medicine can have the exact opposite effect on a child – instead of calming down, it charges up.

Last pre-departure airplane tips: you can book most seats in advance if you say you are traveling with children, so be sure to do so. Make sure your seats enable you to see the movie screen, especially if you are traveling with teenagers who will be very upset if they can't see the movie. Not all seats afford a good view, so make sure you ask.

As for booking bulkhead seats when traveling with young children: the jury is divided about how great an idea that is. With babies, there is no question that the bulkhead area provides room for sky cots. With toddlers or young children, bulkhead seats create other problems you should consider. For example, all of your carry-on luggage must be stowed overhead because you can't stow it under the seat in front of you. That provides many headaches when your child wants something you can't get because the plane is in lift-off, or turbulence grounds you to your seat. Your children may also see the extra space provided by the bulkhead as extra play space. On most long-distance flights these days, passengers are usually advised to stay strapped in, something you can't do when you're playing in that lovely space in front of you.

Ever notice where the bathrooms are located? They are right in front of the bulkhead. That may sound handy, but wait until there are continuous lines for their use. Perhaps you'd like to be further away. Final food for thought: bulkhead seats come with attachable trays. You can be sure you won't be able to get a flight attendant's attention when you need that tray most.

Flight crews are truly the luck of the draw. Friends will recommend this or that airline to you as being good for children and some truly are better than others. However, it most often comes down to that day's crew.

The pilot may be in control in the cockpit, but remember who is in charge in the passenger area: it is you, the paying customer. Don't let yourself be controlled by a flight attendant.

6. Children Traveling Alone

Your decision to let your child fly alone to a new overseas assignment will depend entirely on his age and travel experience. It is rare – unless both mother and father are being posted – that two parents are required to come out ahead. But if that situation arises, and your children are still young, it would definitely be best for one parent to stay behind to ensure that child has a travel companion.

It's true that airlines offer chaperone services, but like everything else to do with airlines (in my book anyway) you should never count on it. I've heard too many stories about so-called airline assistance through hectic airports that somehow never materialized. If your children are traveling abroad for the first time to a place they have never seen before, don't heap any more trauma on them by putting them on a long-distance flight by themselves. For short hops, or in cases where a close friend or acquaintance happens to be going the same way and can act as companion, the situation may work.

7. Fear of Flying Far

If children are boarding an airplane for the very first time a 747 or equally large long-range aircraft may seem a forbidding place. Fortunately, there are so many distractions on board, including the obligatory tour of the cockpit, that their fears are usually gone once the excitement begins.

Fear of moving and fear of flying sometimes get all tangled up together, although in a child's mind they are quite separate and nothing will convince them otherwise. Don't be surprised if the child who resisted the idea of moving is the same child who is suddenly afraid to fly.

Never show fear in front of your children, especially about airplanes. Your fears transfer so easily onto them. Trust me when I say fears can be hidden. I am the world's worst flyer but my children still remain unaware of this. Of course my daughter has become suspicious of the 'water bottle' (referred to as mommy's fire water) the children can't drink from.

ARRIVAL: YOU MADE IT!

After what has seemed like days, not hours, your flight finally touches down in your final destination. This is it. The traveling is over. You are here to stay. Isn't that great, kids? Everyone is comatose from too much eating and flying. The last thing you need now is a chaotic foreign airport and an equally chaotic drive into the city. So here's some advice to help smooth your arrival.

1. Being Greeted at the Airport

It need not be a chauffeur-driven limousine, but most organizations, embassies, even the hotel you are booked into for the first week, will make sure that someone, even if it's just a driver, is on hand at the airport (or train station) to greet you and your family and whisk you into the city. Of course, they can't provide such a service if you haven't advised them of your arrival time, so make sure you do so if you would like airport arrival service.

Being greeted at the airport is not a sign of weakness. Don't dismiss this assistance with any travel macho sentiments. ("We don't need to be met, we'll just hop in a cab.") Parents who have been world travelers before having children, who could most certainly navigate themselves around the world on a shoestring budget and with only a knapsack, must remind themselves that traveling with a family is a new game altogether. Your children will likely be exhausted – and you too – and any assistance which can ease you out of the airport and into the city should be most appreciated. Time enough later to be on your own without an official minder.

2. Jet lag

When the entire family is awake at 3:00 a.m. – new local time – hungry for room service or take-out pizza, you know you are all suffering from jet lag. When your stomach and bowels can't figure out what time it is, when you suddenly become tired and disoriented after several lucid hours when you were positive you had adjusted to your new time zone, you can be sure you are still jet-lagged. You are fatigued not only from time zone travel (the 'lag'), but from sitting in an airplane for too many hours eating too many meals at the wrong time (the 'jet').

There are so many new ways of combating jet lag (from your sense of smell to the amount of light you allow into your eyes) that you could exhaust yourself and your children just experimenting with new formulas. The only surefire way of getting over jet lag, however, is simply time. A few days and sleepless nights and jet lag will lift with or without special scents, diets, or light therapy. You simply have to live through it. Some parents prefer to take a sleeping tablet the first few nights to ensure they get eight hours sleep. Likewise, you can try getting your children back to sleep at 3:00 a.m. by using the same baby antihistamine or anti-nauseant you used to make them sleep on the flight.

75

Just remember with the fatigue of jet lag will come mood swings and changes in eating habits – both completely predictable side-effects of sleep deprivation. Children do eventually snap back to normal, but parents just have to force themselves to live through it. Patience and a few extra catnaps will help.

3. First Impressions

Jet lag combined with culture shock (see Chapter Four) will definitely color your children's first impressions of their new surroundings, so try not to over-expose or over-stimulate them before their brains are ready to absorb the new information. For instance, don't rush out from your hotel room upon arrival and look at your new house or apartment. That's OK if you know you'll be living in a villa with swimming pool or something equally luxurious. If you know you're moving into a rundown diplomatic compound which resembles a low-income housing project somewhere, it might be best to wait until your child's head clears before rushing headlong into a situation you just know is going to make a bad first impression.

EARLY SURVIVAL TIPS

DO let young children run around the hotel room a little bit (as long as they don't disturb neighboring rooms). Trying to restrain their energy is like trying to control the Tasmanian Devil. The children will have energy to be worked off. Find a swimming pool, go for a long walk, or engage in any other activity which will help burn off some of their excess energy.

By the same token, DO let teenagers work things out for themselves (humor their bad mood for a little while) and DON'T ask them every few minutes what's wrong. That's a hard reflex for a parent to control, but try to respect their right to privacy.

DO plan family activities which include some sightseeing and are not just housekeeping chores. Your children will only put up with furniture selection or lineups for a driver's license application for so long. Plan something for children, like a local park, zoo, market, or anything else which is of interest to them.

DO allow older children to make suggestions or wander off, if they are game, by themselves. Try to avoid hectic activities, though, in the heat of the day if your posting is in the tropics. Plan for activities either first thing in the morning or later in the afternoon. Also, DO take a lot of pictures at the beginning. Later on, things which seemed remarkable will hardly be noticed. Encourage your children to take notes in a journal or write letters to friends back home describing their early impressions.

DO establish a routine as quickly as possible. Once jet lag has disappeared, lay down the law about bedtime and stick to it. Children without routines are like a ship without a captain. Throw them a few anchors – established mealtime, bedtime, rest time, and so on, and they will get their bearings a lot quicker. The sooner they discover the new rhythm to their life – even their hotel life before moving into permanent quarters – the better off all of you will be.

DO your children and yourselves a favor. Book a babysitter for a couple of hours and then go out for a dinner alone in the hotel. Babysitters can often provoke certain fears in children (also discussed in Chapter Four) but a quick two-hour outing (in the hotel or nearby) can only have a positive effect on everyone because you as parents have had your own short 'time out' to enjoy a meal quietly.

By the same token, DON'T proceed to book yourselves out as a couple every night with a babysitter in charge for hours on end. If the company, embassy, or other organization requires informal cocktail chatter from you, as the mother, assure them you will certainly provide that – in a few weeks' time, after your children have grown used to their surroundings.

DO check out the local bookstore as quickly as possible for books on the local culture, and the local expatriate handbook (most foreign communities have some local version of where to buy things, what organizations are around, etc). Books on culture can help everyone focus on the new country; books on the foreign community can help you organize your new life.

DO discuss things on a regular basis, perhaps over dinner each night. Allow each child to have his or her say about what interested them that day. Likewise, present the opportunity for problems or dissatisfaction to be raised as quickly as possible so the air can be cleared or misunderstandings sorted out. At the same time, DO reassure your children as often as possible that these unsettled days are going to pass quickly and before anyone knows it, it will feel like you've been living there for years.

As the mother, DON'T expect much emotional assistance or input from the father in the early days. He has likely already vanished into his new position only to return nightly to the hotel to check in and change his clothes. You as mother (that is, if you are the non-working mother) are the emotional rock for your children. So DON'T you race out either the first week to find a job. Right now, your children don't need both parents working and preoccupied with everything but them.

THE BEST IS YET TO COME

The entire family may be suffering from the fatigue which goes with packing and travel. But it doesn't take long for that exhaustion to lift and for life to take on some semblance of routine and order.

Remember that complete adaptation to the new environment can often take up to six months, so don't worry if everyone's view of life is just slightly off-center during that time. The picture eventually corrects itself.

There are just a few practical and emotional hurdles to get past first, beginning with culture shock. Let's move along to the next chapter.

QUICK TIP SUMMARY

- Try to leave home with two of everything, especially parents.
- Plan a fun holiday if you can for along the way.
- Travel light, but don't forget to bring a few things to tide you over at your new post in case your shipment is late arriving.
- Allow your children to see your house empty to prove you really are moving.
- Do something special your last night at home.
- Have a strategy for the airplane: make as many requests as you think you will require, from special meals, to beds and seating arrangements.
- Be sure to advise someone of your arrival time you will be greeted.
- Jet lag must be endured, like a bad cold.
- Don't overload your children with too many first impressions.

Chapter Four

FAMILY CULTURE SHOCK
And How Mommy's Own Shock Affects the Kids

> SHE DID THIS BACK HOME TOO... DID SHE HAVE CULTURE SHOCK THEN?

> BATHROOM

"I didn't mind when my parents went out when we first moved overseas. But I had my baseball bat hidden behind the couch. Just in case."

—11-year-old boy, taking no chances

If I could read minds, I would have loved to climb inside the head of my fair-haired little boy who, until he was 2-years-old, had only known the wide-open space of our rural Canadian home. I would have loved to have read my son's mind when he was yanked from his perch on his precious sandbox – where he could sit and dig for hours enjoying the gentle, sweet-smelling breezes blowing off his meadow of wildflowers – and dropped into a half-finished apartment hotel in the polluted, hectic downtown core of a densely populated city like Taipei. His sweet-smelling meadow had in a flash been replaced with a sour-smelling bathroom drain. Gone were the wildflowers. Hello, raw sewage.

Before the endless journey between Ottawa and Taipei – his first time ever on an airplane – was even halfway complete, Jamie had been jostled by crowds, pinched by strangers, had his white hair touched incessantly by everyone, and been openly stared at. He must have felt like a freak.

To top it all off, on his first full day in the strange new place called Taipei, the very day after a stressful arrival had probably made his head spin with strange new thoughts, his entire family had jumped into a hired car and whisked away to do 'errands'. I know he must have wondered: Couldn't I just sit and play with my Lego for a few minutes? Or if I can't play here, why not go to a park or something fun? He couldn't have known yet that the concept of green space was unheard of in the rapidly developing capital of Taiwan.

The day of errands had been disastrous for him, because his parents resembled frightening strangers. He'd been happy fighting with his older sister and climbing all over the car seats since there was nothing to restrain him. But his parents were stressed out from being dragged all over town in 100° heat by a Taiwanese businessman who was renting them furniture, appliances, even bedsheets and anything else not nailed down, all of which had to be selected from half a dozen locations. It had been sheer torture to select furnishings for an apartment viewed only long enough to determine there wasn't going to be nearly sufficient space to accommodate a family of four people used to the wide open space of a rural Canadian home.

It shouldn't take a mind reader to figure out the result. We were no sooner back at the half-finished apartment hotel where we were staying, when Jamie started 'acting up'. He whined, he moped, he cried. He would have banged his head against the floor but he remembered he had stopped doing that before his second birthday. He wanted to do everything and nothing. He wanted to hide in the bathroom but his mother wouldn't come out of there. Most of all, he wanted to go home. So did I.

There wasn't any difference between my son's behavior and my own except that I'm more than thirty years older.

JET LAG AND CULTURE SHOCK

It is only hindsight which teaches me that pure exhaustion and stress propelled the tantrums from both of us. None of us had sufficient time to get a decent night's sleep or had time to unwind from the long journey. Without rest, and in a frazzled state of anxiety, it was no wonder that neither my son nor I even remotely resembled our pre-departure personae. We were exhausted. Who had the strength to cope with anything?

In the first 24 hours after arrival at a new posting, parents suffer less from culture shock and more from being wiped out and disoriented from jet lag. It is exhaustion which distresses families and frays tempers. The adrenalin is pumping away, but the inner strength has faded with the jet stream. The entire family, not just the children, acts up.

FAMILY CULTURE SHOCK

Other issues besides exhaustion soon come into focus. For instance, as the images of downtown Taipei and distraught reaction to those images were struggling to be absorbed by myself and my son, we were also beginning to interact at an emotional level. Our emotions were bouncing off each other as sound waves do off a satellite. If the sound waves could have been translated, they would no doubt have been heard screaming: Out of control! Separate us, please! Somebody save us!

Once again, it is only now, looking back, that I have come to recognize that I was experiencing what all families go through in some form or another. It was the beginning of the interplay of my family's various levels of culture shock.

Eventually we would adapt and reach the period of readjustment in culture-shock-speak. But before we could reach that final stage, we needed to understand a few basic ideas.

We needed to understand that culture shock is more than just a reaction to new food or a nauseating feeling from the smell of a crowded marketplace. Those are just some of the physical responses. Culture shock is also about emotional reactions. The new culture can't help but have an impact on our feelings in many ways, both positive and negative. We're not made of stone.

Extend that notion beyond individual reactions. Bring together an entire family of separate individuals (and their feelings) and you begin to understand that for families making international moves (and not just traveling on holiday), the concept of culture shock includes emotional considerations. Family culture shock is vastly different from the kind of shock experienced by individuals who are just visiting a country for a few weeks and then going home. It is even different from the shock felt by a single person moving abroad, although a married couple without children will have more in common with the family than the single adult.

Family culture shock is a collective experience. It is initially about loss of control over new surroundings and then, later, over each other's behavior. As each separate person struggles with the shock of regaining equilibrium, the traveling family's culture shock also includes the feeling of losing control over the actions and reactions of the other family members. Factor in conditions like constant physical and emotional proximity in the early weeks, and family culture shock can't help but produce a confusing, unsettling interaction between the parents' (especially the mother's) shock and the effects their own uncertainties and helplessness may have on the children, regardless of their age.

WHY IS MOMMY SO SHOCKED?

From a child's perspective, the shock appears to begin with daddy because he is suddenly absent (at work) and mommy is doing everything and not liking it. Perhaps only daddy can speak the local language so mommy, who is trying to get everything organized for everyone, is frustrated because she can't explain what she wants. She gets angry with daddy for having had the chance to learn the language; what she once considered his achievement now turns into a source of resentment. While she's at it, she's mad because she doesn't have a job anymore and he has a career. In short, the marriage has changed.

The children, meanwhile, are innocent bystanders to their parents' marital adjustments and squabbles and, at the same time, have to cope with their own reactions to the new country. They don't understand a word of the language either, but they are often left with babysitters with whom they can't communicate. Nobody understands the local customs as yet so may be offended, or in turn offend someone without knowing why. Day-to-day life has a different, unfamiliar hue to it. Until the new environment becomes the reality and not some dream-like trance, the picture will seem slightly out of focus. Children looking to their mother as a lifeline find her looking for her own supports.

As I wrote in *A Wife's Guide*, in the early days after arrival in a foreign country, it is the mother who experiences the most jolts to her existence. Her role at home, her marriage, her role in the new foreign community change the most dramatically. Her day is unstructured while her husband goes off to his new office and her children start up in the controlled environment of a new school. If they are pre-school-aged children, she may be dealing with a care-giver over whom she has no control whatsoever due to language and culture gaps. If her children have grown up, she may be facing the empty nest at the same time she is worrying about boarding schools, universities, new marriages, or unseen grandchildren. Or she could be dealing with either a houseful of servants if she has moved to a Third World post, or the shock of a household of no servants if she's used to living where help was inexpensive. Her life circumstances have definitely changed dramatically. Her self-confidence and self-image have probably taken a battering too. She feels out of control.

But her children? That's a different matter! If they are with their parents overseas, they are still under her wing – and control. But are they?

In the case of a 2-year-old child, for example, you are dealing with a loose cannon on an hourly basis. There is no controlling a child that age, no matter how hard you try. Believe me. During our year in Taiwan, I lost my temper more times than I care to remember. And what about young school-age children? Sure, I can try to control my daughter's life, but only to a point. She will still want to select her clothes, decorate her new room, and have opinions on everything from the new cuisine to the lack of television.

And a teenager? One who may already feel too controlled by parents on whom he now is even more dependent with no escape valve like a nearby mall? The last thing he wants is a mother trying to control *his* life just because *hers* is out of control.

CULTURE SHOCK DENIAL

One further complication is what I like to call macho denial of the experience of culture shock. If there is one common thread to the many conversations I have had with parents and children about culture shock, both in reference to this book and when I've spoken with women about to participate in my culture-shock workshops, it is this popular response to my inquiry about culture shock: Who, me? I never had culture shock. No, not one bit. My family never had culture shock. My children adapted perfectly. No culture shock here. We took it all in without any problems whatsoever.

Openly admitting to the experience of culture shock has become politically incorrect – a bad move in the worst kind of competitive travel game. It's not as though a person is confessing to murder, but owning up to culture shock seems akin to admitting to failure rather than the validation of the normal experience it truly is. It reminds me of the days when the baby boomers were hippies competing to see who could travel the world under the worst conditions. These same baby boomers have matured, but rather than escape into travel as they did when younger, they now try to escape by denying their next generation is anything less than unflappable rugged travelers. In other words, perfect. Like themselves.

Like everything else associated with a foreign posting, upheavals and behavior patterns which may have existed at home just become magnified tenfold overseas. The stakes are higher overseas for the father's career. The family holds a higher profile. There's more money to earn and to spend. Cracks in the veneer of a perfectly functioning family must be concealed or they risk losing the sweet expatriate deal. Or so some parents assume: wrongly, in my opinion. To deny is to push a problem aside. One day there will be a reckoning.

If parents choose to openly acknowledge the existence of culture shock in the family, instead of denying it because they are fooled into thinking such an admission will somehow lessen their stature, chances are good that some emotional crises can be avoided in the first instance, or more realistically, dealt with a lot quicker.

Not all parents engage in this macho game of culture shock denial. Some people just aren't aware of the extent to which culture shock can affect their child's behavior and relationship with his parents. Here's one perfect example of culture shock naiveté. An Australian family overseas for the first time had children who were old enough to do things for themselves and be independent, yet not old enough to qualify as teenagers.

One night while playing cards together, I mentioned to them my feelings about the concept of family culture shock. The husband turned to the wife and said, typically, "Well, dear. I guess we missed culture shock."

"So you honestly think your family had no culture shock?"

"No," they both responded, innocently, to me.

"What about your son?" Their pre-teen son, while adapting academically, had gradually become so clingy, so fearful about his parents going out at night, that one evening they had returned to find him huddled on the balcony in cold temperatures watching for their return. On several other occasions, he would not let them go out until they displayed their passports to verify they weren't planning to leave the country without him.

Parents overlook the fact that not only do children react and need time to adjust to changes in weather, food, the people on the street, classrooms, and playgrounds, but also to changes in their parents and their family's new dynamics. Family chaos – and certainly depression and anxiety – can result from just one member's irrational fears, like that boy's fear of abandonment.

Culture shock is in the first instance about reactions and loss of control; never overlook that, in the final analysis, it is about on-going readjustment. As a parent, rather than deny it, be on the lookout for it and the means to facilitate readjustment.

By the way, I'm not saying that parents, and especially mothers already under the strain of having moved thousands of miles from home, should take the blame for all of our children's aberrant behavior during the early days of a posting. Sometimes our children *are* just being difficult and manipulative and not culture shocked. In fact, you can expect to be manipulated by your children a lot more overseas, if only because they so easily pick up on parents' guilt over thrusting their children into a new situation. Before one can understand some of the basic reasons behind culture shock, what triggers it, and how to deal with it, the traveling family needs to have it placed in its proper context.

From my own experience, which I don't think is that unusual, if I hadn't been so depressed about living in Taipei when we did, my young son would have been a lot happier despite being in the throes of the terrible twos.

WHAT CAUSES A CHILD'S CULTURE SHOCK

A child's culture shock is not that much different from an adult's. It is an initial reaction to an uncertain and different environment. But never forget that your traveling child is not just a miniature adult. A child is, after all, a child, and will have more needs which can't be put on hold as an adult's can.

Loss of the Familiar

Traditional comfort items, whether it be a television or granny's voice on the end of the phone, are no longer there. Remember, too, that a child's world can be a limited one. So while an adult will react to what is new outside the door, a child – and certainly one still at home – could potentially experience shock at what is inside the home. This can easily include the shock of a mother who is beside herself with unhappiness, as much as the shock of a new care-giver, new bedroom furniture, and new food on his plate. It may also come as a result of being left all day with a servant who may be the kindest soul in the world, but try explaining all that to the child.

Language Barriers and Unfamiliar Customs

Of course there are many standard issues connected with adaptation which will specifically trigger the onset of a child's culture shock. I've already mentioned language barriers and unfamiliar customs. Most younger children throughout Asia I spoke with on this subject (and many had lived in Africa, too) agreed the biggest shocker of all was being touched all the time. Cheeks poked, hair tousled, being lifted into the arms of complete strangers in stores while mommy can only plaster a fake smile on her face in an attempt to be culturally correct, are all situations which breed a hostile reaction towards the new culture. And make no mistake that hostility is the primary emotion your children will be feeling over this unwelcome tactile interaction with the new culture.

Food

Spicy or unfamiliar-looking glop to a child may also spark feelings of alienation. What on earth is that woman eating, mom? What on earth is that person selling, dad? What on earth has the cook put on my plate? And do I have to eat it?

New School

A new school is also a guaranteed stress point in the early days of a child's adaptation. Where is the 'in' place to eat lunch? Who are the 'in' kids? In fact, what is just 'in'? Personal issues can often be eclipsed by tough academic ones. International schools change from country to country. This one may be tough, that one easy. They all may be tougher than what the student experienced back home. The school itself may be physically laid out differently and that may require adjustment. School buses may be ridden for the first time and the school-bus 'culture' can take time getting used to as well.

Servants and Status Issues

If they are a brand new phenomenon in the household, servants will definitely trigger a form of culture shock. On the one hand, they may be a dream come true for a pre-adolescent boy – "You mean I don't have to straighten up my room? I don't have to clear the dinner dishes? Take out the garbage?" – On the other hand, the child in the throes of this new domestic ecstasy may be brought down to earth when his parents tell him he now has more time for homework or practicing the piano.

To older children, a houseful of servants may also be mistaken as a sign of elevation in status or finances which a child may not be able to absorb. The rank which his father carries, either within a government operation (ambassador), military (colonel or general), chief executive officer of a company, or the community's most influential journalist, may also have a fallout effect on a child. The offspring of these people may find themselves treated slightly differently by their teachers or peer group. If they are not used to it, it can color their perception of reality.

Children of all ages who are used to having servants do everything for them will also feel a shock at the beginning of the post. "Do you mean I have to do these things for myself?"

Freedom to be Independent
What about freedom of movement? Often, in hardship posts, freedom of movement is suddenly curtailed. Even if there was such a thing as a negotiable subway or bus system with drivers who speak English, where is there to go? Where is the mall? The arcade? Suddenly, the apartment walls are closing in, long after a child chooses to use those same walls as a protective cocoon for the first few weeks of his new life. Now he wants to go out! But where? And how?

Poverty vs Luxury in the New Environment
And then he does get out (if he's old enough) and what does he see? If the assignment is in the Third World, he may see poverty everywhere. A child or young adult's reaction to seeing poverty for the first time may be unsettling. Of course Western countries have their share of slums, homeless people, and rundown areas, but never on the scale seen in some of the developing countries. Likewise, the opulent, material West can shock a youngster from the Third World. He can be equally overwhelmed by the sheer volume of goods available in the West and the need to make choices regarding his life if from a culture or country that permits few individual choices.

Loss of Friends
Never forget just how a lack of friends and the challenge of making new ones will make a child feel. Pre-schoolers and children in lower grades can make friends more easily than

teenagers, who have to rely on a sophisticated set of cues and rules of behavior set by that week's consensus. Teens will need more time. That awkward, left-out feeling they may experience while they are trying to connect will most certainly be exaggerated and even mixed up with their feelings of culture shock.

WHO IS MOST SUSCEPTIBLE?

Everyone experiences culture shock in some form or other. But with children, a few groups can be singled out.

First-time Traveling Families

There seems to be general agreement that first-time traveling families and their children are the most prone to stronger feelings of disorientation and alienation from their new surroundings.

Older teenage children are also hit hard if they are yanked out of junior or senior high school. If these teens also happen to be first-time travelers, it can be a recipe for an emotional disaster. Imagine the young man who plays for his high school football team and has his entire ego and being wrapped up in that sport. His academic standing has never been that great but he has scraped by. Now place him somewhere in an international school where there might not even be a football team and where everything depends on scholastics, and you will probably find that same young man locked in his bedroom listening to music for most of the year. And not too happy.

Most neophyte traveling families quickly become indistinguishable from veterans of the expatriate life, but until they do, they struggle. At first the parents are in the dark about what to expect so they can't advise their children in any experienced way. And if they do feel something strange going on, they may deny anything is wrong – the old macho-denial game. Nobody wants to admit to not 'handling' adjustment well. Everyone wants to be settled in *now*, not later. Expectations like these are unfortunately completely unrealistic and will just delay adaptation.

Likewise, the first-time traveling mother will feel she has absolutely nobody to talk to about her problems – especially not her husband who just wants her to get on with things and fit in. She is overseas for the first time and unfamiliar with the cycle of culture shock and adaptation. She could very well be wondering if it ever passes. Her unhappiness and unsettledness just gets passed along to her children who, also with no experience to draw from, take their cues from her. Throw in a few marital problems and you have one very culture-shocked family. If the parents are fighting like crazy over the move, where does that leave the children? Wondering if anything will ever be the same.

Children of Working Parents

Parents' work hours, especially the mother's, are another thorny issue. Children are apt to experience more pronounced culture shock and problems of adaptation when both parents are working long hours and spending little time at home. Obviously, a move abroad has been on behalf of one parent's career and long hours are part of the commitment. When those hours become so many that the children are seen only for a few minutes at breakfast and are left with servants outside of school hours, there are going to be problems. Children feel they need both their parents around, especially a child who has just moved halfway around the world and is already uncertain about his new home. He is only going to feel worse as the days go by.

A working mother – I'm referring here not to a part-timer but to the kind of woman who runs out the door for a full-time job the second the movers have unpacked the last box, and leaves the children with help they have known for about five minutes – shouldn't be surprised to return home to find complete emotional chaos. Attention-seeking devices will abound. Older children will lash out at their new friends or just make pests of themselves. They are desperate for attention and will take any kind they can get, preferably from someone who speaks their language.

Sensitive Children

Sensitive children also have a harder time making adjustments to international moves, even those who have lived all over the world. After observing many foreign service families over the years, and especially after turning a professional eye on the subject, I've noticed just how different each child within a family can be. It's especially interesting when you talk to young adults who spent their childhoods moving from one place to another. When I ask them about culture shock, I get very similar responses: "I never had it, but my younger sister did." Or, "I had it all the time and hated my older brother who just breezed through 10 moves in 15 years!"

The children most affected, it seemed, were the ones who were sensitive to other issues in life. They wanted to be rooted, for instance. They found it hard each time to leave friends or family. They were the children who were *positive* they would not make any new friends in the new place. It usually takes these children longer to get used to a new place.

Children of Mixed Cultural Marriages

One last susceptible group definitely worth mentioning are children of mixed cultural marriages who have returned home to one or the other parent's home country. Perhaps an American father and European mother move away from the United States, exposing their children for the first time to the mother's extended family of relatives and a new culture. A child who has only seen her mother in an American setting may find it distressing to see her mother change as she tries to cope with family who expect different behavior from her.

Fortunately for children of such mixed marriages, most international schools have a high percentage of their enrollment from this mixed-marriage group. The children will quickly find other children with whom they can compare notes and find support.

SIGNS THAT YOUR CHILD IS IN SHOCK

There can be many signs of culture shock, but not all of them visible to the parent's eye. Keep in mind the following signs.

First Signs

A child's first view of how the other half lives could lead to some sleepless nights. Insomnia is definitely one symptom of culture shock. Headaches and upset stomachs are others. Crying is still another obvious sign that adaptation is not going too smoothly for the time being. Crying suddenly and without any apparent purpose can certainly be tied to unhappiness but may also be attributed to jet lag in the early days. When a child is tired and not eating well – not unlike an adult – there is no telling how he will react to certain situations.

"Honeymoon" Stage

Also paralleling the adult version of culture shock, there likely will be a 'honeymoon' phase of the child's adaptation. The new apartment, with a pool or near the ski slopes, may seem com-

pletely enchanting to a youngster. Likewise, local transportation like pedicabs or small shuttle buses with hordes of humanity clinging on the outside may provide just the daredevil treat your adolescent son will find fantastic. The local culture just cannot be embraced quickly enough.

Culture Shock Relapse

Like his parents, the child could be due for the inevitable second stage of culture shock – the crisis which follows the honeymoon. It will be during this phase that you can watch your teenager enter his bedroom, Walkman and earphones in hand, and then not recall seeing him leave again. Given that moodiness is the hallmark of any normal teenager, it may be difficult to figure out what is just normal behavior and what is post culture-shock crash syndrome. If your child has always been well-behaved at school (but sullen at home for the folks) and suddenly you are getting a note from his new teacher that the behavior has reached the classroom, it could indicate that culture shock is taking over. Time for a talk. Learn to recognize the signs so you can help your child recover the after-shocks of the move abroad.

Culture Shock Signs

- Reading all the time is typical escape from culture shock. This 'symptom' provides the proverbial good news/bad news scenario for parents and teachers. On the bright side, any child reading and not glued to the tube or a Nintendo game is a child who you want to encourage. If that same child chooses to read instead of eat, speak, or engage in any form of social interaction, the book may need to be put away.
- Mishaps. An international school nurse told me young children tend to visit the nurse's office a lot at the beginning of a new school year while they are settling in. There is a higher number of minor mishaps in the playground which can be fixed with a bit of reassurance as much as by a bandaid.

- Disrupted naptimes. It's easier to spot a younger child's reaction to the new culture. Honeymoons are shortlived with toddlers. Just when you need a nap in the most desperate way or at the very least quiet time in the middle of the day, your young child will decide it's time to give up naps. But trying to convince a 2-year-old he needs a nap is tantamount to settling the Middle East impasse. He may also be so clingy you will think you've donned lead weights around your ankles. He won't leave your side. Not for one second. No way.

- Separation anxiety makes some children terribly fearful of being left with babysitters in strange surroundings. Many young children will not like it when parents go out in the early days overseas. After arriving at a post, a British woman's 3-year-old daughter would attempt to go to bed at 4:30 p.m. when she knew her parents had to go out, thereby avoiding the babysitter she feared. Children will cry their brains out as you try to walk out the door to a reception because they are terrified you will not come back. If your child did the same at home, expect the tantrums to double when you move abroad.

- Regression is another symptom of culture shock. A toilet-trained toddler may suddenly become untrained, a young girl may start sucking her thumb again, or a pre-schooler won't let go of his bottle no matter what. They are clinging to familiar lifelines and means of insuring their parent's attention.

- Nightmares are the flip side of insomnia. The child eventually falls asleep only to imagine fiery plane crashes, torture by teachers, or equally graphic manifestations involving new interaction with his new culture.

- Anger. Finally, never forget the anger of a child who has been uprooted. He can't tell his father he is angry that he's been yanked away from his old home, but he can hit that child sitting next to him on the school bus or on the playground. Younger children cannot articulate their anger. Watch for it in other forms of behavior, like throwing their toys around.

HELP EVERYONE GET THROUGH CULTURE SHOCK

The good news, which must never be lost sight of, is that just about everyone gets through culture shock eventually. A good sense of humor and a proper perspective (culture shock is not fatal after all!) will obviously be helpful. The bad news is that, as a parent, you should be prepared for some tough times for at least six months. That is the average length of time it takes to reach what culture-shock experts call the 'period of readjust-ment', the final stage of culture shock. I've already discussed stages one and two, the honeymoon and crisis stages. Between those and the end of the tunnel (the period of readjustment) comes the 'flight stage' which should be self-explanatory. In case it's not, that is the stage where some family members (most definitely including mothers) may take it into their head to *escape home*. At the very least, family members may physically lock themselves in bathrooms or bedrooms for unreasonable lengths of time. Emotionally, their mood may turn sullen and cranky. You can identify this stage with teenagers by monosyllabic re-sponses to any conceivable question. Or by children who insist on writing long letters – daily – to friends back home and become distraught when the mail brings them few replies.

With these four distinct stages of culture shock identified and reconciled, there are some means at your disposal to help combat this condition and get everyone through it with a mini-mum of fuss:

1. Do Not Deny Its Existence

Even before you begin to figure out which stage your family is at in the culture-shock cycle, one very important consideration must be paramount: there must be no denial. I have made this point before, but it bears repeating. For many traveling families, it seems that to admit to culture shock is to be considered a wimp, like it's a mark against you somewhere. Perhaps this worry about defeat stems from the personality of the average expat parent nowadays – highly educated, over-achieving, solid, middle- to upper-class social sphere, and ambitious. Perhaps such people think it doesn't look good (where? do your children have emotional résumés?) to own up to a partner and children who are struggling to adapt to their new overseas assignment.

In the days of the British Raj in India, children were referred to as 'outposts of the Empire'. Their mere physical presence was proof that the Raj was firmly intact and, more important, reproducing another generation of colonial rulers. These 'outposts' were perpetually scrutinized and dictated to by arbitrary rules of social behavior which often made as much sense as the Raj custom of calling upon each other at high noon. Back then, however, children were shipped off to England and boarding school before serious parenting issues became important, but not before they had been used for display purposes – to demonstrate the will and might of the British Empire.

I'd like to think we have outgrown those days of Empire, of critical embassy or company officials chagrined over any employee whose wife or family can't seem to cut it. If we haven't got over it, I suggest we start now. I know it's hard to always put children and family first, but I believe we should at least do that for the first six months after the family's arrival in a new foreign place. As a Tokyo-based Western child psychologist stressed to me, parents must be willing, at the outset, to make certain sacrifices when raising children in a foreign country. What good is some fantastic overseas assignment if the family is going to pieces because the adaptation process has been mishandled? A decision to push it aside, refusing to acknowledge its existence, or shuffling it around like a piece of paper will come back to haunt everyone.

Culture shock does eventually go away, but it doesn't disappear by divine right. It can go away without leaving any nasty legacies in family relationships if people are willing to acknowledge its existence, and together work to alleviate it as quickly as possible.

2. Be Available As Much As Possible At First

Here's another issue which has come up in almost every interview I conducted with parents, especially mothers. That is, how much going out is reasonable in the first weeks after the family's arrival? Oh sure, your embassy, company, community of peers, or whomever is dying to get to know you, but to be wined and dined constantly for days on end when you have young children back at the hotel terrified to be left alone with a hotel babysitter (and probably a different one every night) does not provide an auspicious beginning for your children. It's true, I have advised and reassured parents earlier in this book to get out for a few hours upon arrival if possible. But for a few hours, and for one evening. Every evening – and I know this phenomenon to exist – puts too much anxiety and feelings of abandonment onto your children's shoulders. And don't dismiss the stress if it is an older child left minding his younger siblings. He may worry (but never admit to it) that he hasn't got a clue what to do in the case of an emergency. Far from relaxing all evening in front of the hotel television (if there is one), he's been counting the minutes until his parents got back.

Similarly, when you arrive as the school year begins and there is suddenly a choice placed before you, the first school Open House or a cocktail reception for a visiting widget promoter, which do you think you should go to? Opting for the business evening gives your child a clear signal: business first, him second. There are two of you as parents. If the husband decides he simply has to make an appearance at the business party, he can go. As the mother, don't allow yourself to be pressured into doing anything other than putting your child's welfare first. If you don't, you only have yourself to blame when a backlash comes, and it will, in one form or another. It will take a child a long time to forget who came first in his parent's mind. Above all else, be available to your children to the best of your ability. Don't vanish into the night. Every night.

3. Create As Much Stability As You Can

That old saying about a child needing limits goes hand in hand with his need for stability. Uprooting a child from his culture and moving him halfway around the world can't help but create instability. Parents must strive as quickly as possible to replace that instability with a stable environment. This will provide the sense of security in which young children can flourish and allow for the introduction to and enjoyment of the host culture.

It's true that many schoolchildren literally arrive with hundreds of vestiges of their own culture. But these are often just material manifestations of their culture: videos, CDs, computer games, clothing, posters. Like all 'things', they are tangible and replaceable. While they can superficially create a comfort zone which I'm not entirely dismissing, 'things' need to be augmented by the intangibles, like values or emotional guidance from the parents.

Values can't just be packed up like a computer and transported by transworld shippers. Parents hand-carry these highly valuable possessions. During the early days, when nothing seems familiar to your culture-shocked children, you can introduce and reinforce your family's values by talking to them. Make comparisons with local cultures to highlight both differences and similarities, find a church if you need one, or just rely on that old family standby, the evening meal, to discuss issues. Open discussions contribute to stability because they allow for questions that may be circling in a child's head to be both asked and answered where possible. Your family unit grows closer at the same time the children feel that the family is in this adventure together.

Routines are another way to encourage stability. As quickly as possible, establish a new family-life rhythm. This does not mean suddenly changing the rules of behavior you have imposed until your move. If computer games were allowed for so many hours before, don't increase the hours to something completely outrageous just because the child refuses to come out of his room all day. Making allowances for your new circumstances naturally involves a few subjective decisions on the part of parents. But you can still be strict without cutting off amusements entirely. You are still the boss; there are still house rules and assignments. Be consistent, but more flexible. The larger lesson for children to learn is that survival in another culture often depends on a person's ability to bend a little, to become informed about the new culture, and to have understanding, patience, and tolerance.

4. Don't Let Your Prejudices Rub Off

While this point is important in the early culture-shocked days of adaptation, this is really a point that will come up again and again throughout many postings. At the beginning of a new assignment – especially if it's the family's first – not giving expression to your prejudices should be taken even closer to heart so that at least everyone can start off on the right foot.

It's true that when you first arrive, things go wrong and it is easy to blame the local culture. The name-calling can make even yourself blush. Nobody can stay cool, especially a frazzled mother trying to unpack a shipment when the electricity goes off, or the 24 workmen sent over by the moving company are hovering around you or trying to drop your piano. If it happens that your children see you lose your cool in the heat of the moment – you lose it totally and scream at some local person like nobody's business – at least ensure that your child also hears the subsequent apology which you had better make.

Those cases are to be expected. Nobody's perfect, or at least that's what I told my children the day I lost my temper when our shipment to Beijing couldn't be delivered because it was an odd-numbered day and the truck carrying our goods had even-numbered license plates. Yes, I was going insane. Worry more about constant derogatory references to the local culture, often directed against the servants in a developing country, which children begin spouting in direct imitation of their parents.

When I spoke with international school teachers a comment which kept coming up over and over again was the way in which some of the students both spoke of and treated their family maids. Children can be extraordinarily well-behaved in every respect in the classroom, the playground, or the school bus. But for some reason, they dismiss their maids (come to deliver a forgotten lunch or a piece of homework left behind at home) with such disdain it should make any parent blush.

KEEPING THE PROPER PERSPECTIVE

It will be difficult enough as a mother to have to deal with culture shock on so many levels: your own, your children's, and then the impact of your own shock on your children. Follow me? If you are an international traveling mother, as I am, I know you clearly understand what I'm saying because we cope, we organize, and we handle our lives and those of our families on so many levels we must have a brain which resembles a computer circuit board. Be prepared for when the system cracks. As I keep stressing, parents aren't perfect all of the time.

The culture-shocked family of the 1990s is not dysfunctional; our children are hardly suffering all that much. In fact, their lives are so good it is laughable in some respects to be pointing out these 'problems' at all. But like all parents, we just want what is best for them, to be able to make their tears go away if we can. With thoughtfulness and sensitivity, especially in these early days, we can ease their way. It's up to them to do the rest. They are their own person after all. Make sure they understand that.

QUICK TIP SUMMARY
- DO explain the culture shock stages to your children. Regardless of their age, the more they know about the cycle of culture shock, the better prepared and informed they will feel.
- DON'T dismiss every ache or pain or bad behavior as a culture shock symptom or your child will quickly learn he can

get away with acting up under the umbrella excuse of culture shock. You will quickly learn when a child is truly upset or when he's just trying to stay up late to play more on the computer.

- DON'T deny the existence of culture shock.
- DO be flexible when it comes to food. If your child is absolutely hysterical in the beginning about trying the local cuisine, DON'T force him too quickly. If he's really young, DON'T put him to bed without dinner, forcing him to get used to the new cuisine in a negative way. Allow him to have a bowl of cereal or anything else familiar.
- DO try to let your older children have as much freedom as the posting will allow. This does not mean to grant carte blanche entrance into discos.
- DO stick to your own child-rearing values and be sure to establish a foothold with them from the beginning.
- DON'T ignore too many signs of trouble before seeking out professional help. Ask your school for the name of a counsellor if after a year your child is still not settled.
- DO help your children make friends wherever possible by organizing play dates or outings which can bring children together.

Chapter Five

THE NEW LIFE OVERSEAS
Getting Used to a Different World

"My mother was living the 'real life' in our foreign postings. My father's life was his work. He could have been anywhere."

—grown-up foreign service child reflecting on the difference between her parents' lives at post.

Let's roll the videotape six months into your overseas assignment. All of your furniture and clothing shipments have finally arrived and have been unpacked. Your new home is completely furnished and decorated now, and feels less temporary. The children have arranged their bedrooms just the way they like them with posters, bulletin boards, book shelves, or endless stacks of music videos or tapes and CDs. Schools and pre-school play groups have been organized and have settled into familiar routines. A few interesting friends have been made, the phone rings with engagements or work offers for the mother, depending on her interests. Life has settled down into a predictable pattern everyone can handle.

Then, unexpectedly one evening, the father – the working half of the partnership – comes home (early for a change) in a high state of excitement, waving airline tickets for the family's first holiday leave. He's left his office early because he can't wait to tell his family where he's booked the Christmas vacation. The holiday has all been confirmed, he exclaims. There, between the tickets, he proudly displays the hotel vouchers. Breakfast for free, he announces. Isn't that fantastic, everybody?

No one moves a muscle. Not even a hint of a smile appears on anyone's face, except for the children under 4 who may be just happy to see daddy who hasn't been home much lately. Everyone else has been stunned into silence. Finally, one voice ventures to ask:

"Dad, when was it decided we would go to — for our holiday?"

"Well, Mr. — at the office took his family there and raved about the place. I thought we should try it too," explains Dad. But seeing the glum faces, his own face starts to slowly build into a grimace, an early warning signal of his anger.

"I thought everyone would be happy!" His voice starts to rise. "We want to go away, don't we?"

"Of course we do," mother-as-mediator replies for everyone. Before she can get her next sentence out, however, her teenage son or daughter, it doesn't matter which as this scenario is interchangeable, blurts out:

"Why weren't we consulted on this? Maybe I don't want to go to —! I heard the beach there is lousy. Why didn't you ask *us*? Maybe if you were home once in a while, you would have had a chance to ask us about it."

"Dear," says the wife to her husband, still trying to defuse the situation. "Wasn't there time before actually booking the holiday with the travel agent to allow for the rest of us to have a little … input? This is the first we have even heard of it."

Instead of replying, the father storms away, muttering something about 'ungrateful family'. He throws the tickets into his briefcase and closes the door on his home study where he will brood and pretend to work. Eventually, he'll emerge to say he's sorry and try to re-open the discussion. But in all likelihood, the vacation his colleague suggested will be the vacation the family takes because changing bookings overseas can be very difficult and costly. Perhaps for the next trip, the arrangements will be made in a slightly different manner. Everyone will be asked for their opinion. Everyone will have a say in the final decision.

SECONDARY CULTURE SHOCK

Did anyone promise that the adjustments associated with culture shock would disappear completely after that magical six-month period? If they did, they were mistaken. It's true that the initial culture shock – the disorienting, what-planet-have-I-landed-on kind which you feel on first contact with your new surroundings – actually abates for a while after everyone is 'settled' into new routines. Some of its relevant issues (such as family members' loss of control over decision-making) will continue to reappear throughout the length of your posting.

These issues form secondary culture shock, triggered long after the initial move has taken place by a variety of events often associated with family decisions. The father's selection of the location for the first family vacation is just one example. The children – and probably the mother – are angry with the father for just blindly making a decision without consulting the rest of the family. Family problems you could never have anticipated can start cropping up long after the move.

After six months or so, most of the new emotional dynamics of the family have also been established. Then, out of nowhere, a member of the family may suddenly be incapable of coping with new equally distressing issues which will have caught up with the family after six months have gone by. I will identify a few of these issues which I have noted from talking to others and from my own experience. First, be forewarned that whatever the issue, on-going adjustments will be required from each family member, especially from parents, just as would happen at home.

IT'S A DIFFERENT WORLD OVERSEAS

If you haven't already realized it, family life overseas is a whole lot different than it was at home. It's not that you never had to accommodate change at home. New situations and new people just didn't seem to come up as often as they do overseas. Parenting itself, and the interaction of the nuclear family grouping, is fundamentally the same anywhere in the world. But at the risk of repeating myself, any situation overseas – it hardly matters what it is – always seems magnified at least tenfold because it's happening abroad, far from familiar home. This is especially applicable to how the family lives together. Before discussing these differences, I just want to stress that family life abroad can be a happy, positive, and enriching experience for all. Family ties are strengthened, values enriched by the exposure to other lives, and the shared family experience of learning about a new culture makes the posting a unique and rewarding time for all ages. But, like culture shock, the necessary adjustments don't just happen naturally. Careful planning and healthy introspection about one's actions and reactions can make that family experience even better.

Let's start with the fact that so many aspects of family life overseas can be different. How different? Take the family living quarters abroad. Step outside its doors, and you are immediately bombarded with cultural images and icons vastly removed from your neighborhood back home – Buddhas instead of Taco Bells, high garden walls with shattered pieces of glass running along the top instead of wide-open gardens with white picket fences, a much richer or much poorer population depending on your posting, weather as hot as can be, or freezing like the North Pole. And don't forget the different smells, good or bad. There are also changes inside the family home. Your house or apartment could be bigger or smaller than you are used to, lavish or downscaled, filled with servants or with no help whatsoever.

There are also the subtle changes – the emotional ones – which can't be pointed to easily. The biggest difference is a change in how the family functions together as a unit. After all, you are thrown together most of the time whether you like it or not. You travel together much more than you did back home. A shift of loyalties, a realignment of roles, and arguments occur. Here are some specific areas unique to overseas family life which will affect how you as a parent will act and react.

1. Father as Primary Decision-maker

In the vast majority of overseas assignments, it is the father/husband who usually controls most of the major decision-making. Indeed, he typically makes the decision to even move overseas in the first place. In most instances, he will also have the most say (next to the company he works for) in the all-important decision of when the family will ultimately move again.

Not that he has any more control over all events than the next person, but nine times out of ten, final family decisions will still be made by him. If this situation is new to your family – that is, father wasn't such a dictator in the past – there will be adjustments required. His 'power' definitely changes the family dynamics and can have a tremendous impact on the happiness of family members.

Being angry with the father or husband for taking a unilateral decision over something as important as the winter holiday is just one example of feeling out of control, in this case, out of the decision-making process. Be prepared to face it, because that scenario is certainly not uncommon and reflects one very strong reality of family life overseas.

Further, the father also probably controls the bank accounts and family spending. Not only does he and only he know the bottom line for the family finances – which can drive the mother, if suddenly put on an allowance, into the ground – but all banking transactions may be done only through the good graces of his office. In many foreign countries, banking is difficult and the task may be assumed by the father's business. Instant money machines may not be found on every corner. You may be in a cash-only country where your credit cards are useless. As a wife, you depend on your husband's largesse. As a child, your father is your only recourse if your mother can't maintain her own bank account – or access one back home easily. Frustrating arguments are bound to break out among family members.

2. Father who is Rarely Home

While titular head of the family – and all-powerful controller of the lives of his family – too many overseas fathers are rarely home. It is unusual in overseas situations that the father actually has more time to spend with his family than he did back home. After all, the whole point of moving abroad is normally for the father to take up some important, key position which will require much more of his attention at the office. This means he leaves early and returns home late; long after baths, homework, piano practice, and bedtime. He's not exactly a constant presence to answer a child's questions, nor is he around to bolster feelings of security. He's simply too busy working.

He may be expected to entertain a lot more than he ever did back home. Depending on where you are posted, much of that entertainment is done outside of the home. A father who used to be around weekends to take the kids swimming or to other lessons is now squirreled away at the office catching up on

correspondence, or cruising down a fairway with a client. Or, he may simply be off traveling on yet another regional tour of a week to 10 days. If he is working too hard (workaholism is not uncommon in foreign communities abroad) he also may not be in the best of moods when he does finally see his children. He will want to relax, not play with his children.

His prolonged absences can cause a host of problems. The man making all the decisions who is rarely around is bound to have a few fights with children, especially teenagers, when he suddenly issues decrees on something he knows little about. He also risks severing his relationship with his children. I spoke with many grown-up foreign service children who harbor so much resentment towards their working fathers whom they never saw while growing up, that the relationship can never be recovered.

3. 'The King is Home' Syndrome

A group of Singapore expat wives (known locally as the 'bus-stop ladies' because they would go for power walks after putting their children on the bus for school) can take credit for giving this common phenomenon its name. When the King is finally home after still another regional trip, these wives told me, family life must suddenly accommodate the King's needs – be they an urgent golf game or a guilty field trip with his children to a place they are not interested in, or which disturbs their own plans.

The children continue to look to their mother for all answers (since she is likely to know better anyway, being the day-to-day parent) and often fights break out while everyone's respective anger and resentment blows over like a typhoon. It's a storm which definitely provides rough family weather.

4. New Parenting Role for Mother

Someone obviously needs to fill in where father is absent and that duty inevitably falls on the mother. The day-to-day job of raising children overseas is still primarily the mother's. And she must execute this responsibility within an entirely new set of circumstances – a new cultural framework, a state of mind which may have known happier days, and with her better half not around to help out much. Mothers can become resentful.

The mother's status, and likely her attitude, also have the potential to change quite dramatically from home to overseas. This definitely affects the new family dynamics. Take, for instance, a career woman who suddenly stops working and spends her time abroad running errands all day or hanging out at the health club. She may or may not be a happy woman, depending on her feelings about what she perceives as a major drop in her status to 'accompanying spouse'. Mom's new status – and unhappiness with a drop in that status outside the home – will definitely change the nature of the family from what it was before leaving home. She may begin to view her parental responsibilities in an entirely different way.

For instance, if she's frustrated and unhappy, her children may not like this new mom who snaps at them all the time. Children know when their mother feels she is being deprived not only of a life of her own, but respect too. It will be obvious in her moods, her lethargy over family activities, or constant references to the career she left behind. Extremely unhappy women might choose anti-social forms of behavior like drinking, or sleeping all the time. Suddenly, the reliable mother who was always up in the morning to fix breakfast and pack lunches for everyone isn't seen at all until after school or when the maid has come in and started her day. She becomes a different parent than she was at home, and in many cases an ineffective parent.

Similarly, if the mother is enjoying a long-deserved sabbatical from a hectic career and wants nothing better to do than avoid the job market altogether and try something different, even stay at home and try writing or painting, her husband and children may not be happy either. They may want the 'old' mom back in their midst – the interesting woman with a glamorous job, something to say all the time, dressed in a power wardrobe and not a sweatsuit. Instead, the children are being bombarded with homemade cakes and cookies after school that they don't want to eat and a mother, as far as they are concerned, poking and prying into their lives too much. Hasn't there been enough radical change, the teenager may be thinking, without mom suddenly wanting to throw all her energy into motherhood?

The woman who had servants in her own country who moves to a developed country where help is expensive may suddenly be the chief cook and bottle washer and none too happy about it. Once again, the rest of her family may be watching her askance and wondering where the woman they knew vanished to.

Children become more dependent on their mothers overseas. If she is unhappy or insecure about her role and transmits this message loud and clear, her children will not be happy. As one veteran traveling child put it to me: "If mom's OK, I'm OK."

5. Working Mothers

Mothers who work overseas create different problems for the family. If their hours are too long, their children are left for too many hours with servants. It is easy to spot these children who are crying out for the attention of parents who are not there. If the father is working long hours as well, where does that leave the children? With servants from morning until night.

Of course, mom may have worked back home so working abroad shouldn't be all that different. Except it is. A mother working at home has a different support system, as do her children. In a foreign country, when a mother is not at home, children are greeted at the school bus in a language they can't understand, they are likely deprived of easy after-school play dates at the neighbor's house, or they can't begin their homework until a parent arrives home to help them.

I'll return to the subject of working mothers overseas later in this chapter. For now, it's enough to say that overseas, a working mother has the potential, along with the other issues I'm identifying, to have a significant impact on family life and on her children's happiness.

6. The Single Parent

Single parents raising children in expatriate communities which are very conservative, two-parent family situations, will face difficulties. A single mother of two girls told me the first challenge for the parent is to examine his or her own motivation in choosing to live overseas as a single parent. Is she running away from a bad marriage? Travel is an ancient means of escape. But the children are also essentially conspirators in that flight of fancy and may resent leaving the parent left back home.

Another single mom reported her children didn't really notice their unusual household configuration until they attended church or other expatriate gatherings of family units. It was at such events that her children missed having both parents around.

Safety issues (many of which I'll be discussing in Chapter Eight) also become very critical to a single parent, especially those who do not move to a foreign city with the medical benefits offered by a government or corporation. Emergency situations, always the nightmare of parents, are fretted over a lot more by the single parent who may have to cope with one on her own one day. Extra precautions must be taken, even if it's writing down the number of a taxi that whisks a child away.

7. Parents are Out to Dinner All the Time

Back home, parents likely went out on the weekends to movies or parties with friends. They were not out every other night at a diplomatic cocktail reception, National Day celebration, or dinner party. Children were not left with babysitters night after night. Parents were around for help with homework and all other evening-related activities. Suddenly, overseas, parents are social butterflies.

Don't assume for one minute that constant evening entertainment doesn't affect family life. Children may resent being left often with babysitters whom they don't like. Or, if they are young, they may be afraid of the babysitter. One mother confessed that in the early days of her overseas assignment when her children were still very young, she was a 'wet rag' from the guilt she felt over leaving her children, and especially a daughter who clearly was frightened of being left with the babysitter. Her children, said this mother, couldn't verbally express their fear of abandonment, but as a mother she felt it 'right down to her pores'. Any way you look at it, too many nights out is too drastic a difference from what children may have experienced at home.

8. Servants

Drastic changes in the domestic help situation can also wreak havoc on the rest of the family. Besides the fact that they are babysitting constantly, they may also be doing too much for the children. This can upset the mother trying to establish a routine to encourage her children to take responsibility for themselves. When there is a newborn baby, a servant is always a mixed blessing. Just when you want to be with the baby, the child wants to be with the servant and not its natural parent! If there are no servants, mother may still be upset, and have dishpan hands. Father, meanwhile, is happy there are servants around and conveniently disappears after supper or on weekends. He may even drop his clothes in heaps around the house.

9. Lack of Immediate Family

All the immediate relatives you rely on in a pinch back home – where are they? Thousands of miles away, available only by mail and expensive long-distance phone calls. Granny is not there to take the children for a weekend when mom and dad have had enough. The family unit is smaller overseas. There are no relatives for holidays and celebrations. A family can feel quite lonely unless a new support group of friends has been established. A mother still may be stinging from her own mother's parting reminder that she is taking her grandchildren away.

10. Only Children
Family life can change dramatically for the only child who moves overseas. In families with more than one child, siblings who normally treat each other like dirt or with indifference suddenly become the best of pals. There is nobody else to play with – yet. The only child doesn't have a built-in friend to sit with on the school bus or hang around with while getting settled. If both parents are working, the only child will spend a lot of time with servants and risk becoming too much the focus of their attention. The only child may never have minded his singular status back home where he had cousins and lots of friends as sibling substitutes, but now he feels the pressure to have a companion his own age. He may apply pressure to parents to have another child when he had never even suggested it before.

11. Marital Problems
Within the smaller family unit divisive issues may arise that can potentially break up a marriage. Mom and dad may have marital problems which weren't as pronounced at home but now everyone feels the tension. Or children may watch their parents arguing more than they did at home over new overseas issues. They feel insecure and suspect all the arguing is going to lead to divorce. Siblings may also be divided in their opinions on everything – from which place is best (home or overseas) to which food is best. Children's loyalties may be challenged. One child may side with the mother, another with the father.

12. Lack of Distractions
Diversions – going to a movie or a mall, for a bicycle ride, or just going for a long walk – may be difficult if not downright

impossible. So the child (or the parent) who wants to escape for a few minutes may have absolutely no place to do this, except a bedroom or the bathroom. Family members are thrown together whether they want to be or not. Or if the family does want to be together, they may be living in a place where there is literally nothing to do as a family or nowhere to go that doesn't bring on a headache at the thought of logistics and foreign road signs.

SECOND LANGUAGE PROBLEMS

English is the lingua franca of foreign communities around the world because it is the language of international business. So in addition to their native tongue, most parents usually will arrive overseas with some fluency in the English language as well. Not so their children, and this can create some family tension.

The parents may tell their children to run along and play in the new playground at their housing complex. When their children balk at the idea – mostly because they don't have the language or don't want to speak with an accent – the parents can't understand their hesitation. Parents familiar with this situation say it takes at least a year for most children for whom English is not their first language to gain the fluency and slang to help them function as a regular kid in the playground.

Similarly, a mother without English language skills or the same opportunities to gain fluency as her children may have some problems with them. They may be embarrassed at her lack of skill or inability to communicate with other mothers about play dates or birthday parties. All family members must be sensitive to this communication issue and recognize its potential to disrupt family harmony.

BEHAVIOR PROBLEMS WHEN ISSUES EXPLODE

With all of these new family issues at work, something is bound to give. In the case of the parents, it could be the marriage. With children, it is typically behavioral and academic problems, general unhappiness, and the possibility of long-term estrangement from a parent. *But these things do not necessarily happen.* They might or might not happen to everyone and they certainly won't appear overnight.

There will be signs – and it's up to the parents to be on the lookout for indications that all is not well. By identifying some of these problems and their origins, parents can help guide children out of their malaise or avoid the problems in the first place. Here are some of the key problems that can crop up in response to the new family-life dynamics.

1. Anger and Resentment

Not all children are going to thank their parents for dragging them around the world. Children rarely thank a parent for anything but you can bet a child of any age is not going to be grateful if he has given up his spot on the varsity team (if he's a teenager), his friends, or a spacious backyard, only to watch parents fight all the time over stupid things or to eat strange things. Never underestimate a child's anger. It is usually not articulated because a child just doesn't have the facility to express himself. There may also be deep-seated resentment towards the parents for obvious reasons. Where is my backyard? the three-year-old asks. Where is the library? cries a teenager. Small issues, perhaps, to the parents, but large ones to a child. Since it is the parents, and especially the father, who is responsible for their overseas assignment, children will target their resentment accordingly.

The mother might be pretty angry too. She directs her own share of resentment towards her husband for dragging her halfway around the world or towards her children for making life so difficult, complicated, and exhausting. Anger and resentment are natural emotional responses to being thrown into a new situation. There's nothing wrong with feeling. Don't think you are harboring some deep, dark secret which nobody else has.

It is when you see it getting out of hand with your children – a toddler starts biting, a young girl starts lying all the time, an older boy starts fighting on the school bus – that you know the anger must be checked by an open discussion of the reasons lurking behind such behavior. Likewise, when that anger and anti-social behavior spill over into the classroom, so the child is too angry to want to do any school work or make any new friends, there is an issue looming.

2. Over-protectiveness, Manipulation and Guilt

When a mother becomes over-protective overseas, or certainly more protective and fearful than she ever was back home, a child easily feels her guilt and may become manipulative. He knows which strings to pull. When he's been acting badly, for instance, he can pretend to act sick to avoid punishment. He knows that his over-protective mother (who would gladly put her children into a protective bubble) assumes it's a deadly foreign virus and goes into instant sympathy. Or the child throws a tantrum in a toy store until he gets what he wants.

This behavior has many forms, depending on the age group, but the outcome is the same – the mother gives in. She has been manipulated. She moves one step back to anger and resentment towards everything associated with her life abroad. And she likely remains over-protective, encouraging the cycle to begin all over again.

3. Inability to be Disciplined

A guilt-ridden parent being manipulated by her child is going to be hard-pressed to discipline when necessary. Or worse still, will discipline at inappropriate times and then feel guilty about it. Again, the cycle keeps turning round and round. Unfortunately, inconsistent disciplining serves no useful purpose for the child. The mother is distraught and the child knows he can get away with murder.

4. Over-dependence on One Parent

You see this over-dependence a lot with the pre-school age child overseas. A clingy toddler, who may have had a tendency to be clingy at home, now is fearful to leave his mother's side for an instant. Older children too may suddenly want mommy around all the time and that's not healthy for either child or parent. Of course this dependency goes on at home too, but once again, in an overseas setting, it becomes exaggerated because the child has been uprooted and put into an unfamiliar environment.

HOW CAN PARENTS ALLEVIATE PROBLEMS?

I've painted the *worst case scenarios*, but most families will, at one time or another, feel the impact of any or all of these overseas issues with children of all ages. Knowing about them, watching for them, and coming up with strategies to deal with them is the first step in dealing successfully with them.

In the case of a traveling family, everyone's shock, everyone's moods, everyone's happiness affects the whole family. If the balance is off, the family rhythm is off. And you can only sweep this under the table or ignore unhappiness for so long. Eventually, someone's unhappiness will effect everyone. It must be dealt with head-on.

Family life affects just about everything else. For that reason, maintaining a happy family life should be the most important and critical goal for parents raising children in a foreign setting.

COMMUNICATION IS THE KEY

When you live overseas, an inability to communicate can become your *bête noire* as you try to explain even your simplest need to someone who just nods his head, smiles and says 'yes' when he really means 'no'. I know this for certain. I have absolutely no facility for any language other than my native English. In my next life I hope I can speak any foreign language.

I have, however, worked hard on my emotional communication skills with my children – that is, talking about feelings. In that area, I have had a lot more success than I have had with French, Thai, or Mandarin, the three languages I have tried to learn. I believe that without talking with my children on a daily basis, I can have no understanding of what is going on in their minds during their days, nor can I learn what they dream about at night. Without listening to them, I can't understand what is bothering them, what questions they have about life or just their immediate surroundings. Without talk, there would be a vacuum between us and no opportunities to learn from each other.

Overseas, that vacuum has the potential to become a canyon when parents forget to talk to their children. It is one responsibility which cannot be handed over to servants or ignored due to a prior social engagement. In a foreign country, your children, like yourself, are over-stimulated experiencing the new surroundings, the new culture. If a child is notorious for asking questions at home, he will become even more curious when everything is new and strange.

An overseas assignment is the time to be available for more talk, not less. There will be more questions, more issues, more reactions. A parent needs to be there more of the time, not less. Now is not the time for the silent treatment or to abandon this basic parental duty.

Talking with a teenager, parents have assured me, is not any fun when the child simply opens his mouth to criticize or be nasty. But that should never stop a parent. And often a younger child just doesn't have the words yet to express what he's thinking. Remember who is the adult and who is the child. As the adult, you have both the ability and the maturity to initiate communication regardless of whether it's fruitful. It's up to you to use both that ability and maturity as often as possible. And wisely.

WHAT EXACTLY ARE YOU COMMUNICATING?

Communication is a two-way street, but since this is a guide for parents raising children overseas, I am assisting in the parent's 'talking points' on these important issues. Every child is different, so the responses to these messages will naturally be varied. As a guide, I only wish to offer from my own experience some of the issues which I have seen come up in my own family and the many families I have interviewed or met during the last 10 years. These may or may not apply in everyone's case

1. Family Should Be the Priority Whenever Possible

Family is not always the priority to the employee posted abroad. The job is the priority. That message is transmitted in hundreds of different ways to the accompanying spouse and family members. When we were living in Bangkok, and I was pregnant with my daughter Lilly, I just about murdered my husband when I discovered that, after a week away working at a refugee camp, he had checked in with the embassy every day to ask what was new. His pregnant wife, back at the apartment sweating her brains out and wondering just how big her stomach could actually get before making it into the *Guinness Book of Records*, received a single, cryptic phone call. We have since worked out our family versus embassy priorities in favor of the family whenever possible. It is up to individual parents to decide on their own family priorities in order to come up with compromises and their own workable solutions to what will be an on-going conflict and tugging in both directions. As they like to say in the culture shock business, in some matters there is no right or wrong, only different.

My personal belief, and that of child psychologists I spoke with, is that insecurity, unhappiness, and the child's perception of a neglected childhood result when traveling children feel their own needs are clearly *never* deemed to be number one. Of course, there will be some instances when the child's needs will have to be placed on the back burner. But when it becomes the norm, you will have a lot of explaining to do to your children. Start communicating from Day One.

2. When Mother Works

This is another thorny issue, but at the risk of raising the shackles of working mothers worldwide, I have to go on record here and say I believe that when a family moves abroad, and if there is any choice, the mother should not work for at least the first six months. And then, if she does choose to work, it should be only on a part-time basis.

I have watched the effect that working mothers overseas – especially those who run out and start working full-time the minute they arrive – have on children abandoned to servants either all day or after school when they are struggling with homework and dying to tell someone in their own language what happened at school that day. The children feel abandoned, al-though they may not say that straight out, and they devise all sorts of ways to seek attention. Television and computer games become high-tech babysitters and their improper use will eventually become an issue. Overseas, as I noted earlier, the pressures on children are different. Issues which may have been easy to cope with back home, now need more attention – from a mother who is at home when they come home.

I am aware of the old argument that women shouldn't give up their own lives for their children; it just doesn't carry any weight with me in an overseas situation. Staying home with a toddler because of a difficult overseas setting totals up to just a few years out of the mother's life, *which she can recover from, professionally and emotionally*, but which her child may never recover from. School-age children in a foreign country deserve a parent at the end of the day especially during the critical six-month period of adjustment. After that, mothers should be *part-time, flexible* working mothers, available to their children when it's at all possible.

I have heard it said, and it definitely applies here, that children need their mother home after school not only when they are in pre-school, but all the way through high school. Overseas, with cultural differences, limited recreational facilities, and numerous opportunities to get into trouble, this thinking applies tenfold.

Working mothers are often unaware just how much their children use their school work to compensate for the mother's absence. They become high achievers in school, trying to use their grades as a means of impressing their parents. These mothers then console themselves by pointing to the high grades as an indication that there is nothing wrong with their children and their absence is clearly having a positive effect on the children's development. Scholastic development may be on track perhaps, but the wider emotional issue – the fact that children felt bad but found that studying was good – has not been resolved.

And what about children left all day with a maid? Chances are you think yours is a gem, but as one Danish mother pointed out to me, you don't really know what that maid is up to all day. This mother found out her maid had been hitting her young son to get him to sit straight in his wagon. An object of fun had become a nightmare for her son. Evidence, or just fears which can be just as bad, of sexual abuse and other forms of mistreatment are told by some parents, too.

An overseas mother should think hard about her decision to work. Consider the number of women you know back home who don't have the option of staying home with their children, for financial or emotional reasons. Traveling mothers are given a rare opportunity to take a sabbatical from the superwoman role. Often, this is because working in some foreign countries can be difficult, if not illegal, and openings directly related to a particular profession may be zilch. Here's a golden opportunity to be with your children now and go back to work later with the experience of living in a foreign country under your belt. (Yes, living does count for something.) It's worth giving a bit of thought to before racing out for one of those locally-hired, low-paying jobs which many expatriate women accept.

3. Social Butterflies are Just as Bad

Just so working mothers don't think I'm coming down hard on only them, consider the mother who feels noble that she has chosen not to work but can hardly be labelled a 'stay-at-home' mom. She's off every day – all day – at the expatriate club playing bridge, out shopping, at her health club, or just anywhere but at home when her children come home from school. Toddlers can be left all day with maids to accommodate this specimen as much as the mother who goes to an office for the day. Older children will feel just as abandoned. All the issues I mentioned pertaining to the working mother most definitely apply to the mother who is absent due to too many social engagements during the day.

4. We're Special Enough to Do Things Together

If the father is working all the time or away, then be sure to schedule family time together. Evening meals are a great place for families to exchange the news of the day. But if daddy is stuck at the office or out with a client, the meal is eaten on the fly. So plan a family outing, a family meeting, or any other 'special' family time. Vacations are good, but don't occur often enough to sustain good and effective family communications.

A drive in the country, a board game, a picnic, or Sunday brunch – the setting is not as important as the act of sitting down together to catch up, to hear about what's happening at school, in the playground, and on the school bus. These occasions don't always have to include the entire family. Split up – mother and son, father and daughter, and vice versa. Don't become strangers. Take time to talk to each other. Don't let too much time pass between conversations or it will only make it harder to resume them. As one child said, overseas there are so many more stimulating situations which the family can share. Don't cut your family out of the action. These outings are the perfect setting in which to explore and learn more about the local culture.

5. Create an 'Extended' Family Overseas

Some of these family outings can be shared with other families. In the absence of family members like grandparents, aunts and uncles, cousins and siblings, it is up to parents to create a new 'extended' family overseas. Together, these new overseas families can find all sorts of ways to have fun, see the local culture, and be together as a 'family'. This type of family networking is especially useful when there is an only child. It also happens quite naturally once you have settled in and met a few people because everyone is without their immediate family. Parents usually befriend other parents with children the same age so this makes those Sunday outings or holidays easy to plan.

Within overseas foreign communities, it is easy to find that your circle of acquaintances covers a wide age group, which I see as a bonus of friendships overseas. At home, your group is usually limited to old classmates or other people of the same

generation. Abroad, there is a lot of cross-over between generations and while this is good for you as a parent, it is especially
good for the children. Your new friends become representatives
of aunts and uncles or grandparents. Of course they are not
really an aunt or uncle, you will patiently explain to a young
child, but for the time you are overseas, they will likely take just
as much interest as a real one. After all, they miss their nieces
and nephews or grandchildren, too. This community support
system of family is good not only for holidays and outings, but
works wonders in the case of emergencies too.

6. Respect Your Children's Right to Privacy

Living in such close quarters physically and emotionally means
everyone in the family feels crowded and smothered by family. A
child – especially an adolescent – needs his space even if it's just
to blank out by listening to music and to brood for a while.
Overseas, bedrooms become sacred. Be sure to allow your children
to set up their bedrooms whichever way they want it. There
should be no arguments over this one. Likewise, a child's right
to privacy – diaries and any other assorted vestiges of what he's
thinking or up to – should be left alone.

Similarly, if a child asks to go on home leave ahead of the rest
of the family – let him go if he is old enough to handle the
responsibility of traveling alone and there is family at the other
end to meet and accommodate him. I've watched parents struggle with this issue as natural fears of disaster run wild in their
heads. But in the end, parents who have done this agree their
children appreciated the time they had to themselves. It helped
to build a much stronger bond between parents and encourages
independence. (There will be more discussion on this issue in
Chapter Nine.)

Younger children, even pre-school children, also need time
away from their parents. I like to think of this as giving your
youngster his own agenda, separate from mommy's. It allows

him to build his own sense of independence from an early age and, if it is the case, give him a break from a smothering home life. Formal pre-schools abound in foreign communities and often begin at a much earlier age than in Western countries provided the child is toilet-trained. A child who goes off a few mornings a week by the age of 2-and-a-half or 3 by himself not only develops a sense of himself, but has his private time away from parental supervision.

For the pre-teen set of 8- to 12-year-olds, sleepovers are a good device to help them feel they too are getting away from the family for a night to pursue their own life. Sleepovers overseas are an easy form of entertainment to arrange, especially if you are all living side-by-side in a foreign housing complex. Teen-agers should be allowed to go away on school field trips, or tag along with another family on holiday if the situation permits.

7. Help Them Respect Themselves and Others

Overseas, parents seem to do more for their children if only because many things are impossible to do in the foreign culture without some kind of assistance. In order to counteract the resulting helplessness and dependence, parents should try to encourage some activities which give their children – of all ages – a sense of responsibility for their own person.

In younger children, this can mean teaching them to dress themselves. (It's surprising how many children don't know how to dress themselves because a servant assumes the responsibility.) Little things help. Despite having servants overseas, for instance, I've always made my children (even my son by age 3) make their own bed. Naturally, mom could re-make the effort, but it was important to me that my children do it in the first place if only to create some sense within them that everything will not always be done for them.

Similarly, school-age children should be encouraged to make their own lunches, babysit for other foreigners, tidy up rooms and dressers, and so on. Let children go to the school bus by themselves when they are old enough. These sound like small things indeed, but it's amazing how many children on foreign postings are incapable of even simple tasks like tying their shoelaces. Money, while beyond their grasp or even use, should still be introduced in the form of allowances and savings. I believe you teach children to respect themselves by giving them responsibilities for looking after themselves.

This respect, in turn, can encourage respect for others and especially those in the host culture. I have heard numerous horror stories of how children talk to the local maids. When you consider that these maids were likely dressing and feeding these children (many beyond the age where such tasks should be done by an adult) is it any wonder the children were not showing proper respect? Our children watch us for cues. Especially when it comes to the local culture, it's critical to present the proper example.

8. Make It Clear You Won't Tolerate Bad Behavior

It may seem hard to discipline a child you've just uprooted, but probably more than ever, a child needs to know his limits overseas. You make these clear by indicating punishment can be handed out overseas just as easily as back home. Be consistent, follow through, do not let a child of any age get the upper hand. Young children can be given time out, older children can be grounded, videos and computer games made off limits. Do not think you should go easy on a child just because he's moved far away. Obviously, common sense should prevail in the early days. But once everyone is settled, be sure your children know who is in authority.

9. Learning to Create New Distractions

Those special family outings I mentioned earlier can go a long way towards not only becoming new substitutes for old distractions, they may indirectly introduce your children to the host culture – and create an appreciation and stimulate a life-long fascination. It often seems impossible to find something to do on a long Sunday but who better than your children to suggest ideas for a weekend afternoon? Listen to what they suggest. If it's bowling, go along with it. A long drive and winter picnic? Why not? Sharing outings and suggestions for those outings brings parents and children together and reinforces the sense of adventure.

10. Form Parent Support Groups

Parents overseas can definitely learn from each other. I found the greatest support group of my life during our posting to Bangkok. An international mothers' group helped me get past all my anxieties about having a baby. There's no reason that parents of pre-teens, teenagers, or whatever the age group, shouldn't get together to exchange views and experience.

YOUR CHILDREN'S FAMILY LIFE WILL BE DIFFERENT FROM YOUR OWN

Do not measure your values and expectations of the family life your children will have against those of your own. Your children are probably growing up in an entirely different set of circum-stances than those you experienced. So expecting they will be close to cousins as you may have been or any other childhood fantasies you may wish to impose on them is not realistic and can damage your relationship with your children. You love your children for whom they are; now love them for the life they are fortunate enough to lead.

Don't get yourself all twisted up in emotional knots trying to carve out a family life in childhood for your children which may be impossible to create in a foreign country. Enjoy and appreciate the differences between your childhood and that of your son or daughter.

A GOAL OF MAKING CHILDREN FEEL SECURE

Children go forth and do great things when they come from a family which makes them feel loved and secure. Parents should make sure their children know they love them and support each other in whatever they are trying to achieve. The goal of all communication between family members should be the reassurance that the love and appreciation – and respect too – are forthcoming and unconditional.

This is not drastically different from parenting techniques for children growing up in one's own setting back home. Feeling abandoned or ignored by parents in your own culture with friends and relatives a stone's throw or phone call away is a lot different than feeling abandoned in a foreign country where different people eat different things with different utensils in different homes.

And remember, sometimes words aren't required to express love and affection. A parent's mere presence may be all that is required. The best job a parent can do in this new overseas setting is provide that presence, willingly.

QUICK TIP SUMMARY

- Recognize there will be delayed forms of culture shock pertinent to family life overseas that require on-going adjustments.
- Family life is different in a foreign country than it might have been at home.
- DO let everyone be involved in decision making.
- Make family a priority – ensure that father doesn't become some shadowy figure who is never around.
- As a mother, DO reconsider a decision to work overseas. If it's possible, work part-time or with flexible hours to allow you to be home after school.
- If you are not working, DO try to limit social engagements or schedule them around your children's schedules.
- Recognize the role that servants may have in the family.

Don't let them do too much babysitting or do too much for your children.
- Establish a new 'extended family' of friends.
- Be on the look out for behavioral problems on the part of parents and children alike – like anger, guilt, resentment, over-protectiveness, and manipulation.
- Communication is the key to family harmony and a happier childhood for your children.

Chapter Six

INTERNATIONAL SCHOOL DAZE
Getting a Global Education

"There was nothing I could do to prevent changing schools all the time. It's not like I could run away from home in grade six."

—19-year-old foreign service offspring, looking back in anger

Just before Christmas of Lilly's year at Taipei American School, we received a rather strange note from her teacher. It seemed she had fallen behind in her advanced math class. The notion of 'advanced' math for 6-year-olds seemed odd enough, but the teacher's note seemed even more bizarre. We were being informed that our daughter wasn't keeping up with her extra math homework – independent study with math workbooks at least two levels higher than first grade, to be completed outside of regular school hours and classroom 'lectures'.

We were caught off guard. Naturally, I called to make an appointment to discuss Lilly's 'situation'. At that parent-teacher meeting, I learned the reason she had fallen behind. Her classmates all studied after school with math tutors who not only reinforced the learned math concepts of the day, but were paid by parents to spend hours working through these advanced math workbooks with their children.

Tutors? I asked, perplexed. For first grade students? Math lectures? What was going on at the school? Even worse, from my own cultural bias, was news that any adult would actually pay someone to help a 6-year-old do homework that a parent could so easily have helped with.

The American teacher then offered me a quick cross-cultural lesson. More than two-thirds of my daughter's classmates were Taiwanese (American passport holders of course). Their parents, even as early as the first grade level, were already looking down the road to their children's acceptance into Ivy League American universities. I could only shake my head in wonder (and a little marvel too) that the Chinese emphasis on math and science began so early.

At the same time, I was more than a little annoyed that the school administration had not bothered to point out the possibility of tutors. It particularly upset me because Lilly had seemed quite unhappy for several weeks – an unusual state for her to be in – and I had put it down to a bit of pre-Christmas melancholy over celebrating the holiday without the snow and freshly-cut tree she would have enjoyed back in Canada. The possibility that she was depressed about math had not crossed my mind.

When I followed up with a meeting with the school guidance counsellor, she told me she didn't think informing families of new students about tutors was relevant. I suggested that in the future, parents of new students might indeed find it important to know about cultural differences they couldn't imagine and thus ask the appropriate questions.

My daughter's unhappiness made me realize how much an academic issue, magnified by a distinct cultural difference, could affect a young child's sense of well-being, and especially her self-esteem and self-confidence. It was my first exposure to how emotional and academic issues can converge dramatically overseas.

A directory to international schools, school handbooks, even your embassy or company can provide practical information concerning school costs, size or facilities. What I intend to stress here are the emotional considerations in your child's school career and how they definitely can affect scholastic issues.

BE PREPARED TO ADJUST TO AN INTERNATIONAL EDUCATION SYSTEM

The culture shock associated with a move to a foreign country extends into the classroom. It will bring together not only a high number of different nationalities as your child's classmates, but will affect his behavior and academic performance. Just as everybody feels culture shock in some way or another, so too will your child get a cultural jolt when he starts attending a new school. For various reasons, the school overseas may be vastly different from the one he may have just left in his home town.

Parents are often caught off guard. It seems to be a sad fact that when moving overseas, some parents ask more questions about their housing or recreational facilities than they do about the school their children will be attending. Both your child's education and his emotional well-being – a substantial and significant chunk of his childhood – are on the line here. Never just skim over the school issue. Be prepared by knowing what the issues are going to be so that you can ask the appropriate questions, and truly decide if your child can handle it. If you know your child well enough, you should be able to make a wise decision about whether to move overseas in the first place.

The first mistake parents often make is taking everything they are told about a school by administrators at face value. The school, however, is dealing with the status quo; not your child in particular. That school principal doesn't know your child the way you do. He doesn't know that your child may not be highly motivated, may hate to read, doesn't make friends easily, or has been a constant disciplinary problem back home. They also may place the child in the wrong grade.

This happened to an Australian family I interviewed. They are a typical example of how a family moving to the Northern Hemisphere from the Southern, where school begins in January, not September, can experience placement problems. My Australian friends' two children were both placed in classes where their fellow students were an entire year younger. As both children were bright, they were quickly bored. When it came time to try to adjust the situation, the parents reported they experienced the worst 'interview' of their life with school officials. The mother felt the school had made a mistake in the first instance but was loathe to admit it. When they first arrived, they were bombarded with confusing opinions from different sources. Being on their first overseas posting, the parents were also unsure of themselves in an unfamiliar environment and didn't feel confident enough to demand what they thought was best for their children. It was only a year and a half later that they felt the confidence to challenge that initial grade placement.

Other expatriate parents I have met say that on first meeting, international school educators only want to put the best face forward and often do not inform parents of any negatives associated with the adjustment to the new school. It's like that guidance counsellor back in Taipei not telling me about the math tutors.

I agree that constant 'negatives' can be harmful, but as a parent, I want to know all the facts and especially those negatives. I need to know about those negatives so that I can ask the right questions and help my child face the new challenges.

INTERNATIONAL SCHOOLS

The common choice of school for most English-speaking children will be some kind of international school, which will likely resemble selective private schools at home more than publicly-funded schools. Most of the larger foreign communities abroad will have a local international school (some will have several of them, depending on the size of the foreign community) to accommodate the English-speaking children of Western diplomats, business people and others. This means most students are English-speaking children living in foreign countries with their parents. They come primarily from Western countries like Canada, the United States, Britain, Australia, and New Zealand. Depending on which system they follow, the schools are called International, American or British.

Children from as many as 40 to 50 other countries will also be enrolled in these local international schools since many traveling families of other nationalities often wish their children to be educated in English.

Some international schools are larger than others. My daughter switched from the huge campus of the Taipei American School (school population 2,000 and growing) to the smaller International School of Beijing (population approximately 350 and growing). Most schools divide the grades into the primary level (pre-kindergarten to grade six) and upper school (grades seven to 12). Some international schools do not have enough older students to offer late upper school grades, which is a point a parent should consider when agreeing to an assignment with teenage children. However, most schools now offer the International Baccalaureate program or the equivalent American pre-university program, which prepare children for entrance into universities. Parents with upper school children should ask which program is being offered before making the decision to move.

Traditionally, classes are smaller at international schools, providing a lot more personalized attention. Teachers will often have teaching assistants, which removes much of the bureaucratic burden and allows them more time with their students. Many traveling parents feel that international schools provide the next best thing to private schools given the individual attention their children receive.

International schools are normally co-educational. Many receive assistance from the US Department of State's Office of Overseas Schools, and will be members of a regional council for overseas schools, depending on their location. As part of their accreditation procedures, these schools normally conduct 'self-studies' to evaluate themselves. It is my understanding that those self-studies can be made available to parents. If they are, try to read one, because they describe aspects of the school not normally covered in the handbook, such as nationality breakdown, budgets, future plans and so on.

International schools do not come cheap. Tuition is often extraordinarily high. If you are negotiating a wage and benefits package with your employer (who in most instances pays school expenses), be sure to know just how high school fees will run in case they fall outside of your allowances. I met a self-employed venture capitalist in Taipei who paid for his two daughters' tuition out of his own pocket. At the time, the Taipei American School tuition for the lower grades was US$10,000 and the upper school fee was double that. Being an American, he joked that the thousands of dollars he was paying would prepare him for the day his daughters' university education would bankrupt him.

If parents wish to obtain directories for international schools worldwide, here are few addresses: The European Council of International Schools, Inc., 21B Lavant Street, Petersfield Hampshire, England GU 32 3EL, fax number 44 (0) 73067914; or International School Services Inc., PO Box 5910 Princeton, New Jersey, USA 08543, fax number (609) 452-2690.

FEWER SOCIAL SERVICES AND LIMITED SPECIAL PROGRAMS

International schools are typically governed by a board of directors made up of members of the foreign community or a sponsoring embassy. At some schools, a member of the Parent Teacher Association may hold a seat on the board.

One of the most substantial differences in schools overseas from those at home will be the absence of outside 'watchdog' agencies. Depending on what you call them, such agencies may be social services groups or organizations sponsoring programs for children with learning disabilities. Most international schools function independently and may be answerable only to an elected or appointed board or to a local embassy.

In the absence of any watchdogs, rules or legislation at home which define schools' responsibilities toward children with special education needs, or any other students requiring special assistance, will be noticeably absent. What this means to parents of children with learning disabilities should be made perfectly clear: your learning-disabled child is not likely to be accepted into an international school if his needs are special. There are typically few special education teachers, guidance counsellors, or psychologists.

This notion of non-acceptance of the learning disabled was confirmed by the director of the International School of Beijing, a veteran of the international school circuit, and reinforced by other international school educators I interviewed. They all agree: *parents of children with learning disabilities should not even consider a move abroad. Their needs very likely will not be met.* I was told some parents moved anyway and then expected to receive services they had been told point blank were not available.

In the absence of these support services, most international schools compensate by assigning their teachers double duty as both educators and counsellors. Given that many international teachers have worked around the world in various schools and a variety of situations, their experience should not be dismissed. They have worked with children from varied backgrounds and can claim to have 'seen it all' at one point or another. They should be seen as a resource by parents not only for academic matters, but for any other situations which may come up in the school. They are also an invaluable source as cross-cultural guides, having dealt with so many cultures in their classrooms. Look to the teacher in many cases to foster the cross-cultural understanding and tolerance necessary in a multicultural classroom.

However, parents being parents (that is, ready to have at least one bone to pick as they say), express a few concerns about the recruitment of international school teachers. Specifically, I heard several times the complaint that except for those hired locally, many of the teachers on the circuit are recruited as 'teaching couples' who can be easily housed because – and here is the critical part – they do not have children themselves. Some parents question how a non-parent teacher can identify some of the emotional issues which a child may be experiencing.

Another complaint is that some international teachers have been overseas so long that they have forgotten many issues which come up when someone is new. Take culture shock, for instance. When I asked teachers about how culture shock appears in the classroom, I was taken aback when most answers I received implied they had not really noticed it. The same is true for the subject of re-entry – the going home stage. Many teachers never go home until retirement, unlike many of their students who may enter and re-enter their home country many times. Re-entry shock hadn't occurred to some teachers I spoke to, although to their credit, as soon as it was pointed out, workshops or preparatory seminars were immediately introduced.

The best part about international schools is definitely the small classroom size which allows children to receive more attention and stimulation. A lot will depend on which school your children attend (big or small) but some schools may not have libraries or music programs or the facilities for sports. Others may be so lavish when compared to the previous school you will want to enroll your child in everything in sight, not to miss out. International schools are also active in offering in-country field trips and excursions which will help your children get to places you may not have the time to visit yourselves.

Older students who are preparing to come home to university can usually rely on the international school administration to supply the necessary support system. But like everything else associated with life overseas, you should inquire ahead of time to find out just what resources the school has. If pre-university support (testing, addresses for application forms, catalogues, and so forth) will not be available, be sure to plan your summer home leave around your pre-college young adult. While it's true you can rely on the international schools, or your embassy or government for some matters, in the end, responsibility for education choices rests on the parents' shoulders and never forget that for a moment. If help is there, use it. But you as the parent should think of yourself in charge, and educate yourself accordingly.

THE LANGUAGE ISSUE
AT INTERNATIONAL SCHOOLS

Often, for non-English speaking children, there is a language proficiency test before they are accepted by an international school, followed by English as a Second Language (ESL) classes to bring their skills up to speed. I have talked to children who have been accepted first and learned the language as they have gone along. It is no easy task for a child, so be prepared for at least a year – or more – of both emotional and academic backlash.

A 1988 study sponsored by the Overseas Schools Advisory Council in Washington, D.C., which addressed the fears and stress of moving overseas, pointed to language-related problems as the number one fear unique to international schools. This is especially the case for children who don't speak English.

A child needs to understand the school's common language not only to survive in the classroom, but on the playground too. A normally extroverted child may suddenly turn quiet and shy around her new classmates, not because she is anti-social, but because she hasn't mastered the new language yet. This should serve to remind parents not to be in a hurry to encourage social interaction at school if their child is still struggling to learn the popular slang. Likewise, academic performance will be slower while she learns to understand what the teacher is saying. Generally speaking, reading and expression which lags behind what is offered back home may actually continue to be a factor throughout an international school career.

IMPACT OF LOCAL CULTURE

It was clear from our Taiwan experience that the scholastic expectations of the local culture had influenced the international school. However, not all international schools have members of the local population attending the school. But in cases where the wealthy locals have the opportunity to give their children a 'Western' education, both the school policies and the classroom curriculum will be affected by the local culture.

The presence of local students in the international school system, however, will provide your children with a much-needed exposure to the local population which might only otherwise be provided through servants or the service industry. Your children can get to know the local culture a lot better through friendships which begin in the classroom.

OVER-ACHIEVING PARENTS

Overseas, parents typically place a higher than average emphasis on academic achievement. This should come as no surprise, given the demographics of most foreign communities. An unusually high number of offspring of over-achieving, highly educated parents are brought together in the international classroom. It doesn't seem to matter from what part of the world they come, but a cross-section of parents living abroad would likely reveal an abnormally high number of successful individuals, many holding more than one university degree. Naturally, this sense of achievement and emphasis on higher education filters down to the children, and eventually into the international classrooms.

Not only do these parents come from a higher socio-economic background (which their higher education reflects), together they make up a more conservative community, with the life values that go along with that leaning. Overseas, you find very few divorced households. Two-parent families are the norm.

A student population of over-achievers is not necessarily a bad thing if it spurs on high academic achievement. At the same time, it robs the classroom of a mainstream flavor. That is, everyone is more or less at the same level, despite the different nationalities. Sometimes, it does a child good to have a broader academic cross-section of classmates. However, the multi-culturalism of the classroom offers positive compensation.

HIGHER ACADEMIC STANDARDS

Along with over-achievement comes the perception that the school curriculum abroad is generally more difficult. Teachers I interviewed on this topic are in agreement that it may not in fact be the case that school is harder, just that expectations for success – fueled by the over-achieving expatriate parents I just mentioned – are higher. Children are more motivated towards success and want to please their parents, who in many cases may be pushing them harder overseas than they might have at home.

There is definitely more homework overseas. That is not just an impression. The level of instruction and class productivity is definitely higher in international schools, for they don't have to compete with too many outside distractions, especially television. As a result, parents should expect to attend more school science fairs or specialized events which will require hours of preparation from children (and you) at all levels.

Children living overseas tend to read more – lots more – when there is no television to watch. Children may also be expected to be able to read and write at a much earlier age, especially as pre-schools overseas are also more advanced, with children beginning at an earlier age. In her introduction to this book, Dr. Herh points out some of the negatives associated with pushing children to read and write when they are not developed enough to absorb such lessons.

Competition can be fierce at international schools. But the competition can often be not so much between students as it may be at home. Rather, children traveling and going to school overseas often have a much higher level of self-motivation and drive. They will be competing against themselves to do the best they can and live up to parental expectations.

Children on a one-time-only posting, or just their first time out entering middle school grades, will find they need to adjust their own powers of self-starting and inner motivation. These children not only will have to catch up with higher levels of world awareness (and, usually, a better knowledge of geography) but also sharpen their own independent work skills in order to keep up.

Children's grades may initially plummet overseas. It can happen that an outstanding student at home becomes merely above average abroad, the above average slips to average, average slips down to below average, and below average is in trouble. Educators will also tell you that grades are typically lower the first semester or year after a child changes school – even within his or her own country – so the phenomenon may not be unique to traveling children.

Many of these comments are generalizations, as they are gathered from a variety of sources. Parents about to move overseas or presently living the experience, still might be well advised to consider these points when assessing their children's education. Your own children's qualifications and performance levels may be affected in some way, so think before merely dismissing the notion that your child will not be affected.

AN AMERICAN BIAS

Many international schools have their origins in the American Embassy which may have started an English-language school for its employees or military contingent. As a result, while the nationalities of international schools may number as high as 50, the curriculum will often reflect a predominantly American bias unless the school is clearly operated by another foreign embassy, such as the separate Japanese, German, French lycee, Indian, and in some instances, British schools. At Taipei American School, for instance, my daughter spent hours on a project learning about Abraham Lincoln until I suggested to her teacher that my Canadian daughter might profit more by learning about Sir John A. Macdonald, Canada's father of Confederation. As a parent of a nationality other than American, you may have to intervene.

Obviously, when the school is actually called 'American School' you can expect a strong American bias. If it's designated 'International', as a parent it is up to you to suggest introducing lessons into the curriculum that reflect your own nationality. International schools are open to this, you must take the initiative.

FEWER DISCIPLINARY PROBLEMS

Traveling children spend a lot more time in the company of adults. This translates in a positive way into classroom behavior where the international school teacher will likely be afforded much more respect than teachers back home receive. International teachers say they spend a lot less time disciplining a classroom, which contributes to more time on direct teaching – one more reason why classroom productivity is generally higher in an international school.

GETTING HIGH ON GRADES

Back home, it may be considered cool behavior to hang around and tease kids who study too hard. Bookworms are definitely out in local schools, but that is not the case in the international school system. Children take their studies seriously, and the cool kids can be those who succeed, not fail.

A teacher told me about two teenagers who entered an international school late, determined to act belligerent about studies. Where they came from (Europe) it was cool to cut classes and put down books. Within six months, says this teacher, they had done a complete reversal. They had discovered it was cool to do well and quickly jumped on that bandwagon. Certainly something to warm the hearts of any overseas parents.

POLITICS IN THE CLASSROOM

International school teachers are always quick to point out just how harmonious is the school atmosphere given the number of nationalities. It's true that children do learn how to live with others from different cultures and become more tolerant. But it can be equally true that they are quick to defend their own cultures and history in no uncertain terms.

Overseas, people hold strong opinions (many represent the views of their countries even at social events) so it is not surprising when their children espouse the same opinions in no uncertain terms. Parents, and others in similar positions, are the only role models children have in an overseas setting. It is worth thinking about just how much your opinions as a parent affect your child. It is all right to be nationalistic, but when their classmates come from all over the world, a few lessons in diplomacy learned at an early age might take your children further.

SERVANTS AND STUDENT BEHAVIOR

Similarly, parents' opinion and behavior towards servants will be equally significant on the development of their child's attitudes.

This is felt probably the most profoundly on the way parents view the local population and especially the way they treat their servants. Teachers all report that when it comes to a child's behavior towards servants, there is definitely a strong influence by parents. For instance, while children will respect teachers and other adults in the school, the same cannot always be said for the way in which some children treat maids or other servants who may bring them to school or handle other responsibilities.

In the younger grades, some children don't know how to dress themselves to go out for recess because a servant has been doing everything for them at home. One teacher told me a child would point to his shoelaces and demand the teacher tie them, much as he would order a servant around. Local staff employed by international schools often don't receive any greater respect.

SEX EDUCATION

In a multicultural setting, where each culture may have a different set of values and means of communicating with their children, the subject of sex education is often relegated to elective study, if offered at all. It often depends on the availability of a teacher willing to teach it, and then on the parents' willingness to allow their children to participate in classes. Given the different religious backgrounds, letters seeking permission for sex education are routinely sent home for approval.

Some parents rejoice in the over-protective sheltering offered by life in a foreign community and would prefer their children to keep their innocence as long as possible. The introduction of sex education, therefore, represents an intrusion into that safe cocoon. Other parents, especially those from cultures that don't openly discuss sexuality or reproduction, will welcome the help of a professional teacher.

A discussion with a former teacher of sex education proved very enlightening, not only for the information about what's offered these days, but also for a glimpse into the related areas of building self-esteem and independence, which are routinely discussed in the context of sex education classes.

This teacher described an exercise relating to independence and self-esteem. She asked her students to list the people who were most important in their lives. When she did this exercise in her native Australia, students automatically listed their best girlfriend or dates as the most important people. Overseas, parents topped most lists. As the exercise was repeated over several months, newer first-tour children continued to list their parents as the most important people in their lives. Once again, it demonstrates just how critical is the parent's role when living overseas.

More directly on the sex issue, this teacher reported that teenagers are most definitely involved in sexual activity but face a problem endemic to a foreign community: where do kids go to have sex? Where, in fact, can they go to be alone and away from the watchful eye of a parent or teacher? More important, is it possible to discuss birth control with a doctor whom they won't bump into days later at their own dinner table, given the socialization within foreign communities?

Cultural differences may also hamper a student-doctor discussion on such issues. In a foreign community, there may be physicians from various religious or cultural persuasions who will offer conflicting views to a teenager looking for direct answers.

Parents must have an open mind and be ready to discuss the issue in the absence of other professionals or to expect that children will take matters into their own hands. In this day and age, this could mean not always practicing either safe sex (with the fear of AIDS) or taking proper birth control precautions.

If you are traveling with teenagers, put all modesty or nervousness aside and get down to discussing the issue regularly. Once your children reach the age where sexual activity becomes a possibility, prepare them with the facts, and help them take the proper precautions against pregnancy and disease. This task, too, may fall to parents in the absence of trained professionals.

EMOTIONAL PROBLEMS IN SCHOOL

Older children, from about 12 years of age and up, generally have the toughest time making the transition to an overseas school. The study I referred to earlier about stress and fears places adjustment to a new school system as the number two fear facing children. Teachers who confirmed this for me say that part of the problem for these children is that they have already established a school pattern and don't relish making changes which can affect their self-esteem and self-confidence.

Younger children are still open to change because it is all a pretty new game to them. But children approaching puberty are coping with many changes in their bodies and minds. A change in school presents a new academic system (which may temporarily topple their traditionally high place in the pecking order) as well as significant new opportunities to make and be accepted by new friends. But more than the mere age factor, there are other situations in which a school-age child may run into difficulty both adapting and learning.

1. The Multicultural Child

International school populations are a grab-bag of many natio-nalities and children of mixed cultures. As many as 20 percent of the students will come from two cultures, often a higher percentage. Many of them have no trouble switching back and forth between languages and customs. But for others, the experience is painful and requires the hand of a professional.

One teacher told me about a young multicultural student who had extreme difficulty living within her two cultures. It didn't help matters for the young girl that she lived in a 'local' apartment outside of the lavish (by comparison) expatriate compounds. She was not a happy girl, especially when attention was drawn to the non-American part of her heritage. Often, she even tried to conceal the fact that she could speak the local language. Her distress did not lead to academic problems, but she was clearly suffering emotional anxiety about her two-sided heritage. When her anxiety reached a feverish pitch, she would simply tune out during class by laying her head on her desk.

The case of this young girl reveals another interesting point about international schools which was substantiated by other teachers who have worked in both Western schools and international ones. At home, emotional trouble usually translates into academic problems. Not so overseas. In most instances, the will to excel supersedes the emotional problems and instead of translating into poor grades, it is manifested by unsettled social behavior outside of the classroom.

Parents in such situations, advise teachers, should be ever vigilant to their child's unhappiness and do what they can to stop outside influences from making a bad situation worse. The teacher of the young girl I just mentioned, for instance, felt that over summer holidays in the United States, her student was being influenced by grandparents there who clearly wanted her back Stateside. Of course they were well-meaning in expressing their love, but when it is too heavy-handed they may only be adding to the child's already confused emotional state.

2. The Only Child
The traveling only child, without siblings to rely on for companionship, also has a tough time adjusting in the classroom. These children are so used to having immediate, undivided attention from parents at home that they expect the same at school. Trouble with a math problem? Teacher! Come here now! Teachers can spot only children very early on from their dictatorial style which they exercise with parents at home.

3. The Average Child
This area is a bit touchy, because with the majority of overseas parents high achievers themselves, they will not easily admit to having a child of average, ordinary intelligence. But psychologists

and teachers point to distinct academic problems for children who range in the average level of basic intelligence. International schools are tougher, no doubt about it. With smaller classes and often more resource facilities like computers, children are challenged much more. An average child who starts out in grade one will by grade five or six feel the burden of trying to keep up with the smarter children. In some cases, such a stimulating environment may enhance the average child's performance, but professionals agree that many of the children facing constant emotional problems belong to the 'average intelligence' category.

It will be up to you to help in any way you can rather than take the average performance to heart. Not everyone can have a genius child.

4. First-tour Child

It is easy to spot the children out in the world for the first time. They have not yet developed those natural adaptation instincts which help the perpetually moving child cope with new situations. First-tour or one-tour-only children are at a disadvantage when they are put together with professional mobile children. The good news, according to teachers, is that it doesn't take long for them to figure out the drill. Within six months, a teacher in many cases is hard pressed to remember that this may be a child's first time overseas.

WHAT OTHER SCHOOL OPTIONS ARE THERE?

International schools are not the only options open to parents. Consider the following options, too.

1. Other Nationality Oriented Schools

In most foreign communities, there will also be other national schools as an option. Japanese children traditionally go to their own Japanese schools, French-speaking children go to a French lycee, Germans to a German school, and South Asian students like Indian, Pakistani or other Islamic students will also have their own schools. In order to find out about these schools, contact the appropriate embassy.

2. Missionary Schools

Many foreign cities will have separate schools for children of missionaries. The curriculum in such schools will naturally offer a religious program as well as a secular one. In some cities where international schools may not be available, Western children will also attend these schools, often for the primary grades. Once again, in order to find out more about missionary schools, ask at the local church.

3. Local Schools

Depending on where you live, and in some cases where there are simply no other options, your children will attend the local schools. Often, parents wanting their children to really escape from the expatriate circle will enroll their children in local schools as a form of enrichment. Language will obviously be a substantial barrier for older children, while younger ones new to their own language may be able to cope better by learning the host language at a young age.

Culturally, these local schools may provide a tremendous shock to your children. Educational methods vary from country to country, so thoroughly investigate the local option before enrolling your children. One parent in Beijing who enrolled her two daughters in a local Chinese school reported that the exercise worked at the younger grade levels, but was not as successful when the children got older. Language problems held the children back so that they were no longer with their peer group.

4. Study Groups

It is also not uncommon to have small, private schools, often known as study groups, where Western children without English language skills will spend a year to bring their language up to a standard acceptable by the local international school. These are usually small, often run by a non-English-speaking embassy. If your children's English language skills don't measure up for entry into an international school, you will often be directed, by the international schools themselves, to these study groups.

5. Educating a Child at Home
Some parents may choose to educate their children at home either because there is no local school available or because they are not happy with the one which is. Regardless of your reason for making the choice, the idea of home schooling is not a new one. There are certainly a few issues, both practical and emotional, to think about before taking the plunge

First consider the practical questions: Are you ready to take on the responsibility? Will materials be available? Is there funding for those materials? Will both parents be able to participate or will one parent alone shoulder the responsibility? Where do you get the materials in the first place?

Start with your own government's departments of education to determine some measure of curriculum equivalency. Consult the Australians, who have a long history of educating children in outback stations and have encouraged professional materials of a high quality. Also try to talk to teachers and see what they say. One mother who taught her grade one son said teachers told her that her son might have been better off without home school for a short period of time because the environment in which he lived, an Indonesian island, was an enrichment program in itself.

Home schooling is not new to the mission communities, but parents wishing a more secular education may not want to follow their programs. The Calvert School is one highly-regarded internationally recognized program and can be contacted by writing to The Calvert School, Tuscany Road, Baltimore, Maryland, USA 21210.

The interesting emotional aspect to home schooling was pointed out by my Canadian friend who 'home-schooled' her grade one son while living on the Indonesian island of Lombok. She reports that home-schooling parents are often caught in a no-win situation: the local population is offended because you choose not to use the local school and your own society considers your child 'school-less' (not unlike homeless) because you are excluding him from a structured education which many take as a child's divine right.

PRE-SCHOOL ISSUES

Many children begin pre-school at an earlier age when living overseas. In some instances, it is because parents are reluctant to leave small children behind for entire days with servants who may speak only the local language. It is also often the case that small children easily adopt a dictatorial style with servants. Pre-schools offer them a structured environment with teachers who will not put up with demands or spoiled behavior the way a maid might.

Not only do children attend pre-school at an earlier age, they embark on more ambitious pre-school programs. Where at home a child may begin nursery school at age 3, attending only two

days a week, overseas, most pre-schools offer five-day-a-week programs which also have longer hours. Additionally, a 2-year-old may go off willingly on a school bus where at home a parent may provide transportation.

Politics are often evident in a pre-school classroom. A teacher in Beijing reports she was reading aloud to her classroom one of the *Babar the Elephant King* stories and when the subject of a gun came up, one of her 3-year-old students from the Middle East launched into a diatribe against Saddam Hussein and the sad facts about the Gulf War! Like the international schools many of these children eventually enter, the standard of education is much higher. Math, alphabet letters, and other concepts normally introduced to a 5- or 6-year-old child in North America are taught to a 4-year-old overseas.

As for parents considering the pre-school option, pre-school teachers advise parents to ask specific questions when checking out a pre-school. What is the pupil/teacher ratio? (At least one adult to seven students is good.) What are the facilities like? Is it bright? Is there a good selection of hands-on toys, manipulative items, climbing equipment, and a playground nearby? Are there limits set for any nationality? Are the bathroom facilities accessible for children? How long will the bus ride be to school? How many days a week will the child go and for how long? Be sure to ask and certainly let your child see the kindergarten beforehand.

Pre-schools overseas can be expensive propositions, so once again, if you are negotiating a benefits package, find out the cost beforehand or be sure to include the pre-school option in your package.

A GREATER ROLE FOR PARENTS OVERSEAS

As with everything else associated with a traveling life with children, parents cannot stand back and just expect somebody else to monitor or encourage their children's progress. This supports a theme which is recurring – on purpose – throughout this book. That is, parents must simply make themselves more available to their children when living overseas, whether it be for playtime or homework time. With servants easing many household burdens, there can be no excuse to ignore your child's cry for help with homework, some extracurricular project, or just more 'quality' time to discuss the emotional issues which may be preoccupying them.

1. Parents and Enrichment

Parents will be expected to get involved more, not only in matters of curriculum, but also in the enrichment and development of the child's learning process. Such direct involvement should not be that difficult for over-achieving parents living overseas, unless they themselves are too caught up in their careers.

However, the type of parental involvement may be different than at home. For instance, teachers I spoke with pointed out that in their own countries (where they pay taxes), parents typically complain to the school about something they feel their tax dollars should be offering; overseas, parents raise different issues. Parents who see their children fight to adapt to the new overseas culture may wonder how that will translate into the classroom. Others may worry that children going in and out of different schools and systems may lag behind in some subjects. It is important to schedule parent-teacher conferences overseas to keep up to date.

With limited bookstores in some foreign postings, parents may also want to meet regularly with the school librarian to discuss what books they should purchase while away on holiday or on home leave. All the teachers I spoke with confirm that the library and its inventory should be monitored by parents.

2. Parents and Participation in School Activities

Likewise, parents should take an active role in extracurricular activities in an international school since they may be the only recreational outlet a child has in some less developed cities.

Unfortunately, many parents don't do this. They talk about wanting this or that club or organization for their child, but are unwilling to offer to take the time to run it themselves if there is no one else offering to do so. Parents raising children in foreign countries must be prepared to take a more proactive role as a parent volunteer because leaving it to someone else may mean nothing happens. I do know this from my own experience with my daughter's Brownie troop in Beijing. My own family and friends literally hooted over the thought of my acting as a Brownie 'Tawny Owl' (assistant leader) but no other mother had come forward. You may be able to get away with little active involvement at home, but doing so away from home may only mean your child misses out.

3. Parent Teacher Associations

The Parent Teacher Association (PTA) is a good way for parents to get involved in the school. As within any community, the effectiveness of the PTA will depend on the parents themselves, and their commitment to getting involved. In an overseas environment, the PTA also provides an excellent opportunity for mothers to form new relationships.

The relationship between the school and its PTA often reveals a lot about the way the school views many of the emotional matters close to any parent's heart, for PTAs may not pursue academic issues as much as those related to the student's well-being outside of the classroom. A discussion with one outgoing overseas PTA president yielded several questions which parents should ask on arrival. Is the administration supportive of the PTA? Does the international school director participate in PTA meetings? Does the PTA have a seat on the school board? (If not, parental input is excluded from school board matters.) What programs does the PTA offer? If it is involved in fund-raising (as most are) where do the funds go? To school equipment? Extra-curricular programs? Local charities?

When parents arrive overseas and feel alien in their new environment, the PTA is an excellent way to connect to the new community, and at the same time demonstrate to your child that you are interested in his school life.

4. Parental Guilt

Parents need to be realistic about facing up to the guilt they may be feeling about uprooting their children and placing them in a new, strange school. Their guilt should not lead them to change their approach to child rearing in critical areas like discipline. Don't change, is the advice of teachers and psychologists. Giving children too much freedom as compensation for guilt is not advisable. Likewise, imposing too high academic expectations on children may also backfire. Children need a few months to settle into the routine of a new school and a curriculum which may seem tougher at first, especially in the area of homework.

SCHOOL, THE CENTER OF YOUR CHILD'S UNIVERSE

In many foreign communities, the international school becomes the major focus for a child because it is competing with fewer outside distractions. As a result, school and school work become everything to a child. At home, a child may socialize with others outside of school – or with cousins or neighbors at a different school – but in an international setting, the school truly becomes the center of a child's universe. After-school activities, play dates, and birthday parties will all lead back to the school. Never underestimate the importance of the school. It is just one more reason why, as a parent, you should stand ready to get involved.

FROM THE MOUTHS OF OUR BABES

It was hard to resist putting a few questions to some of the students I had access to while living in Beijing. I distributed a questionnaire to the 62 upper school students (aged 13–17) at the International School of Beijing, to see what they would say. There was almost a 50-50 split of sexes in my survey and one third were first-tour children. Almost half did not speak English when they first started in an international school and reported it took them as little as six months to as long as two years to become fluent. On the question of whether there was more homework, it was a two-to-one decision in favor of the more difficult curriculum.

More interesting to parents are some of the comments offered when they were asked if they would like to tell their parents anything if they could:

"Parents should be more understanding."

"We are fighting rejection when we move to a new school. Don't make it harder on us by restricting our freedom."

"International schools are harder so parents should not expect so much."

"Family problems can mean school problems."

"If you don't want complaints, don't complain yourselves."

"Living overseas, kids are exposed to more ideas on how kids should act. This can lead to differences between the kids and their parents. I often wonder if these clashes could be avoided."

"Mom, if curfew is extended to 1 a.m., it's no more dangerous than if I came home at midnight."

"Parents should make sure that information on boarding schools is available in case their child doesn't like the school they are at."

"Parents should know that coping overseas is harder on us than for them."

"I think parents should respect their teenagers' decisions on the friends they choose. Just because some people come from different cultures and have different beliefs does not mean that they should be considered 'bad' friends or influences."

"Get to know the teachers and get involved in what your children are doing."

"Some teenagers really don't like to be overseas and really resent their parents for making them leave their old hometowns."

"I think it is useful to have the teacher talk to the parents before and inform them about their curriculum and how they teach it."

"Just sit back and pat yourself on the shoulder and think what a special, exciting experience you are providing your child. Good move!"

QUICK TIP SUMMARY

- DO spend as much time researching your children's new school as you do investigating your housing conditions.
- DO NOT take everything the school administration tells you at face value. Remember they are catering to the status quo. You know your child better.
- DO NOT bring children with learning disabilities overseas and expect a high level of local education and services for them.
- DO recognize that international school teachers are not necessarily qualified guidance counsellors and may stress academic issues at the expense of the emotional ones.
- DO prepare your children for international schools which may be a lot tougher academically and require they do a lot more homework.
- DO NOT expect children for whom English is not their first language to immediately adapt to an international school system.
- DO assume a greater role in the school life of your child, from enrichment to extracurricular activities.
- DO recognize how important school is to your children in the context of their new universe.

Chapter Seven

THIRD CULTURE KIDS
Understanding the Neighborhood Friends

"My father may be a retired foreign service officer, but I can never be a retired foreign service kid."

—Third Culture Kid expressing his reality

My daughter finds it almost bewildering when our conversations turn to comparisons between my own childhood and hers as a foreign service child. One particular point never ceases to amaze her: the fact that I actually grew up living in only one house, in one neighborhood, in one country – indeed in one culture – until I was 16 years old.

"You never moved, not even once?" she always asks, even though she knows the answer.

"No, not even once."

"And you actually could play on the street in front of your house? With the same neighborhood kids, year after year?"

"That's right."

"And you really went to the same school all those years?"

"I did switch after eighth grade to a high school."

"And grandpa's job truly never forced him to move?"

"Honey, when you're a dentist, like your grandfather, the drills don't move around too well. And if you think I haven't budged," I couldn't resist adding, "Grandpa has been drilling people's teeth on the same Toronto street for almost 50 years!"

Too mind-boggling – and if she could express it politely, too provincial – for her to absorb. After all, she is the product of an international upbringing. Born in one foreign country, she experienced four different cultures before the age of 9. My daughter is a classic example of a Third Culture Kid (TCK).

Sociologists, psychologists, educators, and experts from other related disciplines have been investigating the common experience of internationally mobile children. That research, into the lives of children labeled Third Culture Kids, is gaining recognition and popularity through workshops and conferences held by the authorities on this subject. Chances are you have heard the phrase but have never known exactly what it meant.

If you have been moving in and out of an overseas environment for a number of years, exposing your children to new culture after new culture, then your children qualify as Third Culture Kids. Read on.

HOW DID THE NOTION OF TCK START?

Sociologists at the University of Michigan pioneered the notion of TCKs back in the 1950s when they were sent by the U.S. State Department to examine the lifestyle of the American community living in India. When interviewing the children, the researchers couldn't help noticing how different the youngsters were from those of a similar age back in the United States.

The researchers were intrigued, and some, among them Dr. Ruth Hill Useem, the now-retired University of Michigan sociologist reported to have coined the term 'Third Culture Kid', spent the subsequent 30 years looking at the effects of international mobility on children. Now, all sorts of people are equally intrigued by the subject.

From the United States alone, there are more than an estimated 400,000 TCKs roaming the world or settled into university life back in the United States, which should give parents an idea of the higher numbers worldwide. Not only are their numbers significant, but their way of thinking, their emotional lives, and especially their methods of adaptation, hold great significance for the future when you consider that more and more people will be mobile in the next century. In that respect, TCKs offer tremendous potential for more far-reaching sociological research.

WHAT IS A TCK?

A Third Culture Kid – or a 'trans-cultural kid' as the term is now also being defined – is a child who spends a significant part of his life in a country or countries which are not the same as the one stamped on his passport. The child is not, as the term might lead you to believe, the product of parents of mixed cultures.

TCKs are the children of parents who often share the same cultural background and are now mobile professionals such as diplomats, military types, businessmen, teachers, or missionaries among others, who move in and out of other cultures for several years at a time. TCKs are also the prototype, according to some experts, for the world citizen of the next century. Generally speaking, they are adaptable, globally oriented, multicultural in outlook, and in many cases, multilingual. They are also good observers, less judgmental and less prejudicial than their non-mobile counterparts.

What is the 'third culture'? I'll use my own daughter Lilly as an example to explain the concept. Her first culture is Canadian.

Her parents are Canadian and she carries a Canadian passport. That's her 'home' or 'birth' culture – even though she was born in Bangkok.

The second culture, in Lilly's case, is a blend of the cultures of Thailand, Taiwan, and China, where we have lived. From these places, she has gained things which have contributed to the development of her values. These may be intangibles, even just cultural images, but she will nonetheless carry them with her for the rest of her life.

It is from the combination of these first two cultures that the third culture – the universal, global identity – surfaces. It is a unique third culture which she shares only with children who have also international, mobile experiences as she does. I often think of it as the jumbo-jet culture, where pint-sized travelers flash their passports in exotic airports, or smoothly exit in chauffeur-driven airport limousines or embassy cars. It is overnight or week-long stays at five-star hotels or international resorts while on vacation from international schools and diplomatic housing compounds. It is life in a rustic village, with one well for water and no indoor plumbing, or a South American mining village where natives and foreigners share local produce and customs. It might even be some Arabian oil outpost.

Regardless, it is a 'global nomadic' existence which even at my daughter's relatively young age, has already affected her learning experiences, her friendships, her ability to understand and relate to other cultures and the world at large, and of course, her interest in travel. Eventually, say the experts, it will even affect her choice of career, her relationships, and probably her choice of a spouse.

THE THIRD 'EXPAT' CULTURE

I would like to take this idea one step further. I already noted in Chapter Four that I believe the expatriate culture – life in a foreign ghetto – can sometimes cause its own unique form of culture shock for children. In my view, the expatriate lifestyle must therefore also be acknowledged as an important factor in the emergence of this third culture.

With its isolated foreign communities, jet-set travel to exotic places for Christmas vacation, duty-free shopping, international schools, expatriate health clubs and so on, the expatriate style of life provides not only the reference points for everyday life overseas which many TCKs share, but also greatly affects the child's system of values, in good and bad ways. A child whose parents treat local people, and especially servants, badly, for instance, will also likely grow up not respecting indigenous cultures. By the same token, a child who watches his parents enjoy and respect a foreign culture will be influenced in a positive way. An expatriate lifestyle which provides overseas benefits in the form of money, cars, or lavish housing, will likewise lead a child to believe his family is rich. That may be true compared to the host culture, but the true family fiscal reality may be quite different.

Moreover, I can't help but think by our isolation in foreign ghettos and an expatriate lifestyle abroad, my daughter has in some ways been cheated out of a greater appreciation for the cultures we have lived in. (I take full responsibility; my husband at least speaks local languages.) While it is certainly true that living in China or Thailand has heightened her sense of the poverty and despair in parts of the developing world, it is equally true that living an expatriate lifestyle in those same countries has exposed her to the Westerner's code of values and style of living in developing countries.

Often, unfortunately, chances to learn about the local culture are missed because of the parents' reluctance to investigate and participate. Festivals are an easy way for children to jump in and enjoy their new culture. Older children may participate on their own, but younger ones will need their parents to take them or to explain the significance of the celebrations. When parents can't get into the swing of things, they often spoil what could be a lot of fun for their children.

I tell the following story not with any pride but as an illustration of how easily a parent (obviously myself) can throw cold water over something a child may find delightful. From our Asian experience, the absolute highlight of the year is Chinese New Year. When we lived in Taipei and experienced our first real taste of it, I enjoyed the festivities – the traditional red packets of money presented to friends and relatives and those who helped you throughout the year, and the festive meal which admittedly destroyed my stomach for a week, as I greedily tried everything. On the first night, I was willing to go along with the traditional fireworks, watching the skies of Taipei light up and crackle with celebration. A week later, when the crackle, kabooms, and what sounded like ceaseless rounds of shell fire continued to go off day and night, I felt I was trapped in a war zone. As the traditional time for fireworks dragged on, I got grouchier and grouchier from sleep deprivation. (Three o'clock in the morning and they were still being fired off within my hearing.) The fireworks, started out as something we all enjoyed, resulted in a sleep-deprived mother ready to start an international incident by threatening to shoot the next neighbor to light up a round of firecrackers. Not a great example for my kids, I confess.

Over the years, my children have witnessed first-hand, from their vantage points first as infants inside a snugglie, then from a stroller, and finally standing on their own two exhausted legs, my frenzied 'bulk' shopping vacations or on home leave for goods unavailable at our overseas location. I worry that they believe goods must be bought only by the crate-load, not one at a time. They have both become used to the notion of traveling somewhere new and different every time there is a school break, seemingly without regard to cost. And, they too have enjoyed lives overseas of relative ease, with servants to do all the dirty work, as their natural birthright, which it isn't.

In our two-year stay in Beijing, the children never saw the inside of a Chinese home, learned just enough Chinese to communicate with servants, and visited temples only for the markets nearby. Like their mother, they gagged at some of the local sights and smells when they toured other Chinese cities, where, after venturing out, we returned to luxury hotels and amenities.

If all of those factors combined with other quirks and perks of expatriate life haven't had as much impact on my children's values as the sight of a Beijing *hu'tong* (cramped, local living quarters), or local toilets, I would be very surprised.

What I, and many parents like me, have done for our children is over-compensate for what we perceived were the hardships of life abroad, such as a lack of green space or whatever the local equivalent may be. As a result, we deprived them of a deeper and truer appreciation of local cultures. It is an easy trap to fall into and one which we should make every effort to avoid.

One of the foremost authorities on TCKs, Dr. David Pollock of Interaction, Inc., a retreat in upstate New York where families go for briefings before and after their experiences abroad, reported a phenomenon which substantiates my own feelings. In his work, he has talked with children in the throes of the TCK experience, whom he meets by lecturing throughout the world on the subject, and has interviewed grown-up TCKs. Many feel cheated out of a true cultural experience in the countries where they lived because they were isolated from the local cultures and sequestered into expatriate communities. When they become adults, many can say they lived in three or four different cultures, and perhaps retain a smattering of market vocabulary, but they don't have much more than a superficial understanding of those cultures.

Dr. Pollock's advice – and I couldn't agree more – is to expose your children to more than this expatriate culture. Often one finds it difficult to do so, but as parents, we should not cheat our children out of the broader cultural education which is the most obvious advantage and positive aspect of choosing to live overseas. This can include teaching your children cross-cultural skills, helping them learn the local language and make local friends where possible, and actively participating in the scores of local festivals which will be literally staged at your doorstep.

WHERE ARE YOU FROM?

Like his mother who dreads being asked that horrible, unanswerable question, "And what do you do?", a TCK will shrink when someone unfamiliar with the overseas life asks him, "Where are you from?" That one simple question, which doesn't have a simple answer, raises a profoundly confusing issue that haunts the TCK: his feelings of rootlessness. It leaves him tongue-tied – along with that other contradictory question put to TCKs upon re-entry: "Are you glad to be home?"

"Do you mean where was I born?" the TCK may ask, or "Where am I living *now*?" "Where are my parents living?" is another possibility. The answer to "Where are my clothes at this precise moment?" may offer yet another road to an answer.

There is no direct, easy answer unless the listener has a few hours to spare. That is, there is no easy answer until the TCK assigns himself one, then sticks to it. As a parent, you can help your children come up with some of the answers, which they eventually believe because they have said it so many times it must be true. My daughter and I have been through this hoop already. When someone asks her where she is from, she is fully prepared with the answer: she is a Canadian, who was born in Bangkok, presently living in ——.

WHERE IS HOME?

What is 'home' for the parents is not home for the children. This means that when the adults are excited about home leave, the children may not have the same enthusiasm for a home they don't know. Just as your childhood was different from your child's, so too is your concept of home.

I have talked with many parents who get themselves all twisted up in knots trying to provide a home for their children like the one they had, even though they are living overseas. There's a contradiction at work here. Parents can't have it both ways. But with a little insight and a lot of communicating, not all is lost.

For TCKs, home is where they feel at home, according to Dr. Pollock. Other experts agree. Home is less a geographical location, and more an emotional one based on important relationships. For that reason, home is more often than not where the parents are posted, even if the child has never lived there herself because TCKs tend to be a lot closer to their mother and father. Home can also be a grandmother's house enjoyed every summer during home leave; still others have claimed Holiday Inns as home because during an extended home leave that's where they stayed.

Home can also fall into one of three groups: an 'object', like a musical instrument, a diary or a room; a 'memory', that is, an event or something which makes the child feel warm or nostalgic; or a 'person', the mother or a sibling. To many TCKs, home may be memories of the places they have lived or the one just left behind.

Like everything else in their lives, home for TCKs is transportable. It is also cumulative: home may be a mixture of events and places which come together like a jigsaw puzzle. Home is the family, where a child feels as though he belongs.

HOME VS. NATIONALITY

From personal experience, I have come up with a workable solution which I can share. For my children, I have separated the notion of 'home' from the idea of 'nationality'. In other words, to my daughter and son, home is where we are living together as a family at the moment; our nationality is Canadian.

We have taken important steps to ensure a strong sense of nationality by buying a Canadian home for our children. When the time came to buy a house near the Canadian capital of Ottawa, where we live between foreign assignments, my husband and I chose to select a house not on the basis of future market value, but for our children. We bought a home that could be rented out while we were away and to which we can return after each assignment. It is our permanent Canadian home. The children – while away for years at a time – return to the same peer group who live near this home.

As our home is in the countryside, during home leave we are able to rent a cottage less than a kilometer from our own house, so that during the summers the children can rejoin that peer group. Friendships can be renewed over the summers as well as some sense of permanence established. We can also enjoy the fullest potential of a Canadian summer in the country. It was the smartest thing we ever did. That, and renting our dog along with the house so that he too could be there for the children's return to Canada. If there is one thing all TCKs I've interviewed are agreed on, it's the absence of real pets overseas that makes them long for 'home'.

WHAT ARE THE CHARACTERISTICS OF A TCK?
TCKs share a number of common character traits which distinguish them from what Dr. Pollock facetiously calls the OKs (one-culture kids). These characteristics spring from their unique childhood experiences and the many cultural influences at work.

Some of these characteristics can be seen as positive and some can't help but be viewed as negative. Eventually, as they grow older, it will be these same characteristics that will help them 'recognize' each other on university campuses and bring them together because, above all else, they make TCKs unique.

1. Used to Change
With a move to a different country every few years, an ever-changing landscape cannot help but become ingrained into the

TCKs' subconscious. They don't necessarily like all the change, but they become used to it because it is their way of life and possibly the only way they know. Uprootedness is the norm.

As a result of all the moving around, these children and young adults become extraordinarily flexible and adaptable which can be seen as positive. In fact, the experts believe that TCKs are a lot more flexible than their parents whose ideas and ways of doing things are much more ingrained.

A mobile child develops coping mechanisms to handle the constant moving so that when he arrives at a new location, an unconscious process of coping takes place. It is not unlike an adult who travels a lot on business and in each hotel room puts a framed picture on the bedside table to make himself feel more at home and the unfamiliar surroundings more comfortable. Strangely enough, to the TCK, the unfamiliar is entirely pre-dictable, for change is part of his identity. But he too will develop certain routines or rituals to 'familiarize' a new place. I have watched my own daughter set up her bedroom – and especially her desk – in exactly the same style wherever we go.

Some of these rituals will be emotional rather than physical, for even a young child will set up barriers to protect himself from being hurt too early on in the game. That may be one reason why, contrary to what one might believe, TCKs are not overly friendly to new children at school from day one. Every-one plays a bit of a waiting game before taking any plunges into new friendships.

Some researchers have also made the distinction between the adult who 'adjusts to' his new environment and the child who 'adopts' his new environment. The term 'adjusts' implies that you are still an outsider. Adults, with their strong sense of na-tional identity, prefer to remain outsiders even if they finally cope with a new environment. TCKs, on the other hand, 'adopt' – yet remain both 'part of' and 'apart from' – their new environ-ment. TCKs, raised in other cultures, feel 'ownership in none.'

As a group, they complain less than their parents about their environment and 'bad' living conditions, like traffic, lack of hot water, or dirty streets. They can deal with the bad, because it may have been bad before.

2. Highly Motivated and High Academic Achievers

As a group, TCKs spring from a sub-culture. Their parents are high academic achievers – typically from the same higher socio-economic strata of society. As a result, TCKs collectively score well on any testing of general knowledge and intelligence. All the travel doesn't hurt their scores either. They are more articulate and well-read than their counterparts at home. They usually speak or have a working knowledge of several languages.

TCKs will probably not do well at games like Trivial Pursuit, for according to the experts, they don't accumulate much trivial knowledge, especially information that might relate to popular culture like television or movies, which tend to be limited in overseas communities. So while they gather up special knowledge as a result of their international lives, their store of useless knowledge will be small.

TCKs are more self-sufficient and independent. Researchers have found them to have a high degree of self-awareness – they know exactly who they are and where they are going. While their parents challenge their own values later in life, TCKs challenge them at a much earlier age.

Along with self-motivation comes a higher degree of discipline and better control of themselves. That's one reason why international school teachers seldom complain about discipline problems.

3. Greater View and Understanding of the World

Having seen large chunks of it, TCKs have a much broader world view, with a much sharper perspective on international issues, which are likely discussed more in their international classrooms than they might be back home. With classmates from the four corners of the globe, TCKs also often have more racial tolerance and cultural awareness than their parents. They are certainly less judgmental than their elders.

Experts like Dr. Pollock also believe that TCKs have a three-dimensional view of the world, along with good cross-cultural skills. For that reason, he believes they hold great potential for building 'cultural bridges' in a society that is becoming increasingly international.

TCKs easily become world-weary. Upon re-entry to their own cultures their vast view of the world can alienate them from the 'kids next door' whom they are now trying to befriend. Those new friends have not been out in the world and many could care less about it since it is not part of their experience. Researchers studying the re-entry process of TCKs say the ethnocentricity of 'home' cultures bothers even a child of 10 or 11 who has a global view not shared at home.

Unfortunately this can lead to a feeling of detachment from their peer group. Being multicultural can be lonely, and feelings of alienation are not uncommon among TCKs, especially teenagers.

4. Little Ambassadors

TCKs are generally better-behaved and certainly far more comfortable around adults with whom they spend proportionately more time than their counterparts back home. They also get along better with their siblings, whom they may rely on in the early days of a new assignment before new friends have been found.

Also fueling their best behavior are the limits which most TCKs know are out there: they will be shipped home or shipped out of a school if their behavior does not measure up, especially if they do something illegal or questionable in a country whose government won't stand for it.

5. Extensive Relationship Bank

Depending on how much their parents move around and how good they are about keeping in touch, TCKs may end up having friends in every world capital. Friendships are numerous and briefly intense for TCKs. There will be some loneliness until a new network of friends and companions has been established.

Along with this loneliness will come the sense of rootlessness and of belonging everywhere yet nowhere. There has been no stable peer group for the TCK because it has changed every few years. Peer groups – and measuring yourself against them – are very important for children, especially teenagers. When that measuring stick keeps moving, the child's emotions may be equally unstable. Some of these issues will be particularly exaggerated when the time comes for re-entry into their own home culture. The many issues of re-entry – and how parents can help their children through that often difficult process – will be examined in Chapter Ten.

6. Delayed Adolescence and Rebellion

Work opportunities for teenagers overseas may be limited if not impossible to find. The lack of jobs, plus the narrow social network (which may be limited to a small international school) means there is a sharp reduction in the number of chances a teenager has to break away from his family. In fact, in some overseas settings, there is an over-dependence on family from the beginning to the end of the posting cycle.

The lack of work drastically curtails the chance for teenagers to start that process of becoming responsible, independent adults, handling responsibilities or a bank account. It also delays – and often prolongs – their adolescence.

Likewise, with parents around too much of the time, there are no opportunities to get into trouble during the teen years. But when these same TCKs go to college, there suddenly appears the chance of a lifetime to finally rebel and get into trouble.

According to the experts, many TCKs take the chance and experience what would have been adolescent rebellion well into their 20s, while their non-mobile friends have already worked it out of their systems.

7. Migratory Instinct

It has been said that children raised on *Sesame Street* and then MTV have short attention spans. Magnify that one step further for the TCK, who likely moved every two to three years during childhood, and you have created a child with a distinct migratory instinct which carries over into adulthood.

This instinct is usually felt first in college. According to the experts, TCKs are apt to go to at least two colleges to obtain their degree. Later they may change jobs a lot. TCKs turned adult tend to feel – because of their experiences – that things will change anyway so why deal with problems if you can simply leave them behind? It takes them a while to settle down. Once supposedly settled, they then feel the urge to get up and move again.

TRIGG.

8. TCKs Are Told They Are Special

When re-entering their home culture TCKs tend to feel they are weird since they can't relate to their own culture. Parents must work hard at convincing their children that they are not necessarily weird, perhaps just different.

A problem can arise when these children are continually being told they are 'special'. Problems arise when they re-enter, feeling they are special, and discover that perhaps they are not. One grown-up TCK, the daughter of a Canadian ambassador, told me the greatest disillusionment she had as an adult was the discovery that she was not special, after a lifetime of hearing from her mother that she was.

OTHER IMPORTANT TCK ISSUES

Emotionally, there are other issues unique to the TCK childhood. Any or all of them may relate to your child, so read on.

1. Unresolved Grief

Of all the issues related to the study of TCKs, the subject of their unresolved grief is always highlighted by experts on the subject. It stands out as a major issue because it is a level of grief which in quantity and quality is higher than that which others may ever experience, even in a lifetime.

There is so much grief for the TCK because someone is always leaving his life. Such leave-takings may be multiple and simultaneous. There is even grief which is experienced after leaving a place a child may have hated because he is nonetheless leaving a place or people that had become comfortable and familiar.

In most cases, the grief is denied or delayed. TCKs and their parents can be very cavalier about leaving yet another posting and in the process deny themselves the right to grieve because that doesn't measure up to the image of courage everyone is supposed to put forward. There is great pressure for everyone to 'adjust' and the sooner the better. Worse still for the child or teenager is the feeling that nobody else really understands what they are going through. They feel isolated, alone. This unresolved grief, says Dr. Pollock, can be particularly destructive for the younger child because it can have life-long results.

In the olden days, when families would move around by ship rather than by 747, the long sea voyage provided a suitable grief period between one post and another. Now, too short a time elapses before a grandmother or sibling waits at an airport terminal on the other side of the world, representing the new life that lies ahead.

When that grief stays inside long enough – enough postings go by without ever expressing the grief – resentment and anger can grow, especially a child's resentment and anger towards the parents who have created the situation. There will be a delayed expression when the dam eventually bursts, as it must.

2. Friendships and Relationships

Deep, long-lasting friendships can be problematic for TCKs given their time restraints and the traditional waiting period of evaluating potential friends at the start of a new school year. It may be a few months before a newly arrived TCK feels confident enough to even start making friends and then the school year is ending – and possibly the person they have targeted for friendship is leaving for another post. In some cases, knowing their time is short, some children prefer not to make any friends at all, if it means leaving them too soon. Parents need to help out with their TCK's efforts at friendships by facilitating visits, sleepovers, picnics, play dates, or whatever works.

With the moving cycle associated with life as a TCK, some children also never learn some of the life skills necessary for satisfying interpersonal relationships. In so many instances, they can leave a post without dealing with or settling a problem they may have had with a friend. They can just leave, which is hardly a good method of dealing with a bad situation. Once again, parents need to help out and force their children to deal with problems in friendship head-on rather than just fleeing the scene.

Long-term relationships will also be problematic for TCKs, especially if they cross over into what Dr. Pollock calls a 'mixed marriage', that is, a TCK marries an OK (one-culture kid) who plans to never move around. The partner can't understand many of the ingrained instincts and feelings of the TCK and this can cause problems in the marriage.

TCKs, say the experts, tend to seek out one another, especially on university campuses where they may also befriend the local population of foreign students, with whom they feel a lot more comfortable. It has been said, in fact, that TCKs are really foreign students in disguise.

3. Career Issues and Role Models

I have already noted that TCKs tend to delay decisions about careers and likely switch jobs a lot. It should be plain how some of these feelings arise; after viewing the world, the career choices for the TCK may seem unlimited. Also, with a closer attachment to parents, who may still be living somewhere overseas, the TCK may further delay career decisions and choose to stay for a while with their parents in still another foreign country.

Another important issue which influences career decisions, indeed influences the road to adult career issues, is the absence of role models from their own culture in the TCKs' life. Educators and medical people alike have noted this unique situation which exists for TCKs. Growing up in international communities, TCKs are exposed to very few types of people outside of middle-class professionals who are likely above average in both education and intelligence.

An international school teacher told me a wonderful story which illustrates this point. A eighth grade teacher of social studies and sex education took her class on a field trip so the students could see some of the sights of the country. Her own father had arrived from Australia and thought it would be great to accompany his daughter and her students on the trip. The father happened to be a stocky, well-built man whose work on construction sites back in Australia had hardened his muscles and his general appearance.

The local sights, reported the teacher, paled in comparison to her father. Instead of marveling over the examples of local culture, she overheard her students commenting to each other, "Did you see his hands?!" It had been so long since the students had seen a regular hardworking bloke with hands roughened from hard work.

IT CAN'T BE TOO BAD A LIFE

The experts say that 10 percent of TCKs, when adults, look for some small town and choose to hug a tree – in other words, put down roots. The other 90 percent of TCKs choose to return to international life.

So parents of TCKs agonizing over the childhood they are providing should stop to consider: international life must be a great life if so many children choose it for themselves when they grow up.

Chapter Eight

KEEPING THE MINDS AND BODIES SOUND
Health and Safety Issues

> **"Don't think you are sitting in a safe haven just because you are part of a protected foreign community. Eventually, you will have to take your children home, even for a holiday."**
>
> —international school nurse, dispensing sound advice

Not long after we moved to Beijing, my husband and I experienced every parent's worst nightmare. It happened late one autumn night. We had been out enjoying a late supper with friends. When our car pulled into the driveway of our diplomatic compound, the administration officer of our own Canadian Embassy was there to greet us.

"Hi there!" I said, jumping out of the car. "What are you doing standing around here at this time of night?"

"Now don't worry," began our friend, trying to smile, "but Lilly has had a little accident."

Hearts leaped into throats. "What ... kind ... of ... accident?!"

Lilly had jumped off a chair and snapped a bone in her arm. The babysitter fortunately had the presence of mind to call one of my husband's colleagues whose phone number was on an embassy list by the telephone. He, in turn, had contacted our own embassy doctor. By the time my husband reached the hospital (while I stayed home with our younger son, who was fast asleep and so fortunately couldn't watch his mother frantically pace and cry over not being there for her daughter at a critical time), the nasty work had been done. Lilly returned home with her father, a fresh white cast on her arm, shell-shocked from a late night visit to a Chinese hospital which my husband reported would give an adult nightmares. She was ready to be put to bed by a mother racked by guilt I still feel even writing this now.

The lesson learned that night? Leave a phone number where you can be reached. And if you are out for the evening at a restaurant with no phone number to leave behind, as we were that fateful evening, call in as often as possible, no matter how ridiculous you may feel calling home from every nearby phone. At the very least, leave emergency numbers for a babysitter to contact, especially in a foreign country where communication can be difficult.

I was given one rationalization to assuage my own heavy guilt about that night. When our doctor tried calling our friends in an attempt to find us, she kept getting babysitters who didn't know where our friends were either. We weren't the only parents who learned a valuable lesson the night my daughter broke her arm.

KNOW YOUR EMERGENCY PROCEDURES

Since this event occurred about two months after we had arrived in Beijing, we had been allowed a grace period before having to deal with our first emergency. Others haven't been as lucky. Children often fall sick upon arrival, given the restlessness and exhaustion from a long airplane journey.

If you are still in the hotel when this happens to your children, your first option is to contact the hotel doctor. He may not be a specialist or even a particularly outstanding medical practitioner, but he is a good first stop. He can normally recommend the nearest hospital. If there is no hotel doctor for an emergency consultation, call your own embassy to recommend a hospital. In some instances, parents leave their own country with the name of a local doctor already in their phone book. A doctor back home providing the pre-departure physical may know of someone where you are headed. It can't hurt to travel with names.

Emergencies that happen while you are out for an evening for dinner or with friends are fortunately rare occurrences. But that doesn't mean any parent – especially one living in a strange country where medical care is sketchy at best – should feel it won't ever happen to their family. Be sure to leave the house with all bases covered. This means that when you go out for a social evening, especially to a place with no phone or you don't know the number in advance, always leave some forwarding numbers even if it's the name of a nearby friend or neighbor who may be planning to be at home that evening.

More importantly, as quickly as possible after arriving in a new city, learn where the nearest hospital emergency room is and the quickest route there by car. If there is a language barrier, try to identify a native speaker who can be relied upon in an emergency to accompany you to the hospital to help translate.

Draw up an emergency phone list (and relevant insurance numbers) as soon as possible and place it by the phone. Write down your doctor's number and have it handy in case he has to meet you at the hospital. Also, find out if you need to have a deposit ready to cover the cost of care. In some countries you must pay before you will be treated. Parents should have a letter which authorizes a designated person to make decisions about emergency care for their minor children in case they are not available or can't be contacted. This may be required – if it is not a life-threatening condition – before treatment is given. If your children are in school, make sure you have supplied the school administration with all the emergency numbers where both parents can be reached during the day, and especially where your family doctor can be contacted.

Be sure to know exactly what you should do in the event that an evacuation to an outside medical center is necessary. It's best to sort that procedure out before you go overseas in order to know exactly what contingency plans your company or government offers. Then, reconfirm the existence of those plans shortly after arrival. Medical evacuations should be handled immediately, especially in countries where air travel can be difficult or fraught with bureaucracy. Do not wait any longer than necessary. If a child's condition continues to worsen and no relief is in sight, arrange to get out while he can still travel.

One last word on the subject of medical evacuations. Be sure to know if your medical insurance covers such events, and if necessary, sign up for a regional medical evacuation service to facilitate an emergency air lift.

The 1990 edition of *Travel With Children* from the Lonely Planet travel series lists addresses for two organizations which you may need in matters of medical assistance and emergencies.

Lonely Planet reports that the non-profit International Association of Medical Assistance to Travelers (IAMAT) offers a directory of English-speaking doctors in 1,440 major cities abroad whom the organization endorses for travelers. Write to them at: Suite 5620, 350 Fifth Avenue, New York, N.Y. 10001, U.S.A. For a donation of at least US$25, they also provide information on other related health issues. Similarly, INTERMEDIC provides lists of English-speaking doctors in 200 cities and provides information on immunizations and medications. Write to them at: 777 Third Ave., New York, N.Y. 10017, U.S.A.

Finally, consult your own insurance company about medical insurance while traveling and coverage for emergency medical evacuations. Your own company may provide this information.

KEEPING EMERGENCIES AT BAY

The most important point to keep in mind is this: *when medical resources are limited, parents' medical awareness should be higher*. At home, when a child's fever is high, you can usually rest assured that a good children's hospital is not far down the road. When you live in a foreign country where hospitals may not be that great, the nearest suitable, reliable hospital may require plane or train travel. Now this does not mean parents must overreact to every cough or flushed face, but it should mean keeping in the back of your mind that illnesses should not be allowed to go on too long without consultation and evaluation.

There will always be emergency medical situations which cannot be foreseen. Many situations are the same ones you would have at home: accidents, poisonings, appendicitis and so on. But in addition, parents can take preventive action to keep their children in good health.

A lot depends on where you are posted in the world, but in Third World countries it is always sensible to be on guard by educating your children and your household staff about precautions they can take when you are not around (more on that to follow). This does not mean building a glass bubble in which to put your children for the duration of the assignment. That is completely impractical if not downright impossible. Children are going to get sick regardless of your thoroughness.

Younger children especially, who may be going to pre-school for the first time in their lives, are still building their immune systems. Pre-school or play groups may be their first exposure to another child's runny nose and illnesses, so they are bound to go through a cycle of illnesses until their own ability to fight off viruses develops. The most useful suggestion I can make in order to keep healthy children, is to practice good preventive medicine.

PREVENTIVE MEDICINE
The best medicine is the kind you don't have to take. Preventive measures can help ensure the family's general good health so that when trouble strikes, you at least have a healthy foundation.

1. Inoculations
It should go without saying that inoculations should be kept up to date, but it's surprising how many parents don't even take the

time to find out precisely what is required before leaving their own country. Never rely on a school nurse or embassy doctor to tell you what shots are needed and when. They may be knowledgeable, but are usually responsible for too many people to keep your children's medical book up to date. Inoculations and general immunizations are your responsibility as parents, and don't ever put them aside for another day.

If you are not sure what immunizations are required for a specific country, never assume you will find out when you get there. It could be too late, as some inoculations should be done before you leave. Call your own government's Department of Health or even your own foreign office to find out what shots government employees receive before being sent overseas. You might want to check what information is available from the Disease Control Center in Atlanta, Georgia, U.S.A., either to individuals or through their doctors. They have an international reputation in this area.

The most important immunizations are the routine childhood shots which children receive regardless of where they live in the world, such as polio, measles, and whooping cough. These diseases are often more difficult to treat overseas; do not forget about them when moving abroad.

Vaccinations against diseases unique to foreign postings, typhoid, for example, do not in all cases provide an outright guarantee that your children (or yourselves) will be safe from disease. Some common diseases like malaria don't even have a vaccination yet, and people traveling into malarial areas still rely on pills and a good mosquito repellent. Some vaccinations will not even be offered to children under the age of 12.

The ones that have proved effective and are still widely in use include:

- Tetanus and Diphtheria: This combination shot is not a mandatory entrance requirement into a country, but it is one normally given as a precaution, especially for children who take a lot of tumbles and have lots of cuts. Boosters are recommended every 10 years.
- Typhoid: This immunization requires two doses and is given to children over the age of 2. Protection lasts for three years and can be useful for people moving or traveling through rural, tropical areas. There can be side effects from this shot, such as some pain around the injection site as well as some fever, headache, and a general feeling of sickness.
- Infectious Hepatitis: Gamma globulin injections provide a ready-made antibody to reduce the chances of infection for Hepatitis A. It is normally given intramuscularly at the last possible moment before departure. This is usually given to children over the age of 12. Many people falsely believe one shot will do, but it wears off within six months and must be renewed regularly, especially if you plan any holidays into particularly poor areas where conditions may not be hygienic. A vaccine has recently been made available.

- Hepatitis B: This inoculation, which comes in a series of three given over a six-month period, is absolutely necessary for travelers in most parts of Asia. Children are given this one as a matter of course.
- Tuberculosis: This vaccination, sometimes given at birth, is rife with controversy and conflicting medical opinion. I suggest you consult with your own doctor or health service before leaving home to get their opinion. TB is still rampant in many Third World countries and chances are your children are going to come into contact with it. Opinion is divided over whether the vaccination, known as a BCG, is effective or not. An American doctor suggested children (and adults) should receive what is known as the 'tine' test once a year. This is a skin test which will indicate whether contact has been made so appropriate action can be taken.
- Meningitis: This vaccine is recommended for visitors to parts of Africa and Brazil and for anyone about to trek in Nepal. Even so-called First World countries like Canada have been administering one form of this vaccine to school-age children after a rash of outbreaks in 1991.
- Japanese Encephalitis: Like the TB question, there is considerable mixed opinion on the validity of this one. At various times this inoculation was popular and then fell out of favor for travelers to Third World countries. It comes in three initial doses, followed one year later by a booster. Children can receive this one.
- Yellow Fever: This shot provides protection that lasts 10 years and is recommended where the disease is still rampant, mainly in Africa and Latin America.

2. Water

For families assigned to Third World countries, water quality is a major health issue and one parents need to familiarize their children with as soon as possible after arrival. For younger children, it may mean a general ban on drinking from water fountains (outside of their international schools which normally have purified water) and avoiding any drink with ice in it.

One of the most foolproof systems of purifying drinking water at home is to simply boil it for at least 10 minutes. Once it has been sterilized in this way, it should be stored in sterilized (rinsed out with boiling water) containers in order to avoid contamination. While boiling eliminates potential diseases, it produces drinking water which doesn't taste the best. For that reason, parents can buy any number of water filter systems now available. These usually come in the form of a jug with charcoal filter attached through which water is poured and then stored in the refrigerator.

If you are in a situation where you cannot boil water, then it should be chemically treated to remove harmful elements. Chlorine tablets or even household bleach are effective in most instances; iodine is also effective. Always be sure to follow all directions issued with chlorine or iodine tablets used for water purification because too much iodine, for instance, can be harmful.

The mass market of bottled water should be approached with caution, especially bottles bearing obscure brand names. For instance, when we lived in Bangkok, the all-purpose bottled water sold to the foreign community was tested and discovered not to be as clean as thought. Especially if you are giving water to a baby, be sure to boil even the bottled water first.

3. Hygiene: Personal and Household

The safety level of your household water has a major role to play in household hygiene. It's not enough to have boiled water on hand and then not use it when cleaning food and vegetables. Opinions always differ on the amount of care you should take in preparing food, but if you live in a country where cleanliness is a problem, you must never take any chances with your children's tummies. Mishandled food is a major source of related stomach troubles like diarrhea. Fruit and vegetables need to be soaked not only in clean water, but in water which has been prepared especially for treating foods, with substances such as the popular Milton's sterilizing solution. In the absence of that product, a few capfuls of household bleach in two liters (approximately four quarts) of water should do the trick. Always rinse anything soaked in that combination with clean water. Even some meats should be soaked. Poultry should be soaked or have its skin removed before cooking. Eggs should be kept refrigerated, even if this is not all that common in some countries.

Household staff should have physicals that include chest X-rays on a periodic basis. Household staff and children must be taught – and reminded – to *always* wash their hands after using the toilet. Likewise, it wouldn't hurt to use bottled or purified water for brushing teeth. And if you live as I have in cockroach-infested apartments, it is a good idea to boil your toothbrushes from time to time. While you're at it, boil your cutlery and drinking glasses or any other dish which may have had a midnight visit from an insect. Go ahead and think I'm crazy, but why take chances? In fact, in two years in Beijing, no one in my family had stomach ailments. Other than a broken arm and one bad bout of flu, we were extremely healthy. Perhaps being overzealous on health issues had its point.

Household staff, especially those working in the kitchen, should be brought as close as possible to your own standards of hygiene. In hot countries, for instance, they must be trained never to leave food sitting out for very long. Often, cooks must be made aware that once thawed, meat or poultry cannot be re-frozen unless it has been cooked first. Think of yourself as the hygiene police: your family's health is at risk if you adopt a lackadaisical attitude and just assume the cook is continuing to wash vegetables in boiled water. Make regular inspections of the kitchen and oversee their food preparation as much as possible to be sure they are still following your rules.

Children must be taught never to eat anything from a street vendor, and especially meat or fruit. Likewise, tell them not to eat at a friend's house unless it is someone that you know is adhering to similar rules of hygiene as yourself. Small, out of the way restaurants with flies and mosquitos buzzing all around may look terribly exotic, but should be avoided at all costs.

Dairy products are other foods to be wary of. Train your children – and yourselves – never to eat any pastries or baked goods with creamed fillings unless they come from a completely reliable source. Milk can be a problem if there is no freshness date on it somewhere. Long-life milk, while not the best-tasting (although it has improved immensely), is reliable for its safety, as long as its expiry date is observed.

Some advice which may lead the reader to think I am a complete fanatic: in countries where spitting is a popular pastime, make sure every visitor removes his shoes at the door. Walking barefoot outdoors in some tropical locations could also result in parasites finding their way into the body.

4. Regular Checkups

A discussion on preventive health measures would not be complete without pointing out the advantages of health maintenance through regular appointments with the doctor. Especially before you leave your home country, be sure your children have complete physicals, including any lab work like blood and urine tests. If doctor's appointments are not going to be a simple matter at your posting (see 'Going to the Doctor' on page 194), then I suggest you begin your own growth and development chart for your children which can be measured against professional books on the subject to alert you to any discrepancies.

After the doctor, be sure to stop at the dentist and eye doctor before leaving home. It may be a while before you can make contact with those specialists.

5. Good Nutrition and Vitamins

Good eating habits begin at home, so be sure to enforce mealtimes. Consider vitamin therapy, especially vitamin C if the winter is harsh and the air polluted by not only dust but other viruses, and a fluoride substitute if the water is not already fluoridated. A child is going to get sick regardless of many precautions, but keeping your own children home when they are sick will not only be considerate of classmates, but also prevent your child picking up an even more severe virus when resistance is lowered by the first illness.

Before you leave home, be sure to check with your own doctor about good dietary requirements and then stick to those basic food rules while overseas. There will always be local food substitutes that supply protein – for instance, tofu, eggs, beans, and nuts all provide the necessary protein. Just remember that a growing child cannot live on rice or pasta alone. Infants especially should not be allowed to indulge in common local foods unless they clearly fall within the guidelines.

In very hot climates, ensure your children drink a lot, even if they say they are not thirsty. When going out on excursions, be sure to pack your own water bottle. When I travel with my children throughout Asia, I even pack a package of straws for those days when everyone gets thirsty, and the only option is to drink from a bottle with a less than sanitary top.

TREATING COMMON ILLNESSES

Just as at home, children will run through the various childhood diseases and minor aches and pains. I can't possibly cover all the potential health hazards, but here are a few of the most common.

1. The Most Common Illnesses and How to Treat Them

- Fever: A child's normal body temperature is 37° Celsius (98.6° Fahrenheit). If it rises more than two degrees, that is considered a high fever and should be brought down with any of the fever medications available on the market such as Tylenol or Panadol. A child's fever can suddenly rise out of nowhere for no obvious reason. When your children are young, always travel with a thermometer. If you don't have any fever medication handy, keep your children cool by dipping them into the bathtub or washing them with cool water. Treat fevers seriously – they are often a sign of infection – and always seek medical treatment as soon as possible.

- Diarrhea: Depending on where you live, this is one of the most common illnesses to afflict your child. It may be a lightning bout of food poisoning, or it may be something more serious. For slight stomach upsets, ginger ale and dry soda crackers usually bring relief. For more severe diarrhea, Imodium seems to be the best means of control. If the symptoms persist for longer than a few days, and blood appears in the child's stool, seek medical help.

- Cold, upper respiratory ailments and allergies: After living in Asia, I feel I could write a book just on this subject alone. Polluted, dusty air is a major source of these ailments combined with a variety of bugs which seem to work their way naturally through a classroom. Often (I know this from my own daughter) there is no infection or virus, but merely an allergic reaction to the air which doesn't only mean blocked noses and throats, but phlegmy coughs as well which can be treated with antihistamines like Benadryl or Seldane. If chests start to sound rattling, be sure to have your doctor take a listen. Expectorants bought over-the-counter are a good way to get your child to cough up the phlegm that is blocking his chest.

- Fungal infections, minor cuts, and skin infections: These are common in hot tropical countries where children sweat a lot and fungus is allowed to grow, especially between the toes, as in athlete's foot. Good personal hygiene habits (bathe as often as possible in hot countries and apply baby powder after) will help keep them at bay, but when they do occur, fungal infections should be treated with such anti-fungal creams as Desenex. Minor skin infections should be kept clean and treated with anti-bacterial ointments such as Neosporin.

- General infections: In many Third World countries, antibiotics are handed out like party favors at a birthday party and are often prescribed in cases where they will have no use whatsoever. Viral infections will not respond to antibiotics and will only lower your child's resistance. So don't be hasty in accepting antibiotics just to feel like you are taking some action. Penicillin is definitely not a panacea; in fact, for many infections, especially upper respiratory, penicillin will not work. Ampicillin or what is known as broad spectrum antibiotics are better. Tetracyclines are never recommended for children. Be sure to consult your doctor when fever and general unwellness persist for longer than a few days.

- Tropical ailments: Prickly heat is a common ailment when you live or travel in hot climates. Children develop an itchy rash as a result of sweating too much, and the perspiration gets trapped under the skin. Calamine lotion is more effective than dusting powders in fighting these rashes, but if a rash persists, see the doctor.

- Heat stress and heat stroke will result when children stay out too long in the hot tropical sun. Do not let your children go out without wearing a hat and be sure to dress them in loose, cool clothing. Make them drink plenty of water when dehydration occurs, and adding a little salt to their food will help combat other side effects of heat stroke such as headache and stomachache.

- Snake bites can occur in some countries, but are given less of a chance when children wear boots in areas where snakes may live. Snake bites are not immediately fatal but be sure to get some anti-venin medicine as quickly as possible.

- Mosquito bites: To avoid mosquito bites, always travel with a lot of mosquito repellent. And be sure to use it.

2. Overseas Medicine Cabinets

If you are uncertain what kind of pharmacies may be available, be sure to put together your own first aid kit for home and car. Before you leave, buy medicines to last a year, if that's the length of time you feel you may be stranded without access to a regular drug store. In places where the local drug stores have remedies like ginseng and antler horn and offer medicine for esoteric ailments but not the common cold, be sure to have your own supply of baby or child anti-fever medicines or cold remedies and cough medicine. Vitamins should also be bought beforehand. Thermometers, bandaids, creams, antihistamines, and other over-the-counter drugs should most definitely be brought along with the furniture. Just be sure to check all expiry dates at the time of purchase. Then be doubly sure to put them at a safe distance from young hands.

It would be impossible to list every drug you may need to have on hand for home treatment, but here's what doctors

recommend to help you stock an overseas medicine cabinet:
- A thermometer and infant analgesic (and dropper to administer) – you will need this for fevers and other ailments so be sure to have lots of Tylenol or Panadol on hand.
- Antihistamines – Benedryl is a popular choice for children and serves a dual function of being a good medicine to administer to children before traveling on airplanes (it makes them sleepy and keeps their ears clear at the same time).
- A cleansing agent like Dettol or Phisohex for cuts.
- Calamine lotion for mosquito bites and prickly heat.
- Anti-diarrhea medicines like Lomotil and Imodium.
- Syrup of ipecac to induce vomiting if a child accidentally eats something poisonous.
- Anti-bacterial ointments like Neosporin, which also makes a Neosporin ophthalmic solution to cleanse eyes.
- Anti-fungal ointments.
- Rehydration tablets.
- Over-the-counter cold medicines (both cough suppressants and expectorants).
- Antibiotics (which come in powdered form for later use) may be on hand but should never be administered before consulting a doctor.

GOING TO THE DOCTOR

Home remedies are good to a point, but eventually you will need to consult a doctor, if only for reassurance that your home remedies have been on target. In some countries, the simple visit to the doctor can require major effort because logistics can be complicated or appointments difficult to make. Regardless, one of the first things to do upon arrival is to find out where the doctor is located, what kinds of specialists are available for consultation, what kind of lab facility is available, and what form of payment is accepted for those days when you need to see someone but have no cash on hand.

Always travel with – or be totally familiar with – your children's medical history, including their inoculation booklet. The doctor you see overseas will be unaware of previous illnesses or allergies and can't make a proper diagnosis if he doesn't have all the facts. Never conceal information, regardless of your reason at the time.

It wouldn't hurt to make a preliminary appointment before the doctor is truly needed, to introduce yourself and your children and get a general feeling about your confidence level in the medical help. In most large cities there will be English-speaking doctors (most of them trained in Western countries). If your children meet the doctor socially before they are sick, they might not be as nervous about a new doctor when the time comes to see him or her. Women planning on having a child while overseas would also find it useful to meet the obstetrician before getting pregnant, if only to allay any fears about eventual pre-natal care.

Within foreign communities, word of mouth usually helps establish a doctor's reputation. In fact, the best way to find a doctor for you and your family is to ask around and see who is popular. Of course, everyone will have a different opinion based on their own experiences. For some reason which I can't pinpoint, my medical experiences have been a mixture of good and bad. Good, because doctors generally have high level qualifications; bad, because their technicians or hospital staffs usually don't.

In Taiwan, I personally never left the hospital fully satisfied that everything was being taken care of. Yet my best friend had her first child in Taipei and praised the hospital and doctor to the skies. As I said, a lot depends on personal experience. When I lived in Bangkok, and my daughter would see highly-qualified pediatricians at a first-rate private hospital, I never worried a minute. Unfortunately, I started worrying about the pharmacy when a fellow mother came home one day with medicine from the hospital pharmacy that had been mismarked. Medicine for an ear infection had inadvertently been given for her daughter's eye infection. If the mother hadn't noticed, her daughter would likely have been blinded. It can't hurt to double-check.

If you live in a city where medical care is just barely adequate, take no chances and get a second opinion. My daughter's broken arm was set correctly by Chinese doctors in Beijing, but when the cast came off, we took her to the closest medical center with a specialist – which for us was Hong Kong – for a checkup. We had heard stories of arms needing to be re-broken and re-set and other nightmare scenarios so took no chances.

Second opinions in outside medical centers, by the way, need not apply only to broken limbs. When we lived in Taiwan, and my daughter developed a vicious, phlegmy cough as a result of an allergy (which made her sound like she smoked two packs a day), the doctors in Taipei just kept shoving antibiotics at her and diagnosing her condition as "the cough Caucasian children get when they move to Taiwan." I'm not a medical professional, but even a layman is going to question that spotty diagnosis. Sure enough, when we evacuated her to Hong Kong to see a child allergist, it was confirmed that she was, in fact, suffering from a bad allergy to the dust and pollution of Taipei which was not treatable by endless doses of penicillin. We got her on track and her chest dried up, thanks to the second opinion of a specialist.

IF YOUR CHILD MUST BE HOSPITALIZED

When home remedies fail and your child's condition is worse, there will be the possibility that he or she will face hospitalization. You should have previously familiarized yourself with the local facilities and their admission procedures, so you will be working with some advance information.

Many hospitals allow parents to stay with their children within the hospital. If that option is available, take it and your child will be grateful. Being a patient in a hospital in a foreign country, with foreign doctors and nurses, can be an overwhelming experience.

FIRST AID

There are any number of books on first aid, so be sure to have at least one version (I have found the St. John's Ambulance one the most useful) and place it somewhere everyone in the family knows. You shouldn't have to hunt for your first aid book when you need it most.

It might not hurt either for one parent – or both if that's possible – to take a short first aid course before you leave home. Courses are usually offered by community organizations.

My daughter and I had a briefing on first aid during one of her Brownie meetings in Beijing. I didn't give it much thought, although I took note of the contents of an emergency first aid kit for future reference. Two days after our briefing, I accidentally poured scalding water over my foot and more or less knew how to respond (which was *not* to put any ointment on the second degree burn). I kept a cool head as advised and submersed my foot in a cold bath to ease the pain. Then, when I went searching everywhere for our own first aid book, I realized the importance of everyone in the family knowing the whereabouts of that much needed volume! Many families also keep poison control center telephone numbers on hand to call for advice, and one should check if this service is available.

FIRST AID KITS

You may add other items, but a basic first aid kit (for both home and car) should at least include the following items:

 2 one-inch bandages and 2 four-inch bandages
 12 sterile gauze dressings
 20 cotton balls
 12 cotton-tipped swabs
 12 bandaids
 1 roll tape
 1 triangular bandage
 1 pair tweezers

1 pair scissors
1 bottle alcohol or hydrogen peroxide
1 bottle syrup of ipecac to induce vomiting
2 tongue depressors
2 wooden splints
antiseptic cream
thermometer

HAVING A BABY OVERSEAS

My first child was born in Bangkok, my second in Ottawa. People are amazed when I tell them I would pick my Bangkok experience over my Canadian pregnancy and delivery (Caesarian section in both instances) any day. Now granted, Bangkok, with a worsening infrastructure due to rapid development, is not exactly a calm, orderly kind of city, but my Thai pregnancy and delivery wins hands down.

There are many reasons for this, and as they raise the issues of an overseas pregnancy clearly, I will try to elaborate.

1. Pre-natal Care

As many Canadian foreign service wives in Bangkok were having babies when I was there, I did the logical thing: I arranged an appointment *before* getting pregnant to meet the doctor who seemed to be the popular choice among Canadian women, and for much of the foreign community as well. We met in his office so I could see his facilities. We chatted about what he offered as pre-natal care (number of appointments, availability of lab facilities including ultrasound and amniocentesis), pre-natal training courses, and the quality of both the local hospital for delivery and the pediatricians for after the baby had arrived.

More than the practical requirements, I also had a chance to assess personally the obstetrician in whom I was placing my future. It is certainly true that most women fall a little in love with their obstetrician and I was no exception. Mine was a Thai

by birth who had received his training and experience in the United Kingdom (I looked carefully at all the certificates on his wall). I felt completely confident and reassured; so confident, in fact, that I turned up less than seven weeks later already six weeks pregnant. All of my concerns were going to be looked after without any problems.

Despite a dreadful pregnancy (caused by my own body, not the doctor) I gave birth by C-section to a very healthy, *huge* (4.2 kg or 10.5 pounds) baby girl nine months later. Both baby and mother were in the best possible hands.

One of the reasons I preferred my Thai experience was the fact that, unlike in Canada, where several doctors share a practice, I was looked after from start to finish by the same doctor without any last-minute switches. I felt I had an opportunity to establish a good relationship with one individual who saw me through the experience. Not only that, his own wife (trained as a midwife in Britain) offered a pre-natal training course that I attended with my husband. We learned all the relevant breathing techniques, which I then ignored when I finally went into labor; I didn't say I was good at this experience, just that I felt confident.

I recommend to any woman contemplating the idea of giving birth overseas to follow the same steps as I took: that is, check out the doctor beforehand, ask all relevant questions and more if you are interested in home delivery, availability of birthing rooms, natural childbirth, or opinions on breastfeeding, and then decide if you should go ahead and have your baby in the host country.

Not all postings will inspire the confidence Bangkok did for me. While living in Beijing, no expectant mothers I knew were even allowed by their governments or companies to give birth in a Chinese hospital. They went to Hong Kong, or home to their respective countries.

If you are not confident about the hospitals or doctors, there is no written rule that says you have to have the baby overseas. Most companies and embassies have provisions for sending pregnant women home to have their children. Some women find that option difficult because it means a separation from their husband or other children, but if you fall into any high risk categories, do what makes you feel most confident.

If you do choose to stay put and have the baby, I have one more recommendation: if you don't know the local language, have someone write down the phrases you think you will need and have them translated phonetically so you can communicate with the staff. My husband knew I was losing my patience at the end of my pregnancy in Bangkok when together we drew up a list of phrases I was convinced I would need on an hourly basis. My choice phrases consisted of "Get the doctor, now!", "Get my baby, now!", and "I need another painkiller, now!" I admit, I was feeling pretty cranky at the time.

2. Pre-natal, Post-natal and Other Support

In most foreign communities, there is a pre-natal class offered through a school, community services center, or even hospital. They are not hard to track down and I suggest you find one as quickly as possible. Ask your friends who already have babies, and who may be participating in weekly play groups, for their opinions about doctors, hospitals, or training courses.

After the baby arrives, sign up for one of those play groups, or a larger mother's support group. When I lived in Bangkok, foreign mothers organized a large-scale mothers' support group known as the Bangkok Association of Mothers and Babies International, or BAMBI. (It almost became known as the Bangkok International Mothers and Babies Organization – BIMBO!) These groups are a new mother's lifeline – for exchanging information, getting together, offering support for breastfeeding, or just meeting other mothers – so if there isn't one in your city, I can't recommend enough that you take the initiative and begin one yourself. Many of the members of BAMBI – including its honorary chairwoman, the wife of my doctor – became my best friends. BAMBI had its 10th anniversary in 1992, so many women obviously have found it a worthwhile organization.

3. Baby Supplies and Layettes

Despite the high quality of medical care in Bangkok, I was taking no chances with baby supplies. Cribs then did not meet Western standards and were painted with paint containing lead. Not exactly what I wanted for my new daughter. I ordered everything from Canada, including a cheaper supply of disposable diapers. For those who can't order in bulk, there are always Westerners departing and selling extra supplies or baby furniture like cribs, strollers, or changing tables. Don't forget baby vitamins or other baby medications in your shipment if they are not available. While you are ordering, invest in a traveling playpen/bed. These weren't on the market when my first child was born and I would have welcomed one in place of the giant playpen we lugged around the world rather than risk the often unsturdy cribs offered by hotels.

4. Health Issues Unique to Babies

If you are bottle-feeding, take absolutely no chances with your sterilization procedure. The same applies to any water you are giving to a baby. Bottled water must be boiled for infant consumption. Anything that drops on the floor (pacifiers, teething rings, or anything your baby puts into her mouth) must be constantly sterilized. It doesn't hurt to throw all baby toys into a giant sterilizer once in a while.

Any care givers who will be coming into contact with your baby should be sent to the hospital before the birth to receive a clean bill of health from the doctors. Especially check against tuberculosis which remains the scourge of many Third World countries.

Babies born in foreign countries may also require more inoculations than they would receive back home. Do check with a doctor back home if you have little confidence in the information you are receiving.

Fever and diarrhea will be the most common baby ailments, just as they would be back home. Unfortunately, in some of the unhealthier foreign postings, your children may experience these more often. I must have taken a dirty diaper of my daughter's to the hospital for examination more times than I care to remember, despite all our hygienic precautions.

Normal child development and milestones – not unlike those of older children – should be monitored both with your doctor or by using one of the hundreds of good childcare books on the market. At the first sign that something is not quite right, discuss the matter with your pediatrician and, if necessary, take your baby to another medical center which inspires more confidence.

MENTAL HEALTH ISSUES AND CHILDREN

International schools' health programs for teenagers often draw heavily on books imported from the United States or Europe. I gained access to one set of teaching materials called *Contemporary Health Series* put out by Network Publications (P.O. Box 1830, Santa Cruz, California 95061–1830). I'm not suggesting parents order these particular materials as they are designed for classroom exercises, but do check if your particular school is using these materials or others like them. They can provide some valuable insights into sex exucation as well as mental health issues like depression and self-esteem, some of which I can share here.

This particular series is divided into two age groups: *Into Adolescence* for grades five to eight; and *Entering Adulthood* for grades nine to twelve. I particularly took note of a passage in one book of the latter series entitled *Connecting Health, Communication and Self-Esteem* by authors Susan J. Laing, MS and Clint E. Bruess, EdD. In describing mental health, the authors write: "Mental health is a positive state and should not be confused with mental illness. Mental health is the capacity to cope with life situations, grow emotionally through them, develop to the fullest potential, and grow in awareness and consciousness. Mental health is feeling good about oneself, accepting physical appearance, being content with life, and gaining inner peace. It is also the active seeking of experiences that promote peak mental states … People with positive mental health are strongly motivated to build lives that promote self-actualization."

YOUR CHILD'S MENTAL HEALTH

For parents, keeping their children physically healthy can often seem easier than maintaining good mental health and positive, upbeat moods in their children. For one thing, physical health care, like shots or vitamins, often seems a lot easier for a parent to control and manage. Not so with a child's mental health, for regardless of their age or stage of life, children are going to experience mood swings and unpleasant times in their lives. As one parent put it to me, a teenager is apt to complain about life regardless of how good it is because he is a teenager.

A 13-year-old boy I interviewed put it even better. When I asked him if he ever experienced depression, he informed me with a straight face and without any inflection that he was going through that mad-at-the-world stage of life where "everything stinks, you know?" He at least had identified his own problem, but did confess feeling a lot better after talking to his mother about it.

As with so many issues of child development in an overseas context, issues of mental well-being also become magnified in a foreign situation because there are so many new and unfamiliar influences playing a part. For that reason, the normal emotional milestones of a child's personal growth may seem more intense and complicated when experienced overseas. The following are a few of the crises you can expect your child to experience:

1. Anxiety and Fears

In her introduction, Dr. Herh discusses many of the anxieties which result when a child moves to a foreign country. Younger children may be afraid of servants or teachers; older children may be afraid of fitting into a new peer group and can definitely experience anxiety over the new socialization process. Language-related fears, or the worries about adjusting to a new school system are also factors.

A discussion about safety issues would be remiss, however, if it overlooked a child's concerns about physical safety. This can come in two forms: fear of the new environment (a walled housing compound or strangers touching him in the street) or getting to a safe haven in the event of political turmoil. Parents who have experienced evacuations due to political upheaval report their children – of all ages – took many months and sometimes years to recover from the act of 'fleeing' the scene due to revolutions and civil unrest. Not only does the evacuation procedure unnerve the child, but often the preliminaries leading up to the day they escape can also provide material for months of nightmares, especially if they hear shots being fired. Evacuations usually require a few days of preparation, after days or weeks of tension buildup in a politically unstable country. As in most instances, the children will look to their parents for cues. The calmer you remain throughout a political crisis and evacuation, the calmer they will be. It's easier said than done, of course, but remember who's the adult. If months after the fact, a child is still waking up with nightmares and having abnormal fears about going out, it is suggested that professional help be sought.

2. Anger

What child isn't angry about something at some time or other? A 13-year-old boy may be angry at having acne for the first time in his life. A 2-year-old may be enraged by his inability to communicate what he wants; a pre-teenage girl may be exasperated by her body's slow development of the signs of womanhood; a teenage boy may be furious with his inability to secure the affections of a particular girl. Children on the road to adulthood experience anger over a variety of issues, and may experience both anger and recovery from that anger two or three times in the same day. If the mother and father are angry about their lives, too, that can also affect their children.

The child who has been ripped from what he saw as a reasonably happy life back in his home country may be mad at his parents for transplanting him to some strange, exotic locale. Or he may seem happy and excited at first by a new location, but after a few months of frustrating encounters with the new culture or even the new school, his anger may build up until there is a feverish delayed reaction which may come gushing out of him over something seemingly insignificant.

Some ways in which a child will express his or her anger, which a parent can watch for, are fighting, swearing, screaming, crying, breaking things, running out for a walk by himself, arguing, talking about it, or conversely clamming up about it or pouting, or over-exercising.

Parents raising children overseas must be on guard to deal with immediate outbursts of anger demonstrated in those ways.

A U.S. State Department psychiatrist once advised parents that besides the typical developmental reasons behind anger, the traveling child's anger can also stem from a sense of loss – loss of home, friends, family, and familiar surroundings. He recommended that children must be allowed to mourn that loss, much like the loss of a loved one, before they can move on to the adaptation stage.

This means that when you first arrive at your new home and Johnny hates everything about it and hates you, too, for bringing him to such a rotten place, you have to be patient and let Johnny be angry for a reasonable amount of time while he works through the loss of the familiar. With such understanding – instead of orders like *get used to it, kid, we're here to stay* – the child is allowed time to digest the new information and to gradually get used to his new life – and eventually like it. Pushing your child into immediate acceptance of anything new, just because *you* want it and wouldn't it be nice to have everything immediately fall into place, is not being fair to your child.

When life has changed dramatically for the child, as it especially does in an overseas move, instead of pushing the child into a forced instant happiness, it would be better to let the child settle in for a while and let his emotions make the mental adaptation. Obviously, if the anger continues for months on end with no relief in sight, a new solution should be formulated, possibly with the help of a professional. In the meantime, let the child 'grieve' for the loss of his old life. Most children get over it within a few months.

3. Frustration

If you as the parent are about to rip your hair out because of the inefficiency of the new host culture, you can hardly expect that your children won't experience the same frustration in managing their daily life without television, a nearby mall, pinball machine, soda fountain, library, theater, or any other reasonable facsimiles of their previous life. They are imitating you in miniature, so be as patient with their cultural frustrations as you are with your own.

A traveling child may also be experiencing frustrations unique to his own life, primarily his new life at an international school. He may have been extremely popular back home and wants the same instant recognition or friendships he enjoyed at home. These friendships need some time to grow and won't happen instantaneously. But like his adult counterpart, a child may grow frustrated and insecure over his inability to make instant friends. Parents need to remind their child (and themselves) that some things take time to nurture and that eventually, with a lot of effort and overtures towards new children, they will likely develop a similar group of friends. As a parent, you can encourage their efforts at friendship in order to prod things along. If children are out there trying to meet new friends, these efforts are bound to pay off. If they are sitting frustrated in their bedrooms, reading a book or listening over and over again to their favorite singer, not much is going to break their way. Help them take action which will eliminate the source of their frustration. And exercise as much patience as you can.

4. Loneliness and Alienation

Many of these symptoms go along with my discussion of frustration and have the same root cause. The child has left his friends behind and hasn't made new ones. He's terribly homesick. He feels frustrated by his efforts at friendship and consequently feels that he's alone and will never have friends again. He may also feel that he'll never belong and will be a misfit forever. He writes endless letters back home and can't wait to escape the new life and return to his old one. A few weeks or months is forever to a child. He is on the other side of the world – friendless – and retreats into himself, the only person he feels he can rely on.

Parents should watch for children in the throes of these

feelings. Obvious signs will be children who hide out and refuse to participate in the activities which will eventually help them feel less lonely and alienated. Your own reliable availability as parents will also help alleviate the situation because despite your child's efforts to hide his feelings, he won't be able to do so forever, and eventually he will talk about them with you. If he feels he doesn't have any friends in the world, now is not the time for the parents to be unavailable as well. A lonely child needs his parents very much, regardless of his age. Be there.

5. Stress

Schools overseas can often be much more difficult and set a much higher standard of academic achievement than your child is used to. School stress can be the result, as a child either struggles to keep up, or to surpass even himself.

The *Contemporary Health Series* I referred to on page 202, in its volume *Understanding Depression and Suicide* by Nanette D. Burton MA, suggests some negative ways in which a child might cope with stress, including drug or alcohol abuse, driving too fast, promiscuity, self-mutilation, isolation from others, or excessive risk-taking. She also recommends some positive and healthy ideas for coping which include talking to someone who cares, exercising in a positive way like jogging or sports, reading a good book, listening to music, going shopping, doing something nice for yourself, talking to or spending time with pets, watching a good movie, spending time with a friend or friends, going to a special place to think, developing a sense of humor, and finding the humorous side to predicaments.

SIGNS THE CHILD ISN'T COPING AND HOW YOU CAN HELP

During the initial six-month settling-in period, there may be both visible and invisible signs that your child is not adapting. Keep an open eye and mind.

1. Depression

Your child is unhappy – with everything. He doesn't want to socialize, his appetite may decline, or he may have headaches and nightmares when he finally falls asleep. The child is obviously depressed and the condition is manifesting itself in both physical and behavioral symptoms. This is a crisis of huge proportions and must be dealt with with sensitivity and love by the parents.

One good piece of advice offered by child psychologists is to put a name to the condition for your child. Tell him he's homesick instead of just feeling rotten. It's amazing what assigning a name to a condition does for a child; it helps in the recovery once he knows it's a temporary condition, like a cold.

Besides allowing for a grieving period for the loss of the previous life and friends, parents should work hard at stimulating their children to help them overcome feelings of alienation and its partner, rootlessness. Developing a child's interest in the new environment and all the possibilities it may offer, helps to not only distract the child, but moves her forward into her new life.

For parents trying to understand a child's depression, *Understanding Depression and Suicide* notes that early symptoms of depression can include general feelings of anxiety, panic, or fear and also offers these other signs of depression:

- negative or anti-social behavior
- wanting to leave home
- restlessness, grouchiness, sulkiness, aggression
- unwillingness to cooperate in family projects
- withdrawal from social activities
- hiding out in one's room
- school difficulties, including poor grades and not getting along with teachers and peers
- inattention to personal appearance
- extreme or sudden mood changes
- sensitivity to rejection, especially in love relationships
- abuse of alcohol or other drugs

- sexual promiscuity
- weight loss or weight gain
- sleeplessness or sleeping more than normal
- physical agitation or restlessness

2. Flirting with Danger: Drugs and Alcohol

Children living in overseas environments are very sheltered. When I surveyed through a questionnaire the 62 high school students at the International School of Beijing, more than half of them noted that parents would be well-advised to give their teenagers more freedom. Now granted, that kind of feeling can be expected from any teenager living anywhere in the world, but once again consider your teenagers' unique situation: they may live in separate compounds, are likely driven everywhere by a driver or parents because a driver's license may be forbidden, and generally live a life which to them borders on suffocation.

They also travel with their parents, are constantly surrounded by an endless procession of adult friends of their parents or high-ranking individuals, and are expected to be perfectly behaved. Any self-respecting teenager searching for himself or just for kicks is bound to find the idea of busting out of this sheltered life to flirt with danger appealing. Drugs and alcohol provide a perfect opportunity to act out their feelings about being under their parents' thumbs and respond to the peer pressure.

Many parents I spoke to believe that overseas the dangers of drugs and alcohol are pale compared to some inner city school in the Western hemisphere, but never discount the dangers – especially alcohol which may be as accessible as a parent's liquor cabinet. Some postings are good hunting grounds for illegal drugs. Some international schools help parents by running routine drug tests on the students.

Flirting with danger can also mean busting out onto the disco circuit, which, believe it or not, attracts children who at home wouldn't even be capable of securing a driver's license. Foreign hotels and their obligatory disco centers provide perfect opportunities for these children looking for action – dangerous action.

Parents cannot be expected to be policemen, but the child who is not under constant or at least regular 'surveillance' by parents is the child who will find both motive and opportunity for these dangerous thrills. It comes down once again to the availability of parents in their children's lives. Children who are left constantly to fend for themselves while the parents are forever out on the cocktail circuit may eventually decide they need some entertainment too, regardless of the inherent dangers.

A secondary issue is the parent's willingness to lay down the law and stick to it. I heard once from an American expatriate friend in Tokyo who was appalled that her 13-year-old daughter wanted to join the disco circuit with the rest of her friends. At the risk of the mother-daughter relationship, the mother simply laid down the law (call it discipline, for that is what it is) and told her daughter she was forbidden to go out to the disco with her gang of friends. It didn't make her popular with her daughter (what 13-year-old daughter takes her mother's advice easily anyway?), but rules were set. All parents should establish the rules and stick to them, no matter how difficult it seems.

SEEKING HELP FROM PROFESSIONALS

Fortunately for all parents of children experiencing any problems of adaptation or teenage adjustment overseas, there are usually professionals around who can help when a lifeline is needed. The school is the best place to start. If there is not already a counsellor on staff, the school can likely put you in touch with one practicing privately in the city. Don't waste any time worrying about stigmas or repercussions from taking the plunge into psychological counselling for your children. Consider the choice: a child who is under the care of a psychiatrist or psychologist, or a child who gets into serious trouble with the law or hurts himself as a result of self-destructive behavior.

You as the parent should be the first choice for counselling your own child, but when it's clear you are making no headway, and your child is unhappy, sullen, showing poor results academically, or any other symptoms of maladjustment, go to the experts.

BOOKS TO HELP YOU DOUBLE-CHECK

I have an older brother who is a physician. Rather than discard his outdated pharmaceutical handbook, he lets me have it. That kind of book has helped me familiarize myself with a variety of medicines prescribed to our family over the years. Bookstores carry stacks of health books that include drug guides and A-Z books of childhood emergencies and illnesses. Books on childhood development can help you chart your own children's growth.

Spare no expense and just buy them all. You may not find them where you are going, so have as many on hand as you can.

QUICK TIP SUMMARY

- DO make a list of emergency phone numbers for babysitters.
- Check out the local hospital emergency room *before* you may need it.
- Practice good preventive medicine, with proper inoculations, regular checkups, vitamins, and nutritious meals.
- Be sure your household environment is healthy, with safe water and properly cleaned and stored food.
- Train any household staff to follow your ideas of hygiene; and have everyone examined by doctors, with a special emphasis on chest X-rays for servants looking after children.
- Know your evacuation procedures and what services your company will pay for.
- Recognize the anxieties and fears that your children have are natural; and seek professional help when they go on too long.
- Travel with your own medical reference library and be sure to have a first aid kit and handbook in your home and car.

Chapter Nine

HOME LEAVE AND OTHER HOLIDAYS
Kiddie Wanderlust

"Where are we going next, Mommy?"

—4-year-old boy's query after deplaning from one trip in anticipation of another one

The 4-year-old boy posing that question happened to be my own world-weary son Jamie. The family was packed into a taxi, barreling along a congested road at the only speed Hong Kong taxi drivers know – fast! Less than an hour earlier, we had stepped off a flight from exotic Borneo where we had spent a relaxing, much needed pre-Christmas holiday. My children had seen every conceivable fish known to nature through glass-bottomed boats. They had shared a beach picnic with monkeys living in the trees that shaded us from the Malaysian sun. Father and daughter had even spent an exhausting day flying to another part of the island to inspect orangutans and to cruise through a rainforest. Now, the beach portion of our 10-day jaunt away from our home in Beijing completed, we were scheduled to spend a few days in Hong Kong engaged in our typical frenzied shopping spree.

To my 4-year-old son and his older sister, there was absolutely nothing exotic or out of the ordinary about either our resort vacation or our shopping stopover. We had made many similar forays into the materialistic jungle of Hong Kong. The hotel we were headed for at a dangerous speed was as familiar to them as our apartment back in Beijing since we had stayed there many times before. The Star Ferry, peak tram and other tourist sights of Hong Kong were now commonplace to them. So, too, were the hysterical shopping habits of their parents.

Boarding jumbo jets and setting out for paradise-like resorts – certainly the one we had just left in Kota Kinabalu in Borneo measured up – was simply nothing out of the ordinary for my children. Indeed, traveling to far-flung places, with lavish hotel rooms, room service breakfasts served on balconies covered in bougainvillea, and any of the other extravagant trappings of hotel life, had become a pattern of their early childhood.

TRAVEL IS A FACT OF LIFE

One of the major perquisites of life abroad is the opportunity for family travel to distance places. Airplane tickets to return home or for regional R and R's (rest and relaxation) are typically part of the wage and benefits package. As you are already *out there* in the world, the general feeling is to go ahead and explore the country where you live. Also tempting are the numerous regional flings there for the taking. In some instances – depending on the hardship level of your post – there is also the need to get out, take a break, and bring some color back into your eyes and some moisture to your skin.

And then there's home leave, that annual pilgrimage to your country of origin which is less a holiday and more a life experience which I will describe in more detail – with advice on how to get through it – later in this chapter.

Whatever the reasons for your trips, the fact is you will do a lot of traveling. Certainly more than you ever did back home. Travel is simply a part of life when you live overseas. And the twist, never to be forgotten, is that you will embark on these huge journeys – with endless flights, layovers, itineraries which look like they are written in secret codes – with children in tow.

Traveling with children can never be the same as traveling without them so never expect it to be. There will be pressures, stress, seemingly endless rows of luggage, toy bags, diaper supplies, and the infamous strollers which never fold up when required. There will be pre-ordered children's meals, cribs, and any other accessories you can remember to arrange before departure. There will also be crowded hotel rooms, cranky children in waiting rooms, and never enough time for the parents to share a quiet meal. What a holiday!

Despite all those problems, the family which travels together and shares the experience of a new country or even just some hectic journey, is the family which has a long-shared, happy memory. My memories of some of the countries I have visited with my children would not be the same if I had been there without them. They see things you don't, make comments, wonder aloud, make friends, and generally add an entirely new and unforgettable dimension to the travel experience.

As with everything else associated with life overseas, it pays to know what you are getting into beforehand. The better prepared you are for the small things associated with travel, the freer you are to enjoy the bigger picture.

DIFFERENT TYPES OF JOURNEYS

Your journeys will come in different sizes (with matching prices), but generally speaking, they fall into three categories:

1. Short Hops

The first type of journey will be the short hop. Depending on where you are posted – and the air or other transportation fare structures – there will usually be a lot of spots in the immediate vicinity to investigate over a regular or extended weekend. In tropical countries, these weekend retreats usually mean the beach and a break from a congested capital city. In colder climates, ski weekends are popular. In vast countries like China, there are famous ancient cities to be investigated. In Africa, it could be a game park, in other countries, a hike or camping weekend in the mountains. Any or all of these short hops may be scheduled around a particular local festival. In fact, sometimes you don't even need to travel. You can celebrate a local holiday with brand new cultural traditions without leaving home.

Regardless of the destination, these quickie trips also provide the perfect excuse to get away with another family, usually with children the same age as your own. Your children will enjoy traveling by train with their friends, or in a convoy of cars loaded up with picnics for along the way. Parents can enjoy the fact that their children are distracted with friends and at the same time enjoy other adult company.

When Lilly was a baby and we were living in Bangkok – a congested city which one liked to escape from as often as possible – we would 'break away' to nearby beach resorts with other families, also with new babies. It became the custom during our assignment to Thailand to 'break away' at least once every three months for these beach weekends. Being the spoiled 'madames', we could all take our maids with us – a definite perk of life in Bangkok – and thereby enjoy the evenings without the babies.

These weekend jaunts are a great way to get to know a family you may be forever running into but somehow never spend time with. Your children may already have friends picked out whom they would love to go away with, so ask them for suggestions.

One last advantage to these weekends away: if they are close enough, they are usually inexpensive. You will need your savings to afford the other types of journeys I'm about to describe, for these longer trips will definitely hit your pocketbook and credit cards, and hit them hard.

2. Regional Holidays

Next comes the shorter 10-day to two-week regional journey which coincides with the Christmas or Easter break from the children's school. These are the holidays you blindly believe are going to be cheap because you may have been provided with air tickets by your employer. All I can say on that score is that while tickets may be free, there is a huge hidden cost in resort or hotel fees and all the other uninhibited spending you feel obliged to do once you escape. But it is all worth it, for your children will thrive on these holidays and be able to enjoy the fact that they are living away from their home country. Ask a child what he thinks is the advantage of overseas versus home life, and he will likely tell you it is the chance to take all these wonderful trips.

Destinations for these 10-day to two-week jaunts will once again depend on your assigned country, but holidays in the sun or extended ski holidays are popular with families and there are enough resorts worldwide that will cater to your every need during these escapes.

The golden age for children on these trips is apparently under 12 years, when they still want to be with their parents and aren't bored sitting around at some posh resort. If your children are older, it might be wise to ask a friend to come along.

When you select a destination, never ever forget that you have children. Resorts which cater to plane-loads of European or North American tourists out for a week in the sun may not be

suitable for children anxious to do something other than lie in the sun. Ask your travel agent key questions: Is there a beach nearby? Does it provide water sports? How expensive will those sports be? Are there boats available for touring around? What about bicycles or any other form of transportation which your child might want to use? Is there a coffee shop? (Most hotels have one but be sure to check so that your children will be able to find food that fits their less than exotic tastebuds.) What about the rooms? Is there television? Closed-circuit video movies? Will there be a crib available for a baby? Never assume anything when traveling with children. Always ask beforehand.

Once you are at your destination, be sure to find some activity which can be planned for each day, usually in the morning when children are at their best. Children can be persuaded to hang around in the afternoons – and let their parents put their feet up and read a book for a few minutes – if they have had some distraction in the morning. As a parent, it is up to you to constantly negotiate with your children. It is everyone's holiday.

Since our children are young, whenever we travel on beach vacations, we arrange for a babysitter to arrive at our hotel room promptly at 6 p.m. By that time, our children have usually exhausted themselves and we have fed them with something from room service. We have trained our children that since we are with them from dawn until dusk (which fortunately comes early in tropical countries) the evening is mommy's and daddy's time to be alone and unwind. My children have never protested because we have explained why it is important for everyone to feel they are getting a holiday. Dragging children out for dinner is not our idea of a fun night, although it may be for others.

If you are staying for a week or so, you can often arrange to have the same babysitter every night who then becomes familiar to the children. Since you are usually just eating at the resort, a babysitter can always find you quickly if there are any problems. For my husband and me, a few hours free at night to linger over quiet dinners is our way of 'going on a date' and is good holiday therapy for a traveling marriage.

By leaving your children on their own at night, they learn an important lesson about the give-and-take of family holidays.

3. Home Leave

Then there is home leave. This is the journey many families make during the long summer break from school. More than any other journey you will make together as a family, home leave will tap all of your emotional resources and physical energy. These trips are exhausting from start to finish but they can still be fun and useful for the entire family.

Taking a home leave with children provides a unique challenge because of both the distance involved and the length of the journey. The age of your children influences this type of journey more than any other, because, of all the traveling you will do while overseas, home leave will be the most hectic, the most complicated, the most emotionally dangerous, and the busiest – since in addition to visiting family and friends, there is shopping to do. Trying to amuse children, pick up everything you need, *and* visit with everyone who naturally wants to see you after a year or two away, is, in a word, draining.

Remember this fact: the purpose of home leave is more than just shopping until overcome by fatigue and shopping mall burn-out. It is time to reconnect with family and your own culture. It is extremely important in planning your home leave to include the opportunity for your children to soak up some of their national heritage. Build in a few days for just the family on either end of the journey. Make plans to fit in some sightseeing to reacquaint – or introduce – your children to the country stamped on their passport.

It's also important when planning the journey to arrange a few days holiday along the way, not necessarily in-country, but a vacation destination. I recommend this stopover be on the return portion when the family needs the time and space to 'chill out' after the exhaustion of seeing so many people in so short a time.

As a result of making these annual pilgrimages, and the other types of journeys I just mentioned, I have managed to compile a few travel tips which have worked for me.

KEEP IT SIMPLE

Once, when we were planning a home leave from our posting in Beijing, our travel plans became so unbelievably complicated that we just threw the itinerary our travel agent had given us in the nearest wastebasket and started over again. The plans had become so complex, with one- or two-day stops here, there, and everywhere, that we couldn't sort out what we would be doing at any given time.

When children find themselves waking up in a different bed – indeed a different country – every three days, you can bet there will be trouble controlling them along the way. Factor in jet lag, travel exhaustion, and too many airplane meals, and you are cooking up a disastrous home leave which will make everyone crazy before they even arrive at your family's doorstep.

By the way, the same advice should apply to regional journeys as well. You may spend a fantastic, relaxing week at a beach or ski resort and then make a brief stop to 'buy just a few things'. Suddenly everyone becomes frazzled trying to do too much in too short a time, and you manage to completely undo the point of the holiday – to relax. You return home needing another holiday.

Sure, go ahead and plan stopovers on the way to and from home, especially if you need to break up the long distance flying. But try not to exhaust your children – and yourselves – beyond emotional capabilities. Give yourselves a few days before and after the journey to stare at a wall if that's what you want to do.

TOO-HIGH EXPECTATIONS OF CHILDREN

This leads naturally to my next point. You get home to your birthplace or wherever the family is, and then you put your children on show for the family. After flying for days and camping out in waiting rooms or hotels, parents then expect their children to act like angels with people they've not seen in years. It's true that our children are good with adults, and can be expected to act reasonably adult themselves around swarms of distant relatives even when they are only age 5, but it can all be too much for the little ones.

We arrived to visit my mother-in-law one summer when my son was barely 4-years-old and then included him in a week of tea parties, lunches in restaurants, and other forms of get-togethers where he was expected to be sociable and sit politely and nibble on a biscuit.

Not surprisingly, he did what any self-respecting 4-year-old would do: he ran and hid upstairs in his granny's house and wouldn't come down for the first few days to see anyone, no matter how much we coaxed or how angry we subsequently became. We finally left him alone, and he appeared all on his own one day mid-visit.

Do remember how tough all the visiting can be on your children – of any age. Don't expect miraculous behavior all of the time, even from the most well-behaved. For instance, aunts and uncles who haven't seen them in years may choose home leave time to bombard them with belated Christmas or birthday presents. Suddenly, every visit comes to mean a gift to your child. Then, when a visitor doesn't show up with one, your toddler starts to scream for a gift and you want to crawl away and hide. It wasn't his fault, so don't be too harsh.

Intersperse errands and visiting commitments with activities your children enjoy. They simply won't put up with being dragged through malls and trying on endless outfits that may fit them six months later, or sit smiling at adults they don't know.

THE IMPORTANCE OF RULES AND ROUTINES

You don't have to be dictatorial about routines when traveling – after all you are on holiday – but it helps your children to know that trips aren't just a giant free-for-all in the behavior department.

Bedtime is particularly critical, so establish one and then stick to it even when traveling (after the first few days of jet lag have subsided). The quicker your children know that certain things remain the same – like rules of behavior – the better they will act during all the free time a vacation affords.

By the same token, teach your children how to be good house guests. Make sure your children know how to be sensitive to your hosts' needs. Build small chores into their daily routines, like making their bed or cleaning up the guest bathroom after they use it. Be sure they know to ask before helping themselves to food in the kitchen.

Even the business of flying can be orderly. Make children responsible for their knapsacks of toys and their own change of clothes and travel supplies (juice boxes, water bottles, and snacks). When we fly long-distance on night flights, my young children put their pajamas on (or something comfortable to sleep in) after supper has been served. In this way, they know they are 'going to bed' for a few hours when the window shades are lowered and the cabin quiets down. If you also train them to respect the other passengers' right to a relatively quiet journey, you will make friends with flight attendants worldwide.

PREPARING THEM TO SEE FAMILY

Travel preparations with children – especially for home leave – require more than just making reservations and packing a suitcase. It's a good idea to begin the task of 'briefing' your children a few weeks ahead on those family members they may not remember. We have always had lots of family pictures stuck up on the refrigerator door to remind our children of the family back home.

If you don't already have a family rogues' gallery somewhere in your overseas home, take out the photo albums and go over all the people they are likely to see when you are home. Nothing disappoints a grandfather or aunt more than finally seeing the children they have missed and the child looks blankly at them and says, "Who are you?" Prepare your children so they can put faces and names together and at least have something polite to ask their relatives when they see them.

WHERE TO STAY

When other mothers ask me how we managed on our lengthy home leaves, one of the best survival tips I can point to is our annual habit of renting a summer cottage. Try to have your own space if it's at all possible and economically feasible. As you will likely want to invite people over to visit, having your own place prevents imposing yourself and all of your visitors on a sibling or close friend. Too many visitors can be hard going on even the most gracious hosts. Resentment can slowly build up to a high pitch over the days you are together and tempers can fray.

We find that our summer cottage rental works beautifully, especially as the cottage is less than a stone's throw from our permanent residence. It means we can be in the vicinity of our old neighbors, enjoy our countryside, and reunite with all our friends in the area. It also means I can phone our old babysitters and drop into the local grocery store to stock the kitchen – another invaluable asset on a holiday with children.

By the way, if it's financially affordable, rent a car to facilitate all the visiting and sightseeing you want to do without imposing on family for transportation.

HOME LEAVE CULTURE SHOCK

Just because you have gotten over the shock of the new culture at your posting doesn't mean your children will be immune from it if you stop over somewhere they have never been before or make a regional trip to some exotic neighboring country. Culture shock can crop up on holiday and hotel culture may take some getting used to for first-time traveling children, but this vacation shock is much easier to handle since you won't be staying long and won't have to deal with this new foreign culture on a long-term basis.

REVERSE CULTURE SHOCK

This is the shock you will most likely have to deal with on a home leave (and upon re-entry, the subject of Chapter Ten), especially if you are returning to a home country which is drastically different from where you are posted.

This works both ways – from Third World assignments back

to your developed country and vice versa. The more profound the differences in the places, the more everyone will feel it.

Our home leave in Canada after our first year on mainland China threw our entire family into shock. We were in Winnipeg, a Canadian prairie city which couldn't be more different than Beijing if it tried to be. Winnipeg was in the throes of a Canadian recession and could hardly be labelled a city of conspicuous consumption, but the difference in the level of materialism took our breath away.

One day I took my children to a mall near my mother-in-law's home where we stocked up on running shoes. (I was taking no chances of running out of shoes in China.) We were enjoying some ersatz ethnic food when my daughter – 8-years-old then – put down her fork and said:

"That shoe store was pretty strange, wasn't it, mom?"

"In what way?" I asked.

"The selection of shoes. I didn't know you could pick from so many types." She had been indecisive, and so had I, when confronted with so many styles and colors.

"And that woman in there ..."

"The saleswoman?"

"Yes. She ... well ... she helped us."

"Yes ... so?"

"She *helped* us."

After a year in Beijing and the constant refrain of '*mei yo*' ('don't have'), even when you are looking right at the object you want to buy, Lilly had forgotten that salespeople could actually be obliging and useful.

Reverse culture shock is more a phenomenon of the re-entry experience – when you feel like an alien in your own culture because you have lost track of the common reference points. But it can definitely occur during a month-long home leave. It goes away after a few days, but at the beginning it can be as disorienting as its relative, plain old straightforward culture shock.

APPOINTMENTS FOR YOUR CHILDREN

If you have been unhappy with the quality of medical or dental care overseas, home leave or a regional trip to a nearby major city is the time to have your children thoroughly checked over by specialists or the family doctor.

SETTING LIMITS ON SHOPPING

It's true. We all go a little nuts on home leave when suddenly every shop is like a candy store and you feel compelled to go inside and buy everything in sight. Children, following your cue, will expect to do the same and will think nothing of hitting a music shop or toy store and also want to buy everything they see. Limits have to be set, or your children will think a money tree was packed in the luggage along with clean underwear. Never mind that you will likely have to buy an extra trunk in order to get everything back, there should be some restrictions on the amount you allow your children to buy. In our family, book-stores are the only designated shops for over-spending (how can you discourage reading?), but every place else we try to impose limits. Try to control your own spending. If mommy and daddy can't put down their credit cards, chances are the children will be stuck in a spending mode too.

CHILDREN TRAVELING WITHOUT PARENTS

One of the greatest gifts you can give your teenage children is the opportunity to travel ahead of the family. This works best, of course, when you have a sibling or parent back home ready to look after them for you. But if it's possible to arrange it, allow your children this moment of independence and freedom from the family unit. Their appreciation will know no bounds. If younger children are sent ahead, most airlines are obliging and will arrange for a customer agent to whisk them through cus-toms or to a connecting flight. However, from families who have arranged this service from even the most reliable of airlines, reports come of agents not showing up and children relying on traveling good samaritans. If you can arrange it, try to find a friend on board the same flight who can fill in if the agent is a no-show.

OTHER TRAVEL TIPS

Just when you think you've covered every possible contingency about holiday travel, another issue arises. When we were living in China and my daughter Lilly was starting to get excited about home leave to Canada, she came home from school one day in tears. She had upset her school chum from Kenya, who didn't get a home leave. In fact, she had not been back to Kenya in six years.

1. When Travel is Out of the Question

Not everyone living overseas has the luxury of these extended home leaves or regional holidays soaking up the sun at an expensive resort. Many Third World diplomatic families are not given the same travel benefits that you may be given, and you should remind your own children – if they are lucky enough – just how fortunate they are. Many of their friends at school may not be planning such extravagant holidays so if your children are, teach them to be sensitive to those who have to stay put for the entire summer or Christmas holiday.

If you are the mother in this case or a full-time job prevents you from getting away for an extended leave, try to be creative in coming up with some stay-at-home compensation for your children. Be sure to find out who else is staying and contact their mothers and see what you can work out together in the way of activities and distractions. Local inexpensive tourist sites can be explored easily; suggest these as alternatives to your children. Lots of picnics or just special attention may be in order. Summer projects can be initiated. The local international school may also offer some suggestions and often runs an inexpensive day camp.

2. Traveling Together as a Family

You may have finally adjusted to living overseas as a family when along comes the challenge of hitting the road together. Hotel rooms need to be shared – often the beds themselves – and suddenly you have children rebelling at the notion. All your meals may be taken together in hotel coffee shops or at an aunt's dining room table, and each family member is quietly contemplating an escape route from the suffocation of being together without a daily structure.

The best advice I can offer here is to be sure to arrange time out for every family member. A mother's time out is critical, especially if the home leave journey is made without her spouse and she bears sole responsibility 24 hours a day. Find babysitters as quickly as you can so you or you and your husband can get away for a private dinner or a movie.

If you are going to be in one place for a while at home, and it is summer, call up the nearest recreation department and find out what programs they offer. Many mothers line up summer camp at home for their children. Even day camps offer distractions for younger children. Local swimming pools may offer short courses of instruction. Your teenagers may be able to find summer jobs at home as camp counsellors. Don't just arrive home and expect everyone to sit around together or to happily jump in the car as a gang every day to go visiting or shopping. Be sure to ask what activities can be arranged for your children.

3. Stock Up on Small Gifts

This advice goes along with nurturing good house guests. Teach your children at a tender age that it is polite to say thanks to a relative or friend with a small present. These don't have to be expensive gifts. Often, just a color drawing left hanging on your host's refrigerator will suffice. A teenager can offer babysitting free of charge or gardening service. Usually, however, experienced traveling mothers load up on some small gift item which can be bought in bulk and be on hand for their own children to present to friends they are visiting as a token of thanks or just a small sample of the culture where you live.

PARENTS TRAVELING WITHOUT CHILDREN

No matter your children's ages, the issue of traveling without them is bound to come up at some point during your stay overseas. *This is completely natural.* You are not trying to shirk responsibilities and you can still love your children very much, but you and your husband may want to get away on your own for a few days or a week.

Obviously if you are still breastfeeding a baby this won't be possible, but I have known parents of young children to manage a holiday by themselves. When my husband and I were living in Bangkok we spent two weeks in New Zealand and Australia by ourselves when our daughter was only six months old. What did we do with her? We left her with a good friend who absorbed into her household our daughter, our maid, my daughter's crib, and the rest of the baby paraphernalia. I'll admit, it was a gut-wrenching decision for us.

In Bangkok, our particular circle of friends (all having their first child) needed a break away from new parental responsibilities from time to time so we banded together to find a solution. We arranged extended sleepovers with Thai maids on hand to help ease the burden on each other and provide care-giving continuity for our children. A lot will depend on where you are living if you are considering solutions like this. While we were living in China – with spotty medical care – the question never even arose. We just knew we wouldn't feel comfortable leaving the country. But some friends of ours managed it with a happy ending, even though one friend came home and clung to her 2-year-old daughter vowing never to do it again, despite returning tanned and relaxed.

If you feel it's downright impossible to get away for a long weekend or a week when you are living overseas, there are a few alternatives. First, see if you can arrange a side trip for just the adults during home leave. Perhaps loving grandparents or aunts and uncles would love to have your children to themselves. So if they offer to take the children, take them up on it. At least you will feel your children are in good hands. Many traveling couples I know have arranged for 24-hour getaways which don't even necessitate leaving the city. If you have a good maid or babysitter willing to sleep over, check into the nearest luxury hotel for the night. Leave early one Saturday morning and come back after Sunday brunch. It's amazing how even these brief respites from children will make you feel refreshed.

MAJOR HOLIDAYS CELEBRATED ABROAD

Just when you think your children have survived the culture shock experience, along comes a major holiday or milestone which – now that you are living in a foreign country – will be celebrated in a different fashion than at home. Children, especially younger ones, will feel that something is not quite right but will not be able to articulate that sentiment. They may start acting moody or unhappy, and you are at a loss to define why they are acting up when finally their adjustment seemed so solid.

1. Christmas Away From Home

Christmas can be the biggest shocker of all. My own children, experiencing their first Christmas away from Canada, had the shock of their young lives when we were living in Taipei. Where was the snow? The sweet smell of the freshly-cut Christmas tree? All they could see was the ubiquitous fog and a fake tree purchased hastily at Toys 'R' Us.

Obviously, Christmas in a tropical country can be problematic for families from northern countries used to a white Christmas. But there are a few ways to rally everyone out of their homesickness. For starters, when you pull your Christmas box out of the storage closet, and the children see all the decorations they have been hanging on their tree for years emerge, that goes a long way to helping create some semblance of home.

Be sure to pack everything associated with major holidays. Whether you celebrate Christmas, Chinese New Year, lantern festivals, or Rosh Hashana – bring all your own holiday paraphernalia with you. Perhaps you would like to bring extras as well, in order to introduce your new local or international friends to the customs of your own country or religion.

While it would be culturally interesting to eat local food, a major holiday is not the time to experiment. Serve your children a meal that comes reasonably close to what is familiar. You would be surprised how easily some substitutes can be found.

At the same time that you are substituting food, find a few stand-ins for family with the friends you have made. Try to invite a few older friends as well, as replacements for missing grandparents or aunts and uncles. Or, if it is possible, invite family who have indicated an interest in visiting you at your foreign post to come at holiday time. It is a good time to entertain guests as everyone is usually off for a few days or there is school vacation. My mother-in-law chose to visit us in Beijing at Christmas time and she made a wonderful house guest at the perfect time for our children.

Some families select their major holidays as the perfect time to take a vacation. For instance, many regional resorts cater to the traveling family by putting on wonderful Christmas spreads. If you can't leave town, try the local hotels for their Christmas dinners. If you can't be home, these lavish buffets often fill the gap.

Fortunately, presents are handy reminders that Santa Claus has not lost his way over the International Date Line. Opening a present is fun no matter where your children are in the world.

2. Birthday Parties

Birthday celebrations are easier to arrange away from home. Your children will have many new school friends they will want to invite and chances are there is a local club or nearby park where the celebrations can be staged.

Most traveling mothers buy up the necessary birthday paraphernalia, loot bags, party favors, and party games during home leave. Once again, it's amazing how substitutes can be found. When my young daughter insisted on playing pin-the-tail-on-the-donkey at her 7th birthday party in Taipei (and a ready-made game was nowhere to be found), we came up with a new version called pin the flag on the map. The children enjoyed it just as much as the original.

While you are loading up on birthday accessories, be sure to throw in some birthday candles. As a going-away present, good Canadian friends of ours gave us birthday candles in the shape of the numbers for each birthday our children would celebrate abroad. The idea was a lovely one – each birthday, we remembered our friends when we lit the candle on the birthday cake.

CREATING TRAVEL MEMORIES

If you are worried that your children's memories of your travels will get tossed away with old boarding passes, then consider a few ways of ensuring that doesn't happen. Video cameras have been a positive boon to helping parents keep visual records for their children when they grow up and can't remember that Easter holiday spent in Africa or Spain. As prices of video cameras are now dropping, be sure to snap one up at a bargain.

Besides providing the means for creating your own travel memories, videotapes can be copied to send back to family who, I can assure you from experience, will watch them over and over again. Ask your children to say a special hello on the tape to granny or granddaddy. These messages are a big hit.

If you are only using a still camera, be sure to take the time to put together photo albums instead of just stashing all the photos in a drawer somewhere.

Travel journals, long letters home (saving copies for your children), unique postcards, even drawings scrawled on hotel stationary are all assets to a travel memory box. Encourage your children to take the time to write these because years later they will definitely thank you for it.

IT'S WORTH IT

When you are packing and repacking the heaps of luggage, or preparing what seems like endless airplane, train, or car picnics, just remember that although the travel preparations or searching for a nearby laundromat to keep everyone in clean underwear is exhausting, these trips are definitely worth it. As usual, your children may not take the opportunity to thank you for it at the time, but they will when they grow up and can look back on an old travel journal or photo album from some far-flung location in the world.

QUICK TIP SUMMARY

- DO remember that travel is a fact of life and expect to make a lot of trips during your overseas posting; your children will typically love all the travel.
- Your trips will come in three different sizes: short hops, regional journeys, and home leaves.
- DO try to plan some of the shorter trips with other families whose children are the same age as yours.
- DON'T complicate travel plans: the simpler the better.
- Always remember when choosing a destination that there will be children involved, so make sure there are activities on hand or nearby for them.
- When planning a home leave DO make sure to understand your children will not put up with endless shopping or visits with strangers: plan activities for them.

- DO establish bedtime and other routines for younger travelers. DON'T expect them to be on the best behavior at all times.
- DO brief them beforehand about family members they may not have seen in a while.
- Be prepared for the children to suffer more culture shock on holidays and the more common reverse culture shock where they feel strange in their own country.
- DO make appointments with doctors or dentists when you travel if the medical care is not adequate where you are posted.
- DON'T let your children – and yourself 'shop until you drop'.
- Traveling together as a family will be a challenge but a memorable one, especially if you help your children create travel memories with pictures and journals.

Chapter Ten

THE SHOCKS OF RE-ENTRY
Helping Your Children Return Home

"I had a romanticized vision of what my life would be like as a teenager back home. I thought I would go out on dates. Instead, all of my friends were girls."

—grown-up ambassador's daughter, looking back on a re-entry experience

Throughout the entire three years of our diplomatic assignment to the Far East capitals of Taipei and Beijing, we faithfully dragged our video camera along. From the Great Wall of China to the California Disneyland, from the Costa Del Sol of Spain to a Borneo rainforest, and to other equally exotic points along the way, we religiously recorded the memories of our extensive family travels. We accumulated several 'keeper' tapes, stored them inside a cupboard, and then forgot about them completely once the events had been duly recorded for posterity.

We decided the time had arrived to finally screen our collection of home video memories on the night my husband received official word that we would be leaving our post in Beijing for a headquarters assignment. Re-entry to Canada was about three months away.

When the first tape began to roll, we discovered it's absolutely true what they say: the camera never lies. Beginning with Act One, Scene One – our very first departure early one hot summer morning from the Ottawa airport – one whopping truth jumped off the screen at all of us gathered in front of the television set.

"Have we ever changed!" the entire family shouted almost simultaneously.

GOING HOME AS DIFFERENT PEOPLE

The truth of the matter – substantiated right there before us in living color and with a soundtrack to even record the differences in the children's voices – was that individually, and collectively as a family, we had changed during our years abroad. We were not returning home the same people who had left Canada three years earlier.

During that time, for example, our son's 2-year-old temper tantrums for the camera had mercifully eased off to almost none, his white blonde hair had darkened, and his squeaky baby voice had vanished. His parents' faces had visibly relaxed. After a hectic settling-in period, we got over looking like we were on the verge of nervous breakdowns. Our daughter had become a lovely young girl even though her mother had insisted on having her long hair dramatically chopped off in the interest of neatness.

Besides physical growth, the rest of the changes – the emotional ones – were not visible to the eye. They were inside all of us. The entire family had undergone very personal changes as a result of our respective experiences abroad, especially after living in the world's most populous country, China. Our physical

236

surroundings had affected our attitudes, our tastes, our outlooks, and most of all, our values. There was also no denying that time marches on. We were all older, especially, it seemed, the parents, but who wants to admit that? And the many emotional changes would be completely unexplainable to anyone back home.

While we were viewing our own transformations on tape, we also had glimpses of all the friends and family we had left behind, caught by the camera during home leave holidays. There, too, were shots of our house, our dog, and other nearby locations. The videotape was bringing 'home' home to us, through the medium of video. At our own separate levels, we escaped into our thoughts for a few minutes and were reminded where we were going back to, and as whom. Subconsciously, we were receiving the message that if we had changed so much, the people and places in our videos would likely have changed too.

Before I even begin to offer advice on how to better understand the ways in which those changes are going to affect your re-entry experience and that of your children, allow me to suggest that you pull out those home videos from the cupboard. If you haven't jumped on that particular technological bandwagon, dig out your photo albums or any other visual records (clothing now too small will do, or a collection of ear picks or any other esoteric collection started abroad). These activities will help you begin the process of understanding the changes which time and the overseas life have brought to your own family, and to the people and places you will be rejoining.

MAKING THE DECISION TO GO HOME

The decision to go home for some expatriate parents is thrust upon them by the government or corporation for whom they work. The decision for others may rest entirely with themselves, so there will likely be many serious issues to consider.

There may be the obvious reasons for returning home, such as being fired from a job, or when the economic advantages of being abroad disappear. Sometimes, a political crisis or the threat of one forces an expatriate family out of the country.

But more often than not, the needs of the children – usually the educational needs – help sway the vote to go home. Suddenly, your son or daughter is entering high school and you as the parent have to decide whether you will be able to stay where you are long enough for him to graduate or have to uproot him halfway through. Or, it could be your confidence in the scholastic reputation of the present school is not high enough to ensure your child's future entry into a good college.

In some cases, a decision to go home comes from the recognition that your child's knowledge about his home culture is limited. When you discover your child can speak the local language more fluently than his own native tongue, you naturally begin to worry that you have stayed too long at your foreign assignment.

There are many other reasons. It could be you want to escape the life with servants and the illusion of a wealthy lifestyle which seems to be warping everyone's values. Health reasons often tip the scales. Boredom or disillusionment with a job, or burning ambition to jump ahead via a headquarters assignment may lie behind the decision. Or it could simply be the case that it's time your young child experienced a backyard with a dog running in it rather than the concrete jungle of a claustrophobic foreigner's compound. All of these considerations may surface, and all are good enough reasons to decide to go home.

Whatever the rationale, any or all of them should be discussed openly with the family, especially disillusionment over the monotony with a job. A father, for instance, may not be as willing to discuss such feelings with his children and sometimes covers up that boredom factor with statements like: "It's because of you that we are going home!" Such a statement directed at a young boy or girl can place a heavy burden of guilt on a child for a situation truly not of his making.

Children should not be made to feel guilty when their needs force the family to go home. For even if it is the case that it's time to go home for high school or better medical facilities, that child is also a family member. If the overseas life is not providing what that child needs – educationally or healthwise – then nobody should dispute the decision to go home.

PARENTS' RE-ENTRY ATTITUDES AFFECT THE CHILDREN

Nothing can disguise the fact that all the issues which are facing the parents both as individuals and as a married couple are going to impact dramatically on the family's feelings about going home. It's not that much different from the settling-in period when the family dynamics were in a state of flux. As a married couple, the parents may be wondering how they will adapt at home without servants, allowances, and all the other perks of expatriate life which defused many domestic disputes they used to have at home. Their marital tensions can be felt by their children.

Separately, each parent's attitudes will also pervade the household. Just as at the beginning of the overseas assignment the mother's culture shock can drive her children to experience similar chaotic feelings, at the end of an assignment a father's ambiguities or worries about going home can leave the children feeling something is wrong.

A mother about to re-enter who has shelved her career while overseas may now be faced with the harsh economic reality that she has to go back to work in order to support the lifestyle to which they have all grown accustomed. She may also not only be worried about career prospects, but enduring sleepless nights over practical issues such as child care for young pre-schoolers, or after-school minders for older children. A mother who gets herself all tied up in knots, shopping for things that will never even fit into a house back home, is going to charge her children up too. Her distracted and nervous behavior will not exactly inspire serenity or confidence about the move in her children. Remember how children imitate you, the parent.

A father will have other issues to face which may affect his family's behavior. For instance, a father who starts fretting about the financial difficulties associated with re-entry is going to transfer those worries – his tension and uncertainty about what lies in the future – onto his children. Besides financial woes or worries about what job he will be asked to perform at headquarters, he may also be facing up to deeper, personal issues, and his distraction and depression may affect his children.

One night when we were facing our own re-entry to Canada from Beijing, I managed to wrangle out of my own husband the worries and thoughts which were so obviously consuming him.

He had been ruminating about going home (of course worrying about loss of overseas benefits and money as his counterparts everywhere do) and then, with a sudden clarity, he expressed the notion that in a broader context, re-entry had come to signify a major milestone in his life. He felt it marked both a beginning and an ending. The assignment was ending and a new one back home beginning, but he himself was older, his children older and life had somehow irrevocably changed and moved on.

When you live in the same place all the time, a promotion or change in job may provide this same separation of experience, but not with the same magnification which a dramatic change in location will bring.

In my husband's case, I felt he was expressing an idea many other returning expatriates probably feel: he was conscious of one chapter being closed and time moving on. I made a note to call this milestone of re-entry an 'emotional demarcation line' separating one stage of life from another. I think re-entry definitely provides these passages, and not just for the angst-ridden adults, but for all the members of the family. Our young son certainly left his toddler and pre-school years behind him in Asia to embark on his elementary school experience in Canada.

The positive side to these emotional time boundaries is that they provide everyone with a feeling that a 'fresh start' lies ahead. Children, especially, embrace the notion of having a clean slate. Re-entry can be seen, therefore, as a positive opportunity for new beginnings.

Perhaps this discussion has become too philosophical for those parents just looking for solid, practical advice about getting from here to there with everything in one piece. But I believe that thoughtful parents will recognize that their emotions are re-entering as much as their furniture. And just as inanimate objects may show the test of time, so will parents' feelings about themselves. I believe you will be doing your children a tremendous favor in the long run if you take a good long look at your own feelings in between drawing up inventories or making plane reservations.

And after you have thought about all of these things, put them aside and get on with the business at hand. Once the decision is taken to go home – just as when it was taken to go abroad – everybody must get behind that decision and put the best face and attitude forward, especially parents.

RE-ENTRY CAN BE HARDER THAN MOVING ABROAD

Re-entry is not as easy as it looks. Parents preparing for their first re-entry experience should know that right up front. Those people who were busy denying they ever experienced culture shock in the first place, will likely be the same people denying the existence of re-entry shock. Here's an important news flash: you are not impervious to it.

Re-entry can definitely be a joyful, happy time. Thinking about going home conjures up all sorts of wonderful, nostalgic images. But like everything else associated with the overseas experience, it pays to be realistic and to know what you are getting into so that you can adjust your expectations accordingly.

As parents especially, it is important to recognize the issues that will have a direct impact on your children. Remember that your goal is to make their transition as easy as possible.

Why is it harder than it looks? For some specific reasons:

1. Myths and Expectations about Home

Home is perfect. Home is clean and orderly. People are more efficient and smile more. These are just a few myths that some people believe, and depending on where you come from, it might just be the case that compared to where you have been living for the past few years, home will seem like the perfect place. Many people going home from Third World countries to Western, industrialized nations will definitely feel this. For others making the reverse journey, it may be the case that they are tired of the crass, shallow Western materialism and it is time to return to more fundamental values. Regardless of which way your journey is taking you, understand that your idealization of your home culture will be acute and not just a little romanticized.

Not only do we think that home is perfect, but we often buy into a myth that time stood still while we were away. We believe that despite the changes in ourselves, everyone back home has not changed at all. Forget that myth and realize that places may have also changed while you have been away. Buildings may have been torn down to make way for parking lots, streets may have changed direction, loved ones may have aged dramatically in just a few short years.

Some of us harbor myths about how current we have stayed with life back home, a process virtually impossible overseas except from snippets of foreign news or letters from home. Often we believe that the entire family will fit back into life at home with complete ease and that there will be no problems whatsoever. Wrong!

And here is one of the biggest myths of all: the misguided expectation that people – and for children especially, new classmates – will be interested in hearing about the adventure just completed. Wake up, everybody! See these myths for what they are: part of the idealization stage which can be amusing or comforting to believe in, but are usually far from the truth.

2. Reverse Culture Shock

Feeling like an alien in your own culture is the essence of reverse culture shock. You feel like an outsider looking in, even though the people and places look familiar, and recognition seems as if it should be within your grasp. For a few months after your arrival home – just as for a few months after your arrival overseas – most people will experience the same stages which are associated with culture shock.

There will be an initial honeymoon period when it is so darn great to be back that you are willing to overlook a lot of things. Then suddenly, it will hit you: you are home to stay. No trips, no adventure, no unexpectedness, no excitement.

This dramatic feeling of let-down usually causes your emotions to crash, though not as dramatically as they did in the first instance abroad. The idea of moving back overseas – immediately if not sooner – starts to seem appealing and, in a perverse way, you begin to idealize all the things you left behind at a posting which actually drove you crazy. Then, slowly the period of readjustment slips into place, and you emerge from your shocked system to go on with your life. A new routine – which breeds familiarity – has been established once more.

The reality is that reverse culture shock can be the reactions that surface naturally in response to all those myths about home I just described. When you live overseas for an extended period of time, you do tend to idealize home as perfect and when you discover there are problems at home, too, this can be a shock. You have also lost touch with day-to-day life in your own country. We don't, in fact, know much about what people are wearing, talking about, thinking about and so on. It will take a few months before we are once again plugged into the home culture.

For children, this reverse culture shock will seem utterly confusing unless it is explained to them carefully. The initial culture shock overseas was more or less understandable. Even a pre-schooler understands when things don't look familiar and the country seems upside down with people who don't look anything like him and strange food is on the dinner table. He will find it thoroughly confusing, however, when he experiences those waves of shock in response to something that is supposed to be 'normal' for him.

Likewise, a teenager knows why he can't communicate with a neighbor who speaks a foreign language; he won't understand why he's getting nowhere with his old 'best friend' or with new kids on the block who do speak the same language.

For a few months, when returnees are in the grip of this reverse culture shock, the language, while sounding the same as the one they speak, will have words and reference points which make no sense because they represent events and cultural talking points which you have missed while being away. Children, especially, mimic what they hear on television or in the lyrics to a special song. When your child doesn't have the vocabulary, he won't be able to communicate and will feel left out – of his own apparent culture.

3. Return Shock and Distress are Real

All of the experts who have looked at this concept of return shock agree: it is very real. Nobody is imagining it or making it up to explain away discomfort.

There is a distinct jolt one feels upon returning home, not quite like an earthquake, but certainly an aftershock of the emotional upheavals from moving abroad and then arriving and feeling like a stranger in a strange land – home. What causes some of these shocks and distress signals?

• *Length of Time Away*

The family's reaction – once again individually and collectively – will depend on several factors, often beginning with how long you have been away. Even a few months in a foreign country will offer a share of shocks to the system, but families with children who can never remember living at 'home' will likely face the most readjustments. Many children hear about 'home' only through anecdotes or other family stories, or perhaps from books. The reality may seem so far from what they have been told that they are disappointed at what they discover.

Likewise, a long posting in a country which provided servants may not have prepared children for the reality of life without them. The concept of 'picking up after themselves' may be new to them and not all that pleasant at first.

Depending on the country you call 'home', there may be many social and political changes which have happened while you have been away. For instance, my own family returned home from China to a constitutional crisis in Canada. Another returnee may find a change in government and new social programs. Many may face social problems which they have never seen before, such as homeless people living on the street or food banks for people hit by hard times. Returnees to Third World nations might have missed a coup d'etat or a famine.

• *Physical Reactions*

I cannot remember exactly how many mothers I have spoken to who have reported to me the illnesses their children went through after moving home, but I have heard it often enough to believe it must have some truth. The shock of upheaval on a young child's system, or the physical ache of loneliness and alienation in an older child, often causes a breakdown in their immune systems and subsequent constant colds and aches or other ailments are not uncommon. Sleep and appetite disruptions are other common physical symptoms of anxiety and depression.

• *Mental Health Reactions*

The most common psychological reaction to being home is confusion, which shouldn't surprise anyone when you consider that you are once again adapting to new customs and rituals, even if they are supposed to be your own. The fact is, you have not engaged in them in a while and they might as well be new.

Loss of confidence and issues of self-esteem will also go hand in hand with re-entry shock and distress. Until everyone feels normal again and feels connected to the landscape, there will be feelings of inadequacy. That great existential question, "Who am I?" will start popping up in heads again. In adults, alcohol and drug consumption may rise, and this will of course affect the children they are trying to resettle.

Depression and anxiety over the process of reconnecting and making new friends may also be felt by all family members. These reactions are temporary and usually disappear after a short while so try to endure them. When they persist longer than six months, consider seeking professional help.

• *Marital Problems*

These cannot help but crop up as couples struggle with new issues, like 'flying money' (how much of your savings can be spent in a day on appliances, cars, or houses) or 'decision overload' (every major decision connected to being back must be made immediately). Feelings of frustration and a sense of powerlessness while waiting for a new phone to be hooked up or new furniture to be delivered will also be felt. The parents' frustration can filter down to the children very easily, so be on guard.

4. Impact on Children of Mixed Parents

Where you live overseas, marriages of mixed religion or race may be commonplace. This may not be the case back home. If your children are the product of a mixed marriage, you may have to brace yourself to help your children face a few adjustments.

A lot of these adjustments will depend on whether you are moving home to a large city or a small town. Your children will have their nationalism ingrained in them by you, but peer groups at home may challenge their notions.

Children of mixed marriages who have never lived in the country stamped on their passport may have the hardest time, especially older ones who are at ease with their identity, but now find themselves defending that identity to others who may not always display the same levels of tolerance prevalent overseas. Regardless of any of these factors, you as a parent should be on the lookout to make sure your children are not victims of any racism at school, so you can help them address any that exists.

RE-ENTRY COMES IN THREE STAGES

Re-entry is a three-step process. Think of the experience as having the following three crucial stages, and you will better understand what you and your children are going through.

1. Closure

The first stage is known as 'closure'. Closure is truly what the word implies. It is important for every family member to feel that they have 'closed' the chapter on that particular overseas assignment. I find that each posting we go on is like a 'time capsule' of memories, each one focussed on a distinctive place. Unless you want to pattern your life after a cliffhanger novel (where each chapter never finishes, but leaves the reader hanging on for resolution which doesn't ever seem to come), it's important that each stage of your life be more or less self-contained. That means not carrying over excess emotional baggage from one stage to another without ever resolving the problems which produce the emotions.

Of course life, not unlike a book, will have overlaps between chapters – personalities don't stop at the end of a page. But it is critical that everyone in the family feels that issues, friendships, problems of every stripe have been resolved so there is no unfinished business.

Unresolved grief – a major piece of emotional baggage and one of the biggest issues affecting Third Culture Kids according to the experts – occurs when there has been no closure. The grief caused by the move (saying goodbye to friends, in particular) is denied in the interests of getting on with it, putting the best face forward, and all those other clichés. The result: many children (and adults, too) keep that grief locked up too long inside, leading eventually to an explosion of anger and resentment directed at the parents (or others) responsible for moving them around too much.

Delayed expressions of grief occur when a child eventually breaks down and lets all the pent-up emotions (sadness, grief, the feelings of unfinished business) come at once. The outbursts are often triggered by a vicarious experience, like watching a sad movie or the death of a pet.

The family needs to know it is all right to grieve when another move is thrust upon them. Let everyone do it and know that it is all right to hurt for a while. Reminisce, even if you haven't left yet. Home videos and photo albums are ideal catalysts for this activity. If you never talk about the shared experiences again, never dragged out the photo albums or home videos to remember the textures of the experience, then together you won't ever re-experience much of the joy you felt. Grieving over a move is not that different from losing a loved one. Together, you must work hard to keep memories alive.

As part of this closure stage, children must especially be encouraged to resolve outstanding issues. The child who thinks he can just move away from a troubled friendship, a bad relationship with a teacher, or any other emotional problem, will later become an adult who will never be able to resolve the important issues of his life. He will continue to think he can just walk away from them.

The closure stage is the time for farewell parties and tearful conversations about how much you are going to miss the people with whom you have made your life for the past number of years. Be sure to engage in these and *never* let any family member slip out of town without saying goodbye.

By the way, mentally, do not leave town too early. As easy as it may seem to start distancing yourself from everything in anticipation of leaving, don't put your mind too far out in front of you. Try to avoid the family leaving town emotionally long before they have left physically.

2. Chaos

This second stage is a chaotic limbo. It's the time between packing up *back there*, but not yet being settled *over here*. Everyone feels weightless and anchorless. The disconnection has taken place. You have left the post and traveled 'home'. But the reconnection has yet to happen. Everything seems unknown; there seems to be no structure or routine to life. Your house is half-furnished because shipments haven't arrived. Children may be on an extended summer holiday or waiting for school to begin.

Emotionally, this is the time when everything and every reaction to being home can become exaggerated and overblown. To their family members back home, returnees are hopelessly self-centered and anxiety-ridden – conditions fueled by the stresses of return shock and the feelings of isolation experienced by each family member. Relationships are just being renewed and everyone is more or less uncertain about how things will go.

Self-esteem and self-confidence have vanished, just as they did in the initial stages of culture shock, because the family is once again on uncertain – albeit familiar – ground. There is also jet leg and exhaustion affecting everyone. Both children and adults may finally be suffering from some of the feelings of grief over leaving the post. Panic may be gurgling up to consume everyone.

This chaotic stage should be recognized for what it is – a transitory step on the road to re-entry which does not last long.

3. Reconnection

This is the stage which is the sweetest part of going home. Suddenly, you really and truly feel you are back. Often, this stage is reached only after an entire cycle of seasons and holidays. Or, parents may feel it as soon as the children are back in school; the children may feel it after a month or so has gone by and nobody remembers they are the new children back from that weird place overseas. Everyone is involved with new people and situations. They feel secure again, in familiar surroundings. Welcome home!

TEENAGERS AND RE-ENTRY

Re-entry is not an easy experience for children over the age of 12. In fact, the experts believe that of all the family members, teenagers face the most challenging transition of all, and have the most problems relating to the home culture. After finally 'fitting in' at the post, they must now shift gears and try to 'fit in' at home. They must do this in the midst of one of the hardest stages of their lives.

The issues which typically swirl around in the minds of teenagers – barely manageable for those who never leave home – are magnified for those who have traveled and are now returning. Teenagers, much more than younger children, will need all the support and sensitivity parents can offer to ensure the transition from abroad to home is easier and the hard-to-avoid stresses of return shock are lessened considerably.

WHY DOES THE TEENAGER TAKE RE-ENTRY SO HARD?

There are many reasons unique to teenagers which will make their re-entry more difficult.

1. The Turbulent Teen Years

Let's face it. Even when the environment is supposedly stable and there are no particular upheavals or traumatic experiences to interfere, life is an everyday drama for a teenager. The normal teenager spends hours, if not the entire teen years, completely wrapped up in and fascinated by his or her own image, as seen in the mirror, or reflected by his or her peer group. These are the years when the body is examined in minute detail every morning and evening for signs of adulthood; the face is judged from every angle as if somebody special across a classroom or at a party is also checking out a profile; the mind is working overtime, worrying, plotting, lamenting. In other words, the adolescent is growing up into adulthood.

When life is lived under such intense scrutiny, both personal and from others, a change in the environment can be anathema to the teenage soul. Change either causes a young adult to stand out because he's new (the first curse), or socially vanish (the second curse). From any standpoint, change is not likely to help massage the teenage ego, which at this point in his life bruises very easily. Likewise, the teenage self-image is extremely fragile. A move home not only takes away friendships and other familiar emotional landmarks, but also transplants the teenager to a completely different landscape.

That scenery will look familiar again in a few months' time, but tell that to a teenager whose concept of time is now, today, this minute, not a moment into the future. As a parent, you are capable of seeing down the road and of understanding that, given time, life returns to normal. A teenager cannot share that longer view so must be given help. Or emotional binoculars.

2. Returning TCKs

Upheaval can produce feelings of rootlessness, especially in teen-agers who, unlike their younger siblings, do not necessarily feel protected and comforted by the presence of parents. So for returning TCKs, now in their teens, who are already grappling with the sense of not being from anywhere, the move home is going to exaggerate those feelings, especially if 'home' is merely a place they experienced during hectic summer home leaves.

The search for identity is also serious business when you are a teenager, but the TCK's identity has often been muddled by too many foreign postings. Now add their own so-called culture to the mix, and you have a teenager with a lot of questions on his mind.

3. Desperately Seeking Independence

Besides putting himself under a microscope or mirror daily, this is also the time a teenager's natural urge is to crave independence. Yet throughout the posting, and during re-entry, the possibility of independence continues to be delayed because he must still rely on his parents for the arrangements associated with resettlement. Not only is he still dependent on his parents at a time he should be moving away from them, he may actually be over-dependent, given the unique circumstances.

Of one issue the teenager is certain: if he has been at a 'hardship' post overseas, there was almost no opportunity for an independent social life. It was either being organized by the international school, embassy, or local foreign youth organization, or was being monitored by all his classmates.

An adolescent also can feel helpless and out of control (not unlike his mother) because the circumstances surrounding all the upheaval have been caused by somebody else – the father, or the working partner whose career has precipitated all the moves. This loss of control and accentuated dependence on parents can combine to make the teenager feel miserable. He will especially feel constrained when he returns home and meets new teenage friends who apparently run their own lives without parental interference. These issues will definitely lead to confrontations with his own parents.

4. Breaking into a New Peer Group

TCKs often find it easier to speak to adults – with whom they have spent more than an average amount of time overseas – than to a new peer group whose members are definitely speaking a different language.

Despite being the same age and essentially looking alike, the new peer group at home only qualifies by virtue of age, not experience. Your child may not have been exposed to television, music, movies, and other cultural activities which provide a teenager's talking points. Without television, your teenage child has also been free of the superficial grip of advertising, so is unaware of how high the level of materialism may have risen in the teenage values system.

Since approval for everything at home must come from the new peer group – with whom the process of connection must now begin – the inability to communicate with the group will present a major hurdle.

Your young adult is seeking validation and approval from a group that is not in the first instance open to anyone different (which your teenager most definitely is). Only 'sameness' or uniformity wins popularity contests. It is also a sure bet that a teenager who doesn't know 'where life is at' back home is going to struggle socially for a few months.

Being so wrapped up in themselves, teenagers are not, as a group, very sensitive to the needs of others. They can hurt each other right to the soul. They want to surround themselves with other kids who are 'with it' and in teenage terms that translates into kids who are dressed the cool way, are good-looking (since bodies and looks are a teenage obsession), are in on who's hot and who's not in the world of pop culture, and are plugged in. Run down the list, and you can tell for the first few months your children will hold no credentials for entry into the 'in crowd', which naturally is the only crowd they want to join – immediately.

This completely circumstantial rejection usually rights itself after a year or so when teenagers find themselves accepted once again. Watch how quickly they forget the struggle for acceptance.

5. "I'm Weird"

Cliques are the hallmark of teenage social interaction. Ask any teenager. When a teenager is returning from a foreign posting, those cliques will seem formidable. Your teen may have been the star of the high school musical or held some other role in his international school which gave him status. But when he returns home, he finds the role that gave him self-confidence or bolstered his self-image overseas has already been taken by someone who has been at the school – with the same kids – forever.

In the beginning, before a new role can be established, your teenager can't help but figure he is some kind of freak. Not only that, TCKs have been assured all along that they are special. Or as foreigners, they have had preferential treatment in a host culture for the past few years. Suddenly they are not only not special: they are weird. They dress weird. Their haircut may be weird (as in 'out'). They may sound weird if their language doesn't include the culturally correct passwords of the day. In class, they may be advanced in some subjects which makes them sound like geniuses, or lag behind in other subjects which makes them feel like dunces. Whatever the case, they may stand out, especially if on the first day, the teacher asks them to stand up and say a few words in the language of whatever country they just left. And they barely know a sentence because they never, in fact, had to use the local language, living a cloistered existence in a foreign compound.

Along with the feelings of being weird – hard enough – will also come feelings of disappointment about not being special anymore; or not standing out in a crowd. Worse still, nobody wants to listen to anything your teenager has to say because he might as well be speaking a foreign tongue himself. He may also be seen to be bragging if he mentions the last holiday he took to some exotic spot which his classmates have only heard about in geography class.

If your child prefers to be alone, it may be because he simply cannot find anyone he can relate to. Schools back home are not overflowing with a constantly newly-arrived student population, as were the international schools. Returning TCKs tend to seek out other so-called rejects or misfits because, if nothing else, they share the rejection experience.

6. Dating, Drinking, Driving, and Safe Sex

For teenagers coming from small international schools or locations where the foreign population was small, dating without the scrutiny of the entire student body was downright impossible. Suddenly, entry into a large high school may mean numerous opportunities for dating and sexual activities. Your teenager may not have either the social skills or the information which will help ease this particular transition.

Likewise, your teenager may not have had a driver's license, so the issue of drinking and driving (every parent's nightmare) never arose. You can be sure it will come up at home.

It can be particularly overwhelming and confusing for teen-agers of either sex to suddenly find themselves in situations they are completely unfamiliar with, either sexual situations or parties where young people are drinking and then jumping into cars. A young teenage boy may suddenly feel he has to become a macho man with a beer in one hand and a girl in the other; likewise a young teenage girl may worry about appearing too childish or risking date rape. I am painting an extreme picture here because for your teenagers, these worst-case scenarios are likely to be the view they see.

Dating and sex, like everything else overseas, may have been closely monitored, with all the potential participants protected from risky behavior. At home, you may not be able to protect your children anymore. As a parent, you should sit your teenager down for a major talk on the subject. Not about the 'birds and the bees', which, believe me, they already know about, but about venereal disease, AIDS, safe sex, the dangers of drinking and driving, and any other relevant issues.

7. His Unique Brand of Nationalism

The national identity your teenager nurtured and cherished overseas may suddenly be challenged when he returns home. He finds his patriotism is not shared by his classmates. They actually view him as naive or a hopeless romantic about his country. For the returning teenager, this can lead to complete disillusionment.

International schools are constantly encouraging classroom work related to each student's country of birth as one way of teaching the children something of their home culture. Some teenagers, therefore, may know things about their country which kids who have lived there all their lives haven't taken the time to learn. The returnee won't be able to fathom that people who have lived in a place all their lives don't know some basic facts or hold the basic beliefs which he may have learned overseas. Once again, he'll feel like an alien with his own people.

8. Suddenly, the School and Its Setting have Changed

After the relative elitism of an international school, a large public school in a central city, where classroom size is almost double and threatening-looking local boys are outside the door, may overwhelm a returning teenager who has led an insular and over-protected existence in a foreign community. The teachers are also probably different than the ones he has been used to. In an international school, with smaller class sizes and numerous teaching assistants, the teacher may have had more time to provide individual attention. Not so at a big public school.

And what happened to all the classmates who were interested in good grades? They also may have vanished in the time zones. International schools, which place an emphasis on academic standing, don't allow for too much fooling around during class and certainly there are not the sort of discipline problems there seem to be at home. All of this can throw a teenager into return culture shock. The reverse may also happen. A returnee may find himself with fellow students so keen on entering the 'right college' that competition is fierce.

9. "I Don't Want to Make any New Friends"

He just left behind some close friends, so even if there is a glimmer of hope on the new-friendship horizon, your teen may not want to take a chance of getting close if he thinks he may have to say goodbye. Some children who have moved around a lot simply give up trying to meet new children if they think the friendship will have to be abandoned too soon.

This negative attitude is in keeping with teen attitudes in general. Teenagers tend to focus on the negative side of life. They certainly don't look in the mirror and see anything positive. So it will be natural that it could be some time before a returnee sees the positive aspects of moving home. He will dwell, maybe for months, on the negative aspects of the father's job (the one that's just uprooted him and brought him home) rather than remembering the positive aspects of his life as a TCK (the exotic holiday the family took on the way home).

ISSUES PARENTS OF TEENAGERS MUST FACE

The protective cocoon is lifted from both sides. Teenagers have to face up to a new lifestyle at home which may have been in evidence abroad but very minimal. Parents have to face up to their children challenging them, and adjust their relationship accordingly. I have just described some of the issues which teenagers are going to face. But what about parents? You will have to deal with your children's issues and then some.

1. Designer Teenagers

Since teenagers are so obsessed with appearances, it is no wonder that the clothes they wear take on unbelievable significance, especially those with designer labels. Your returning teenager may not know what the right labels are, but will know enough to recognize that the labels he has are definitely not cool. (In China, strange label-spotting became a local sport. My favorite: 'Boys and Balls'. Imagine how that would stack up against Esprit or Benetton.)

Not only are the labels important, they are expensive too. You may have been trying to encourage a new climate of non-materialistic values, when suddenly your teenager is confronted with this very materialism. He needs designer clothes which carry price tags completely out of this world. You will have to deal with this not only in financial terms with your teenager ("We can't afford a $150 pair of running shoes" might not work) but on a moral level as well. He, on the other hand, will be coming under pressure from his new peer group.

2. Lack of Adult Supervision

Overseas, the number of single-parent families could be counted on one hand. When you return home, in some instances, the dwindling number of two-parent families may be the ones you can count on your fingers. Divorce rates are high and, as a result, there are many teenagers roaming about, without anyone in particular wondering where they are at night, especially where a single parent is working to support the family.

Your teenager, suddenly independent and able to move without a presidential convoy, may view the freedom of his new friends and want some of that for himself. Many disputes are sure to erupt over the question of freedom. There are no more convenient excuses as there might have been overseas where a teenager couldn't get a driver's license. Brace yourself for parties going on at a house where there isn't a parent to be found.

3. Drugs and Rock Concerts

Drugs impossible to obtain in your overseas home are now plentiful. The teenager thinks that since the risk of being booted out of the country has been eliminated he can now indulge where he didn't before. Rock concerts, the kind which are a parent's nightmare with drugs and the possibility of being trampled in a riot, have come into the picture and your teenager – deprived for years – now wants to catch up. Inside his bedroom you hear the voices of rock stars, with their lyrics of destruction and evil, and your teenager is mesmerized. Welcome home.

HELPING CHILDREN OF ALL AGES ADJUST TO RE-ENTRY

Dr. Pollock of Interaction Inc., whom I wrote about in Chapter Seven, works extensively with returning TCKs and offers some wonderful advice for parents which I will pass along.

He advises parents to consider what he calls essential 'touch-stones' to help assist in the adjustment of their children. The first of these touchstones is the relationship between the mother and father, as he believes that is the source of the child's primary roots. If home is where the parents are, then a happy marriage provides a happy home for mobile children. Consider the image you present to your children, and remember again how much you, individually as parents and together as a united front, influence your children. If you are seen as stable and happy, that will definitely have a positive impact on your children; just as the opposite will have a negative impact and make your children, who already feel insecure over the upheavals of a move, feel even more uncertain.

The second of Dr. Pollock's touchstones is the notion that children must perceive that they are valued. He especially stresses the difference between you as the parents valuing your offspring and they themselves truly feeling it.

In other words, do you tell them enough how much you love them? If parents are consumed by their own lives and work and leave out the children, this will definitely lead to problems in adjustments. And more important, do you think they feel that they, too, are consulted over major decisions and are important? For instance, when parents decide that boarding school is the only option for a child's education, make sure the child knows exactly why this avenue is being taken – all of the reasons. Otherwise, children can grow up never fully understanding and resenting their parents for the rest of their lives. They could end up feeling like victims, despite the good intentions of their parents. Communication, once again, takes on special significance for a happier traveling family.

Finally, the last touchstone is to be sure the child perceives that what the parent is doing is valuable. That is, if the parent is not happy with the career, is not entirely convinced that he does valuable work (the work that is precipitating all the moves and travel) an unhappy child will feel that all of the upheaval has not even been worth it.

1. While Still Abroad

Some re-entry experts believe parents should begin preparing for the day they go home from the day they arrive overseas. That is not as silly as it sounds when you consider some simple measures you can take to ensure a healthier and happier re-entry. For instance, DO help your children keep in touch with friends and cousins back home, or even with someone designated merely as a penpal. In this way, your children can keep abreast of events and trends which they are interested in. DO subscribe to any magazines or hometown newspapers that have youth content for the same reasons.

DO plan your summer vacations and home leaves with eventual re-entry in mind. The more often you can take your children home to allow them to reestablish or just catch up with their old friends, the easier it will be for them to reconnect on the day they do come home to stay. If that's not possible, DO investigate the possibility of your children attending a summer camp which might offer new friends whom they can see on each trip home. A summer camp, not unlike a cottage, can provide memories your child can cherish the rest of his life.

2. When You Know You're Leaving

In order to provide the proper 'closure' for your children, DO help them collect all the names and addresses of friends they will want to keep in touch with. At the same time, DO help them create memory aids, like videotapes or photo albums with everyone's latest picture in it. DO NOT let them sneak out of town without any farewells or official going-away parties.

If they have been fighting with any particular friend, DO help them resolve those differences. DO NOT let them run away from relationships or unresolved problems or you may set a pattern for life.

DO be sure to contact the school to ensure you take all appropriate records and samples of school work to pass along to the next teacher. At the same time, if you know where you are headed, DO write to the principal of the new school informing him you are returning and would like to ensure a spot for your child in the school. Likewise, if there are any medical records from your time abroad, DO pick them up from your overseas doctor.

DO talk about all the expectations and myths your children may have about home. While it's nice to rhapsodize about a home or pet waiting there, DO point out all the things they will miss about the post so they will view their expectations in the proper light.

When sorting through your possessions for the movers, DO NOT throw away any items if this will upset your children. Be very careful about what gets given or tossed away. Children have 'sacred objects' like old teddy bears or books or anything which has an emotional attachment. It's all right to clear away some of the accumulated rubble, but be sure to consult your children about things which they may want to carry around for a few more years.

3. When You Arrive Home
DO seek out young people who can help sensitize your children to being home by filling them in on what's hot and what's not in the culture. DO invite over neighborhood children who can help your children get up to date and also explore the new neighborhood. Help your children connect with new organizations or after-school activities which will help them feel connected and make new friends.

Encourage your children NOT to talk about experiences as much as they talk about feelings so they won't be viewed as bragging. Help your children accept the fact that people, with the exception of other children who may be in similar situations, will not particularly want to hear about their overseas experiences. At the same time, DO have a word with a new teacher about forcing your children to talk about the foreign country they just left before they are ready. At the beginning of the re-entry period, some children DO NOT want to be singled out as different. Later, they may find it easier to talk after they feel they know their classmates better. DO encourage your children to listen to others, so they can learn what they have missed.

DO pay careful attention to the entire family's health and nutrition. The stress of re-entry could cause more illness, so ensure mealtimes are enforced as well as bedtimes. DO consult your family doctor at home to see if there are any medical tests which should be done now that you are home.

DO let your children decorate their new bedrooms or family room or any room where they want to relax.

HELPING TEENAGERS IN PARTICULAR TO ADJUST

All of the advice listed above applies to teenagers but there are a few more items I would like to add: DO let your teenagers make a few long-distance phone calls when you get back to speak to the friends they just left behind. It's expensive, but limit the time they talk to an affordable range and they will be eternally grateful. The calls will taper off once they begin reconnecting at home, but in that initial period, let them have a bit of leeway.

DO be more sensitive to the anxieties of the older children. Young ones, especially those still at home, will not begin to feel half as bad as a teenager, so unconditional support and lots of communication are definitely in order.

DO encourage your teenagers' independence whenever possible to allow them to feel they are catching up with the peer group. DO advise them to take their time making new friends by helping them assess common interests. Teenagers may latch onto other teens too quickly with whom they have nothing in common; later they will struggle to extricate themselves from these friendships made in haste.

DO seek professional help if you simply can't control their distress. If it's possible, DO start a support group of teenagers in similar situations.

AS PARENTS, YOU WILL BE ADJUSTING TOO ...

As parents, you will not only have to be sensitive to all of these issues which relate to your children – and help them get through them – but you, too, will be in the throes of the re-entry experience. There will be days when you will naturally put your children's concerns first, but parents are important too – never lose sight of that. A happy, well-adjusted parent will help a child a lot more effectively than one who continues to delay his or her own re-entry.

Above all else, never lose your sense of humor. There is no reason to be glum. In fact, you should feel extremely happy and positive about the experience your family just had. Life could be a lot worse than just getting used to a slower, less exciting lifestyle. You and your children have been fortunate to have participated in an overseas adventure. Never take that for granted. And remember all of the advice that I have tried to offer within these pages – for the next time you embark on an overseas adventure.

THE AUTHOR

Robin Pascoe knows what it's like to be a travelling wife and mother. Since 1981, she has moved to Bangkok, Ottawa, Taipei, Beijing, and back to Ottawa with her diplomat husband and two young children. Her own writing career as a journalist, broadcaster, documentary scriptwriter, and speechwriter has been a mobile one and provided numerous insights which she shares in *A Wife's Guide*. She is currently living near Ottawa again, wondering where her husband's next overseas assignment will take her family.

INDEX

Academic development of children 15–17, 23, 123, 141, 171
Accidents 179–180
'Adoption' of third culture 170
After-shocks 95
Airplane 70–74; convenience seating 72
Airsickness 64
Alcohol 210
Alienation 207–208
Allergies 191
Allowance 128
Anger 61, 96, 117, 205–206
Anxiety 13–15, 82; children's 31, 43–46, 70, 73, 96, 99, 204–205; parents' 13, 47–48, 74

Babysitter (Babysitting) 36, 77, 99, 113–114, 123, 179–180, 219
Baby: health issues 201–202; supplies 201
Bangkok: birth of first child 33, 198–200; medical issues in 195; support group for mothers 201; vacations from 216, 229
Beijing: arrival in 101; health issues 188, 196, 200; school in 33
Birthdays 232
Books 57, 59, 77–78, 155, 212
British Raj 98
Brochures 40
Budget 58, 226, 246, 258

Career 28, 34, 92, 111–112, 177, 239–240
Checklist for parents 32–33, 49
Children: active 25–26; adjustment to foreign culture 10; adjustment to life overseas 28–29; average 149–150; babies 59–61; behavior problems 116–119, 205–207; communication 120–121; comparison

with adults' perceptions 11, 30; culture shock 88–93, 248; dependency of 119; experiences of 29–31; first-tour children 150; hostility in 88, 206; hotels 2, 28, 29; influence of parents in shaping attitudes 11–12; insecurity 11–12, 204–205; intellectual 23–24; lifestyle of global children 27–28; loneliness 207; manipulative 87, 118; of mixed marriages 93, 148–149, 246–247; only children 115, 149; pre-departure tasks 52–53; preparing for the move 37–46; pre-school 44, 84, 126–127, 153–154, 183; pre-teens 127, 148, 205; questions of 39–40, 46; reactions to move 39, 41–43; resentment 69–70, 117–118, 205–206; right to privacy 126–127; sensitive 24–25, 93; servants with 19–20, 88–89, 92, 114–115, 128; stable environment for 100; stress 99, 208; teenagers 16–17, 18, 29, 34, 39, 44–46, 58, 66, 69, 76, 85, 91, 95, 97, 121, 205, 244, 250–259; toddlers 17–18, 34, 66, 69, 80–81; traveling without parents 73, 126, 226–227; traveling with young children 63–69; types of 22–26; see also Third Culture Kids
China 29–30, 31, 36
Clothing 58–59, 60; for travel 68
Club 36, 124
Colds 191
Communicating in a foreign language 17–18
Cultural appreciation 164–166
Culture shock 76, 80–103; denial 85–87, 91, 97–98; escape from 97; family's 83, 106; home leave 224; mother's 83–85, 92, 102; relapse

95; school 134; secondary 106; signs of 94–96; stages of 94–95; those susceptible to 91–93

Depression 87, 133, 209
Diarrhea 188, 191, 202
Discipline 118, 144, 211
Doctor: checkups 189; choosing 194–195, 198–200; directory of English-speaking doctors 182; hotel 180; professionals 211–212
Dressing 127
Drugs 210, 259

Early days 101
Embassy 49
Emergencies 180; first aid kit 197–198; preventive action 182–183; procedures 180–182
Employer 49
Encephalitis 186
Environment, suitability of 36
Exhaustion 69, 74–75, 78, 82
Expatriate: compared with immigrant 10; lifestyle 163–164; perception of reality 10–11
Expectations 129

Family: changes in roles overseas 107–116; discussion 38–39, 78, 100, 105, 260; 'extended' 125–126; history 55–56; meals 124–125; priority 121–122; stability 100, 119–120; time-sharing 125, 129; travel 66; values 100, 129
Father: absent 109–110; decision-maker 108; financial issues 108, 240; re-entry issues 240
Fears: see Anxiety
Fever 190–191, 202
First aid 197–198
Flexibility 101, 170
Flying 63–74
Food 59, 88–89; festive holiday 231; health 187–189, 190; flight 71

Friends: leaving 43, 52–53, 61, 90–91, 248–249, 257; making 40, 43–44, 253–255, 257–258
Frustration 206–207

Gifts 228–229, 232
Grandparents 61, 114–115, 149, 168, 230
Guilt 14–15, 47, 114, 157, 238–239

Heat stress 192
Hepatitis 185–186
Holidays 66–67, 104–105; Christmas 230–231; stopovers 66, 220, 221
Home: concept of 167–169; going home 236–239; permanent 29, 169; vacation 223–224
Home leave 219–226; briefing children on relatives 223; children's routine 221–223; getaways during 230
Homesickness 207, 209
Hong Kong 35–36, 213–214
Hospitals 181–183, 196
Hotels 2, 28–29, 66–68, 70, 76, 180, 214
Housing 40, 49, 76
Hygiene 187–189

Identity 31
Illnesses 185–186, 190–196
Independence: loss of 46, 90, 210, 252
Infections 191–192
Inoculation 53, 66, 183–186
Insecurity 204–205
Insomnia 42, 70, 75
Insurance, medical 182
International school 12–13, 89, 132–159; addresses 137; adjusting to 134–135; advance 'movies' of 45; advantages 139–140, 145; American bias 144; attitudes of parents 15; competition in 143; culture 23–24; disadvantages 138–139; fees 137; higher academic standards 142–143, 145; kinds of 136;

language issue 140–141; local culture impact on 141; major focus of children 157; pressures of 15–17; signs of stress 14, 91; teachers 138–139
Isolation 164

Jet lag 75–77, 82, 221
Journal 77, 233

Language: barriers 88, 116, 140–141; learning 17–19, 21–22, 36, 204; of care-givers 19–20
Laundry 68
Learning disabilities 21–22, 47, 138
Legal matters 54
Luggage, children's carry-on 56, 67, 223

Malls 58–59
Marital problems 115–116, 239, 246
Medical evacuation 181–182
Medical examination 53
Medical history 195
Medical supplies 53, 60; flights 71–72; home 193–194; jet lag 75
Medicine, preventive 183–190
Meningitis 186
Mental health issues 202–208
Mosquito bites 192
Mothers: absent 92, 99, 122–124; as emotional touchstone 37, 78; role overseas 110–112; over-protective 118; re-entry issues 239–240; traveling with children 64–65; working 112–113, 122–124
Motivation 28–29
Moving 36, 38–39, 56; adjusting to the idea of 37–38; necessity for complete acceptance of 38

Nationalism 168–169, 256–257
Nightmares 96

Packing: over-packing 68–69; to travel 67–69; to move 38, 56–61, 69–70
Parents: absent 113–114; accepting their children 26; comparing notes with other parents 48; difference between home and overseas parenting 34, 106–107; responsibility in children's education 155–157; importance of parents overseas 147; influencing children 11–13, 28–29, 31, 37–38, 100, 145–146, 239–241; over-achieving 141–142; questions to ask 32–33; single 113; supervision of teenagers 258–259; time away from children 77, 219, 229–230; helping children adjust on re-entry 259–260; united front 48; withholding information from children 41; working 92
Parent Teacher Association 138, 156–157
Parties 99; farewell 53, 249
Passport 54
Patience 76
Pediatrician 195
Pets 61
Photo album 52, 56, 67–68, 223, 232–233, 248
Plans, making 49
Political evacuation 204–205
Pollock, Dr. David 166, 168, 169, 172, 176, 177, 259–260
Pre-departure: briefing 41, 51–52; checklist 49; stress 43
Pregnancy overseas 121–122, 195, 198–202
Prejudice 28, 101–102
Presents 59
Privacy 126–127
Problems, aggravation of problems overseas 22
Psychology; children living overseas 9

Reality, different perceptions of 10
Re-entry 173, 236–264; changes in own family 236–237; compared to

moving abroad 241–242; helping children adjust 259–264; myths 242–243; reasons for 237–238; stages 247–250; teenagers 250–259, 263–264
Relatives 221–223; *see also* Grandparents
Research for book 33
Resentment 69–70, 111, 117–118
Respect 127–128
Return shock 224, 243–247; factors determining reaction 247–248
Rituals 170
Rootlessness 29, 170, 178, 251

Saying goodbye 61, 248–249, 257
School 132–159; at home 152, 257; boarding 46–48, 260; Calvert School 152; choosing 48; counselling 211; emotional problems 148–150; extra-curricular activities 155–156; foreign language problems 18, 140–141; issues 40, 134–135; new 89; options 150–153; placement problems 135; politics in 145, 154; pre-school issues 153–154; records 54–55; *see also* International school
Scrapbook 52
Servants: and children 19–20, 89–90, 101–102, 114, 122–124, 128, 145–146, 164, 216; and health 188; life without 127
Sex 146–147, 255–256
Shoes 58, 189
Shopping 58, 220, 226, 239
Sightseeing 76–77
Skills of children 15–16
Sleepovers 127
Snake bites 192
Socializing 164–166
Spiritual growth 17
Sports equipment 57
Stress: in children 14, 17; managing stress 15

Support, emotional 31
Support group 114–115, 129, 201
Support system 112, 126

Taipei 34, 37, 56, 87; American School 132–133, 136, 144; festival 165; health issues 195, 196; quality of life 36, 80–81
Tetanus 185
Third Culture Kids (TCKs) 160–178; career 177; characteristics 169–175; concept of home to TCK 167–168; definition 162–163; delayed development 173; friendships 176–177; grief 175–176, 248; interviews with 166; migratory instinct 174; multiculturalism 172; origin of term 161–162; peer group 253–255; re-entry of 251–252; rituals 170; self-sufficiency 171
Tolerance 145
Tours, reconnaisance 45
Toys 56, 61, 67
Transportation 49, 95
Travel: choosing a destination 216–218; opportunities 29, 165, 174, 213–215; planning 220–221; questions to ask travel agents 218; regional 217–219; short journeys 216–217; with children 215; *see also* Home leave
Tuberculosis 186
Tutors 21, 133
Typhoid 185

Vacation 104–105, 125, 213–234; vacation home 223–224
Videotapes 55, 232, 235–237
Visa requirements 54, 66

Water 186–187
Wealth 90

Yellow fever 186

CULTURE SHOCK!
SUCCESSFUL LIVING ABROAD

A WIFE'S GUIDE
by Robin Pascoe

"The book offers tough, down-to-earth suggestions to women who feel they've 'vanished' with the move. ... every expatriate husband who values a happy career and his traveling marriage should listen to her articulate voice ..."— *South China Morning Post*

"Filled with insight – she might have been a fly on the wall in many homes where expat wives reside. ... I recommend it to the newcomer and to the seasoned expat."—*Canadian Association of Singapore Newsletter*

"At long last a good survival guide for expatriate wives has been written ..."—*The Nation*

"What Robin Pascoe has managed to do so brilliantly in her book is to accurately pinpoint every emotion a woman will experience at each particular stage of her adjustment to expatriate living ... This is a book full of honest and practical advice ... It is also a very funny book ..."—*The Beam*

Encouraging and practical, Robin Pascoe's honest and helpful advice helps you to cope with the gamut of emotions and situations experienced by most 'accompanying' wives.

As essential to making it in your new life abroad as your entry visa, *A Wife's Guide* is the first book of its kind offering emotional support for married women who have to make a home away from home.

In the CULTURE SHOCK! series

Culture Shock Australia
Culture Shock Borneo
Culture Shock Britain
Culture Shock Burma
Culture Shock Canada
Culture Shock China
Culture Shock France
Culture Shock India
Culture Shock Indonesia
Culture Shock Israel
Culture Shock Italy
Culture Shock Japan

Culture Shock Korea
Culture Shock Nepal
Culture Shock Norway
Culture Shock Pakistan
Culture Shock Philippines
Culture Shock Singapore
Culture Shock South Africa
Culture Shock Spain
Culture Shock Sri Lanka
Culture Shock Thailand
Culture Shock USA

Success in a foreign country depends on your ability to think, feel and interact in terms of the host culture.

Every CULTURE SHOCK! book takes you through the mindscapes of the country's psyche, explaining the do's and don'ts, social customs and traditions, business and social etiquette. With tips on food, entertaining and relationships as well as explanations of daily sights and scenes which might otherwise confuse or deter the visitor, each book is a mine of information on making any stay, short or long, in a country rewarding.